'Written with great insight and compas
needed book, at a time when suffering has come home to so many. Alison Morgan deftly explores the many ways in which the ancient poetry of the Psalms can speak into our own lives, so that we really understand what it means to say of these scriptures that "deep calls unto deep".'
Malcolm Guite, poet and life fellow of Girton College, Cambridge

'This book is stunningly *beautiful*: as filled with light and shadow, and with energy and life, as the Psalms that form its subject and have power – so Alison Morgan argues – to turn things on their heads. But this is a book that is also *felt*. Alison "sees and sings" these ancient biblical songs, by mapping them onto the here and now of her own and others' lived experience – and she does so with a visceral intensity, that invigorates the senses and discovers meaning in the sights, sounds and textures of places. This is a remarkable book, that brings memory, experience and theology into play with literature, art, music and even neuroscience, and does so with the lightest of touch and the sharpest of wit. It will surely inspire even those who have known the Psalms all their lives, as well as those for whom they are new or less familiar.'
Professor Clare A.P. Willsdon, History of Art, School of Culture and Creative Arts, University of Glasgow

'I found my journey through the Psalms with Alison Morgan eye-opening, encouraging and challenging. It was as though God was inviting me into a deeper level of communication and intimacy with him as Alison shared her reflections. She has given me tools and a desire to engage with the Psalms, and the God of the Psalms, more deeply and honestly.'
Bishop Martin Breytenbach, retired bishop of St Mark the Evangelist, Limpopo, South Africa

'There is so much to enjoy throughout the book. Each chapter offers a stimulating breadth of literature, history, geography and natural sciences easily woven into the narrative. Many engaging stories illumine the text and demonstrate what may be involved in real, visceral engagement with God. There is a catholicity of scholarly perspectives deftly presented without being showy or obtrusive. Alison's style is lucid and lyrical with occasional iridescence. There is evidence of substantial pastoral experience supporting people in different continents and cultures undergoing the common human condition of fiercely personal trials. This leads to realism in facing personal pain and the unreasonable reactions from others that can be so shocking in life's adverse episodes.'
Rodney Green CBE, former chief executive, Leicester City Council, and author of *90,000 Hours: Managing the world of work*

'This book is an excellent companion as you walk through the ups and downs of everyday life. It is a gentle yet deep reflection on personal and sometimes challenging experiences that can only strengthen and deepen one's faith in God. Alison's intercultural writing style will draw you in, whatever your cultural heritage or ethnicity. Her insights during this personal adventure through the Psalms will keep you engaged and genuinely bless you. In this book, you will find something which is critically rigorous, helpfully informative and personally meaningful and that you can use as part of your pattern of prayer. I wholeheartedly commend it to you.'
Rt Revd Dr Timothy Wambunya, honorary assistant bishop in the Diocese of Oxford and former bishop of Butere in Kenya

'This is a deeply personal book in which the author explores how the Psalms, in all their shades of light and dark, have illuminated and given shape to her own journey of faith. A most engaging read, vividly written.'
Canon Patrick Woodhouse, former canon of Wells Cathedral and author of *Life in the Psalms*

'Alison does not shrink either from the difficulties we face in life nor from the so-called difficult parts of the Psalms. Indeed she brings these two together, first by talking openly about the bad things that happen, some of them from her own life story, and then by using the words of the Psalms themselves to face, express and reassess our experience. A particular delight was reading Alison's appreciation of the richness of the natural world, represented in the Psalms, illustrating their word pictures with her own examples full of awe and wonder.'
Revd Dr Liz Hoare, tutor in spiritual formation, Wycliffe Hall, Oxford

'Like the Psalms themselves, Alison's book is refreshingly honest and abounds in insights from her extensive general knowledge and life experience. That makes it a very rich read. Alison draws the reader into their own journey of reflection on what it feels like to be human, with an understanding that we can only truly find ourselves as we discover God in all his multifaceted layers. I found this book immediately engaging, totally absorbing and ultimately healing and restorative.'
Canon Andrew Evans, rector of Broughton Gifford, Great Chalfield and Holt, and rural dean of Bradford, Diocese of Salisbury

'A book focused on pain could be a daunting prospect – and this one does make demands, inviting us to engage emotionally with our experience as well as in our thinking. But it does so with a lightness of touch, bringing numerous stories from personal experience, laced with wise reflection and playful humour. In all this the Psalms provide lenses through which to explore life's hardest times and also words through which to express them. Inhabiting these ancient songs really can help turn our world the right way up.'
Revd Dr Bill Goodman, assistant principal at St Peter's College and director of ongoing ministerial development, Diocese of Sheffield

WORLD TURNED UPSIDE DOWN

THE PSALMS AND THE SPIRITUALITY OF PAIN
FINDING A WAY THROUGH

Alison Morgan

Foreword by Dr John Inge,
Bishop of Worcester

15 The Chambers, Vineyard
Abingdon OX14 3FE
brf.org.uk

Bible Reading Fellowship (BRF) is a charity (233280)
and company limited by guarantee (301324),
registered in England and Wales

ISBN 978 1 80039 166 6
First published 2023
10 9 8 7 6 5 4 3 2 1 0
All rights reserved

Text © Alison Morgan 2023
This edition © Bible Reading Fellowship 2023
Cover image © Siegi Déthune

The author asserts the moral right to be identified as the author of this work

Acknowledgements
Unless otherwise stated, scripture quotations are taken from The New Revised Standard Version of the Bible, Anglicised edition, copyright © 1989, 1995 by the Division of Christian Education of the National Council of the Churches of Christ in the United States of America. Used by permission. All rights reserved. Scripture quotations marked with the following abbreviations are taken from the version shown: **NIV** The Holy Bible, New International Version®, NIV® Copyright © 1973, 1978, 1984, 2011 by Biblica, Inc.® Used by permission. All rights reserved worldwide. **NJB** The New Jerusalem Bible © 1985 by Darton, Longman and Todd Ltd and Doubleday, a division of Bantam Doubleday Dell Publishing Group, Inc. **KJV** The Authorised Version of the Bible (The King James Bible), the rights in which are vested in the Crown, are reproduced by permission of the Crown's Patentee, Cambridge University Press.

Extract from 'The Bright Field' by R.S. Thomas © R.S. Thomas 1993 is reproduced with permission of Orion Publishing Group Ltd through PLSclear.

A catalogue record for this book is available from the British Library

Printed and bound by CPI Group (UK) Ltd, Croydon CR0 4YY

Photocopying for churches

Please report to CLA Church Licence any photocopy you make from this publication.
Your church administrator or secretary will know who manages your CLA Church Licence.

The information you need to provide to your CLA Church Licence administrator is as follows:

Title, Author, Publisher and ISBN

If your church doesn't hold a CLA Church Licence, information about obtaining one can be found at **uk.ccli.com**

Contents

Foreword 7

Preface 9

1 Making sense of life 13
Psalm focus: Psalm 23

2 An anatomy of pain 27
Psalm focus: 107, 88

3 Who am I? 45
Psalm focus: 139

4 Who is God? 63
Psalm focus: 74, 29, 8, 125, 136

5 Connecting with God 89
Psalm focus: 65, 104, 147, 148

6 Travelling with God 113
Psalm focus: 22, 78, 105—106, 135—136, 77, 90

7 A difficult conversation 133
Psalm focus: 119, 51, 32, 35, 109, 23, 63

8 Putting things right 159
Psalm focus: 81, 50, 7, 37, 94

9 A long walk in another world... 183
   Psalm focus: 100, 150, 137, 126

10 Coming home 209
   Psalm focus: 110, 121, 30, 138, 131

For further reflection 229

Index of psalms... 241

Select bibliography... 244

Foreword

'The Psalms take us on a journey; and they take us on foot... in a sense walking is the dominant theme of the entire Psalter.' So writes Alison Morgan in her highly perceptive, reflective and personal exploration of this great repository of timeless wisdom. Alison is the ideal walking companion and guide, walking not racing, never charging on ahead, always taking time to stop, to absorb the view and to ponder. She shares her personal experiences – of pregnancy, of rejection, of confusion, of bereavement, of times when her world has been turned upside down – in such a gentle manner as to invite the reader to call to mind the highs and lows they have similarly experienced, endured or enjoyed. As well as being intimately familiar with the landmarks, Alison is the kind of guide who inspires confidence: she has trodden this path before, she reads the map, she knows the direction, she is not daunted by difficult terrain, scree or scramble, not held back by headwind, storm or fog.

At each stage, Alison's method is to draw attention to a particular feature of the Psalmist's landscape, then, as readers and author together rest their gaze on that aspect, readers come to see how the Psalmist's hard-won insights into the human condition can be a source of understanding, perseverance, faith, and hope in their own lives. In the process they come to know themselves more fully; they also come to know God more fully, the God who has 'searched me out and known me'. The best guides, of course, do more than show people the way; they also enable them to find their own way. Anyone who follows Alison's guidance will be better equipped to return to the Psalms again and again and discover fresh insights of their own – and become a guide to others.

From the very outset of this book, it becomes clear to the reader that this walk is not an amiable, aimless ramble. Rather, the journey on which Alison is the guide is a pilgrimage; indeed, as she points out, several psalms were themselves composed to accompany the pilgrim. As a disciple of the one who called himself the Way, the Truth and the Life, Alison discerns the presence of Jesus every step of the way. What Alison offers the reader here is a *camino* through the Psalms. It is telling that the heading of the final chapter is 'Coming home'.

I hope you will enjoy your pilgrim walk with Alison, that you will marvel at the beauty along the way, and marvel even more at the Creator, Redeemer and Sustainer of it all; I wish you a rewarding journey and a safe homecoming.

Dr John Inge, Bishop of Worcester

Preface

When I was a child I used to go with my friends to our local swimming pool. It was an outdoor lido, and the water was shockingly cold. Each time, I was faced with a question: would I simply sit on the edge in the sunshine, or would I have the courage to dive in? Many years later, I find the Psalms asking me that same question. It is easy to recite a psalm without thinking too much – enjoying the rise and fall of the words, pausing over a particular image, scooping something off the surface here and there. Satisfied, we move on – touched, perhaps, but not changed. But a psalm makes exactly the same demand as a swimming pool: it invites us to dive in, to explore what we find beneath the water, to abandon our landlocked competence and accept that we cannot move through it as we move through other, more familiar texts; that we may have to change the way we see things. As we immerse ourselves in each psalm, we begin to look and feel differently. We may worry that the water is cold and the pool deep; we may find things we do not expect. It takes courage to dive into an ancient text, but if we don't take the plunge, if we are not willing to grapple with the psalmists' rich, unexpected words and learn to make them our own, we will never receive what they have to offer us.

I hope that as you read this book you will accept my invitation to take that plunge. We live in a complicated world, and life throws up challenges we may feel ill-equipped to meet. For centuries the Psalms have served as the primary spiritual resource for both Jewish and Christian believers. Until the Middle Ages, if you owned one book, it would be the Book of Psalms; a few centuries later the Psalter would become the first book to be printed in North America. Embedded in the lives of ordinary people in both private prayer and public worship, the Psalms have shaped and sustained whole generations. Today the Psalms have lost much of their former pre-eminence, and yet as I have prayed them myself I have discovered that when we are at our weakest, when we feel we most need God and yet have no idea how to talk to him, it is the Psalms which leap to our rescue. With the psalmists as our guides, we learn to draw closer to God, to hear his voice in fresh ways, and to identify what it is that troubles us. Borrowing their words, we find that we are able to articulate our most painful feelings and walk through suffering with honesty, hope, and confidence in the God who travels beside us. Here is an opportunity to read the Psalms differently: an invitation to embark on a new journey.

Books on the Psalms tend to fall into three main categories. Specialist works written by academic theologians offer detailed analyses of individual psalms and their contexts. General introductions, often written by these same scholars, provide us with the background information we need if we are to engage with the Psalms meaningfully today. Finally, devotional books written by a wide range of people offer personal readings of selected psalms, encouraging us to adopt them as part of our own pattern of prayer. My aim in *World Turned Upside Down* is to produce something which draws on all three of these genres; something which is at the same time critically rigorous, helpfully informative and personally meaningful. In order to enable the reader to engage fully and personally with the Psalms, a series of pointers for further reflection are placed at the end of the book.

My background lies not in theology but in literature, which inclines me to treat individual psalms as poetic rather than doctrinal texts, and to take a thematic and narrative approach to the collection as a whole – I read the Psalter not simply as a collection of works to be taken in isolation, but as a book which tells the story of a people. Many years of ministry to others, combined with my own experience as an ordinary human being living in a complicated world, have persuaded me that this story is also our story: that the things which provoked the psalmists to pour their feelings into these ancient songs are the very same things which fill our hearts and minds today. This has led me to take an approach to the Psalms which is unashamedly personal. I have come to believe that it is in making connections between our own experience and that of the original authors that we will best enable these ancient texts to fulfil their potential in our own lives, and the primary experience available to me is my own; the Psalms have transformed my ability to cope with the ups and downs of my particular circumstances. But I have also been hugely helped by the many people who have shared their own life stories with me, and their experiences too have enabled me to engage more deeply with the Psalms – although none of them appear here under their real names.

I would like to express my particular gratitude to Andrew, Brigid, John, Katy, Mike, Rodney and Stanley, who have in different ways offered me their encouragement, advice and support during the years in which I have been living and writing this book. And I would like to thank Olivia Warburton and her team at BRF for believing in the book and for their skill in preparing it for publication. It goes without saying that any errors or infelicities are mine alone.

Lastly, I would like to thank my husband Roger, who has walked beside me on the path of life for 40 years: I dedicate this book to him.

Alison Morgan

Making sense of life

The Lord is my shepherd, I shall not want.
 He makes me lie down in green pastures;
he leads me beside still waters;
 he restores my soul.
He leads me in right paths
 for his name's sake.
Even though I walk through the darkest valley,
 I fear no evil;
for you are with me;
 your rod and your staff – they comfort me.
You prepare a table before me
 in the presence of my enemies;
you anoint my head with oil;
 my cup overflows.
Surely goodness and mercy shall follow me
all the days of my life,
and I shall dwell in the house of the Lord
 my whole life long.

PSALM 23

In the beginning

When I was a child I had a friend named Sarah. Sarah lived next door, and she was a couple of years older than me. Sarah had a way of asking questions. 'If you had one wish for your life,' she enquired one day, 'what would it be?' 'To be happy,' I said. 'And if you were going to be run over,' Sarah continued, 'what would you choose to be run over by?' I frowned. It dawned on me that life might not be as simple or straightforward as I had anticipated. Even as I yearned for happiness, there must be a real possibility that things could go suddenly and disastrously wrong. 'An ambulance,' I said.

When things do indeed go wrong, it is to Psalm 23, probably the best known and loved of all the psalms, that we often turn. David begins with a lyrical description of human happiness, and he does it not by articulating a feeling, but by evoking an ancient pastoral landscape: 'The Lord is my shepherd, I shall not want. He makes me lie down in green pastures; he leads me beside still waters; he restores my soul.' Happiness, the psalm suggests, is wandering free of care through green pastures, pausing to sit beside the cool waters of slow-moving streams, relaxing among memories which take us back not just to our own childhood, but to that of the human race as a whole – this is the archetypal landscape of human well-being. As we read the opening words, we find ourselves at peace.

And yet David, like Sarah, knows that life is more complicated than this. Sometimes, he goes on to say, we find ourselves walking through much darker valleys, places where clouds of evil shut out the sunlight and where people who wish to harm us lurk in the shadows. Sunshine or darkness, peace or anguish, refreshing water or menacing rock – these are images which will echo through the Psalter, laid out here for us in the simplest of terms. And as David paints his canvas of light and darkness, I learn something which Sarah did not tell me. I realise that David is drawing our attention to the *order* in which these experiences come. Your wish is to be happy, he says, to find yourself wandering beside the clear streams which trickle gently through lush meadows. But this experience comes not by having the good fortune to avoid things going wrong, but by knowing where to turn when they do. The essential thing to take on board is that when your path does lead through dark valleys, you will not walk alone. You will have a guide, a shepherd, someone who will bring you to a place of safety, someone who will spread out the sunlit picnic from which those who sought to harm you will be very specifically excluded.

True happiness, David is suggesting, comes not before things go wrong, but after they have been put right.

The elephant in the room

Each place and time has its own set of values, its own way of doing things – its own invisible philosophy of life, if you like, a philosophy which among other things determines how we seek happiness and how we handle pain. We live in a very particular place and time – a postwar consumer society founded on the quest for growth and prosperity; a society which has persuaded itself that things can only get better, that money and technology will usher in a bright new world. We wrap ourselves in these promises and try not to notice that what is promised is not necessarily what is delivered. Pain, suffering and death remain persistently stubborn; although we do of course need food and shelter, human happiness does not appear to be related to material prosperity. If anything, the reverse is true: it seems that the wealthier and more technologically advanced the society, the higher the rates of depression found within it. In England, more than 83 million prescriptions for antidepressant medication were issued in the year 2021–22 alone; more than a quarter of us now depend on long-term prescriptions for antidepressants, opioids or sleeping pills.[1] The psalmist would not have been surprised: 'The days of our life are three score years and ten; yet the sum of them is but labour and sorrow,' he said.[2]

One of my favourite contemporary authors is Alain de Botton, a philosopher who writes engagingly and thoughtfully about the undercurrents of modern society. An ideology of optimism, he notes, is released into the air we breathe like a colourless, odourless gas. Embedded in newspapers, adverts and TV, underpinning everything from business

---

[1] Data published by the NHS Business Services Authority, 'Medicines used in mental health – England 2015/16 to 2012/22', 7 July 2022. See also the 2019 Public Health England report, gov.uk/government/publications/prescribed-medicines-review-report.

[2] Psalm 90:10, attributed to Moses. Please note that whereas the Psalms are equally relevant to women and men, I shall follow historical probability with regards to their authorship, and refer to the psalmist as 'he'.

practice to government policy, it claims to assert age-old truths, but in reality offers us a set of values which turn out to bring neither peace nor happiness. 'The single greatest enemy of contemporary satisfaction,' de Botton suggests, 'may be the belief in human perfectibility. We have been driven to collective rage through the apparently generous yet in reality devastating idea that it might be within our natural remit to be completely and enduringly happy.'[3]

For 25 years I served alongside my husband in parish churches, first in a former steel town, then in a growing multicultural city. And for 25 years I listened to people pour out their pain, as the happiness which once had beckoned crumbled into realities of broken dreams. Wives abandoned by their husbands. Children abused by their parents. Chronic illnesses, unexpected redundancies, heart-breaking bereavements. Betrayals, bullying, career-shattering accusations, petty jealousies. Mental ill health, powerful addictions, self-harming hatred. All these things and more – often ordinary things: ingratitude, selfishness, hurtful criticisms, poor decisions. 'The truth of the matter is that all we have to do is live long enough, and we will suffer,' theologian D.A. Carson observes.[4] It's a truth which, however hard we try to dispel it, echoes throughout history and reasserts itself stubbornly in our own experience.

So there is an elephant in the room. Perhaps we should not be surprised. After all, this bright new world of ours was created by a generation of thinkers who wished to confine the pain of the human condition to the past, and at the same time to suggest that we no longer had any need for God. That, they proclaimed, was yesterday; it doesn't have to be like that. Really, we said – how so? Well, we can just start again. Rewrite the story. Think more positively. The 18th-century philosopher Rousseau, the symbolic architect of this new environment of hope, dealt with the inconvenience of pain by rejecting it as the unnatural consequence of an oppressive social and political order. Shining his

---

3 *The School of Life* (Hamish Hamilton, 2019), p. 16; for a more detailed exploration see his *Status Anxiety* (Penguin, 2005).
4 *How Long, O Lord? Reflections on suffering and evil*, second edition (IVP, 2006), p. 16.

philosophical shoes, he consigned his children to an orphanage and got on with creating his progressive new world. In old age he was left lamenting everything he had lost and complaining about the unfairness of it all.[5] We have, in one way or another, been pursuing his dream ever since – often with the same outcome.

Perhaps, as Rousseau's dream begins to crumble, we are gradually becoming more open to the idea that it's time to face up to the reality of suffering – to recognise not only that we need to pay more attention to the pain which rattles around inside us, but also that we are not, after all, immune from the suffering which remains so alarmingly obvious in so many parts of the world. Wars in distant places propel waves of frightened, hungry people onto our affluent shores; a warming planet subjects us to increasing insecurity as storms, fires and floods sweep through places which don't expect them; a new virus cages half the population of the world and unleashes a tide of anxiety among us. It is becoming increasingly apparent that our world is more fragile than we had thought; that pain is not just the unfortunate experience of an unlucky few, but a global reality which affects us all.

When, as an atheist with a firm belief in self-determination, I left an uneventful childhood in a London suburb for a period of study in an ancient university, I was following Rousseau, of whom I had never heard. At university I met the Italian poet Dante, who began one of the greatest works ever written with an acknowledgement that his life had, at the peak of his career, gone pear-shaped. Dante did not put his children in an orphanage. He faced up to reality and travelled through the valley of shadow and death in his search for a truer world, one which would not deny suffering and pain but seek to integrate it into a bigger and more stable vision of reality. Dante, like the writer of Psalm 23, found comfort not in the false promises of a pain-free world but in the discovery that there is another dimension to life, a spiritual dimension, which does not paper over the cracks or close the door on

---

5 Rousseau wrote about his disappointments in his final work, *Reveries of the Solitary Walker*, trans. Peter France (Penguin, 1979).

the elephant crashing around in the crockery, but nonetheless finds the peace which comes only through recognising and embracing pain. The psalmists knew this; and with their help I have come to know it too.

The elephant in the church

Living in a world which has long sought to dull and deny pain, it seems natural, when we find ourselves nonetheless assailed by the slings and arrows of outrageous fortune, to turn to the church for help and support. And yet all too often we find that it isn't only our culture which urges us to believe that all is well; we bring our collective inclination to retreat into denial into the church as well. Gathering in beautiful buildings on Sundays, we sing heart-warming songs and uplifting hymns; we repeat comforting liturgical words and remind ourselves what we believe through the taking of bread and wine; we listen to a short talk and pray for those who suffer in distant places. Then we go home, taking our own doubts and difficulties with us. As biblical scholar Walter Brueggemann remarks, it's as if we believe that having faith means a refusal to acknowledge and embrace negativity; as if that would be some kind of failure.[6] So we sing brightly and sometimes beautifully, offer one another coffee and biscuits, and go home slightly more cheerful, hoping that by pretending all is well it will become so.

And yet two things are true. The first is that one of our responsibilities as the church is to help people navigate life, not as we would like it to be, but as it actually is. And the second is that pain lies at the very heart of our faith: in encountering Jesus, we encounter a man who gathered the suffering of the world into his own suffering, who forged a path from death to life, and who through it all earned the right to offer the uniquely powerful invitation 'Come to me, all you who are weary and burdened, and I will give you rest.' Pain is the inescapable thorn in the flesh of the human condition, and an essential element in the journey of every single one of us towards God. Without pain, we cannot grow;

---

6. *Spirituality of the Psalms* (Fortress Press, 2002), p. 26.

pain is the tunnel through which we must pass if we are to reach the light at the other end. Everything depends on how we respond, and how we help others to respond. Many, at the very point when they most need to connect with God, give up on their faith altogether. Overcome by the darkness of the valley, they never reach the green pastures or rest by the refreshing waters. 'What are you going to write about?' asked an old and wise friend. 'Pain,' I replied. 'Thank God,' she said.

Every morning I read the biblical passages set for the day in the Anglican lectionary, and for the past few years I have focused on the Psalms. And in the Psalms too I have found elephants – not the grey, invisible elephants which mope their way silently through our 21st-century world and hide behind the pillars of our churches, but attention-seeking, violently coloured, lambastingly noisy ones. These elephants cannot be ignored; their trumpeting and bellowing echoes from the first psalm to the last, and they rampage with the energy of animals unrestrained in their expression of pain, of anger, of lament and finally of joy. It's said that an elephant can be heard at a distance of six miles; there is so much sheer power wrapped up in the vocalisation of an elephant that I began to pick up my Bible with a newly cautious reverence. Few people know that the elephants are there, lumbering about inside.

And yet so often we don't pray the very psalms which could most help us. 'Which psalms do I know best?', I asked myself as I began to pray my way through them. The 'nice' ones, of course. Psalm 139 probably tops the list – God made me and knows me. Psalm 46, perhaps – 'Be still, and know that I am God.' Psalm 23, of course, with its first-impression promise of green pastures. And the summer cheerfulness of Psalm 104, which sees God stretching out the heavens like a tent, renewing the face of the earth. In these psalms the elephants graze peacefully in a sunlit savannah, and all is well with the world. And yet closer examination reveals that even in these uplifting verses there is an undercurrent of anger and fear. Psalm 139 ends with a trumpeting imprecation – Oh, that you would kill the wicked, for I hate them! The stillness promised in Psalm 46 comes in the midst of mountain-shaking turmoil. In Psalm 23 the sunlit pastures lie on the other side of a dangerous valley. And Psalm 104 concludes with the fervent wish that sinners be consumed from the earth. What do we do with these uncomfortable parts of our favourite psalms when we read or preach them? On the whole we smile apologetically, and leave them out.

For three years I prayed the psalms set for each day. I crossed them off as I prayed them. Many became familiar as they echoed repeatedly through the months; but at the end I was left with a short list of psalms that had been excluded from the lectionary, in whole or in part. I looked them up. They were the ones that howled in agony, the ones that called down unremitting disaster on those who had harmed the psalmist, the ones that found startlingly vivid ways to explain what he would like to see happen to them. Any painful psalms which did feature in the daily readings were often accompanied by commentaries which completely failed to recognise the reality of the ways in which human beings sometimes treat one another. Yes, the commentators acknowledged as they considered the unseemly behaviour of the rampaging elephants, we may feel this way – not in our own lives, of course, not here in the context of our stable democracies and our polite churchgoing, but as we watch atrocities *in other places* on our televisions. Furthermore, the commentators suggested from their comfortable, book-lined studies (as the distressed elephants set about uprooting trees and tusking competitors), we may helpfully remind ourselves that these lines are about spiritual battles, not real-life experiences; or about the pernicious influence of advertising; or about the enemies within our own heads; or about the fact that we really do need to confess our own vengeful feelings. For we are nice, we are progressive, we don't have enemies, do we? And if we do, it's probably all a misunderstanding.

Of the 150 psalms in the Psalter, over a third contain anguished and urgent pleas for rescue and deliverance, and many others are framed as thanksgiving for God's saving response.[7] Many of these pleas are

---

[7] Carleen Mandolfo identifies 42 psalms as laments: 'Language of lament in the Psalms' in William P. Brown (ed.), *The Oxford Handbook of the Psalms* (Oxford University Press, 2014), p. 115. Walter Brueggemann and William H. Bellinger list 66: *Psalms*, New Cambridge Bible Commentary (Cambridge University Press, 2014), pp. 9–12. Commentators agree that many psalms usually classed under other headings also contain elements of lament.

preceded by sharply worded complaints, aimed not just at those who oppress the psalmist and his people, but, alarmingly, at God himself. For readers who have the courage to admit to the emotions they express, these psalms open up a conversation with God, forcing us to acknowledge thoughts and feelings that we prefer to suppress, and pointing to a healing based not on polite surrender but on real, visceral engagement with God. 'I am here,' trumpet the furious elephants in the traditional African greeting, 'and I have something to say.' 'I am here,' I cry as I borrow the words of the psalmist to make my anguished complaint. 'I see you,' says God simply, in the traditional response. And in those words, my healing begins.

A new language of prayer

Following the insights of Walter Brueggemann, the Psalms are often divided into three types which reflect three distinct movements in the life of faith – although these types are not grouped together.[8] First come psalms of orientation, which celebrate the goodness and stability of life in a world created and ordered by God. Then come psalms of disorientation, which express the screaming agony of the discovery that this bountiful order has crumbled, that evil is triumphing over good, that the world is upside down, and that the psalmist feels angry, afraid, abandoned and lost. And finally come psalms of reorientation, in which the psalmist, after a period of conversation and reflection, emerges to a place of renewed security and thankfulness.[9]

The unique value of the Psalms is found in their ability to help us navigate from disorientation back to orientation – not simply by pointing to the promise of eventual deliverance, but by showing us that God is present in the pain itself. The way through our difficulties is to be found not in denial, or by looking on the bright side, but in being willing

---

[8] 'The Psalms and the life of faith: a suggested typology of function', *Journal for the Study of the Old Testament* 17 (1980), reprinted in *From Whom No Secrets are Hid* (Westminster John Knox Press, 2014).

[9] A more detailed analysis will be given in chapter 10.

to engage in a full and frank conversation with God. Through their startling willingness to share their own pain, the psalmists teach us a new language which enables us to articulate our most private prayers and to listen to the voice of God as he responds. It's a language of imagery and rhythm, in which the created world provides the words for a new conversation, and in which repetitions and patterns serve as vehicles for our most powerful emotions. As we learn, psalm by psalm, to speak this language, we begin to find that God conveys his all-powerful presence to us in the heaving of the earth and the tossing of the sea; that he whispers to us through the song of birds and smiles at us in the upturned faces of flowers. We discover that he teaches us by reminding us of the history of those who have gone before us, that he wraps us in a cloak of guidance as we stumble through our days, and that he surrounds us with promises of salvation. Sometimes, he remains silent, and invites us to examine the realities of our own hearts.

As we listen to God, we discover that suffering and death have the potential to bring life. We begin to glimpse what the mystics have called the treasures of darkness, after the prophet Isaiah, and to understand that the sadness of the world is tinged with beauty, and that it can be transformed into something deeper and stronger than can be found in the illusory comfort of an easy life.[10] By the time we have finished our journey through the Psalms, we feel that perhaps at last we are at peace with ourselves and with others; looking back, we are thankful for the huge strides we have made. We hold up our heads again; we smile; we are ready to walk onwards through this muddled and complicated world, knowing that we are not alone.

Before we start

There used to be a pub on London's Old Kent Road called The World Turned Upside Down. Opened in 1822 by John Offer, it served the people of Southwark for nearly 200 years. It was still there in the 1970s, and

---

10 Isaiah 45:3–7.

we drove past it whenever we ventured into town. The World Turned Upside Down and its sign became a fixed part of the landscape of my imagination. The world is a curious place, I thought, and making sense of it is surely one of the main things we have to do. It was as if the pub were asking me another question: which way up, exactly, does the world go, and why? The question is an old one, and it's explored with wry humour in the 14th-century manuscript copies of the Psalms. Created at a time when the Psalter was the book most likely to be owned by lay Christians, these bear witness to a society seeking for answers to the chaos which lapped at the margins of village life. As barons rebelled against kings, riots and storms swept the country, harvests failed and the Black Death loomed, the English illustrators adorned the cries of the psalmists with surreal images of a topsy-turvy world in which men ride ducks and defend themselves from marauding snails, rabbits fire bows and arrows and conduct funeral processions, and monkeys act as physicians to bed-ridden bears, play organs, or joust with spears – and all of them intertwined with fantastical images of devils, demons and grotesques.[11] The images had left their legacy in the sign outside the pub, which showed a huge, grinning fish hauling up a bedraggled fisherman in a tiny net.

John Offer was almost certainly unaware of these manuscripts. But the concept had winkled its way into the popular imagination. In the 19th century the world upside down was a popular genre of children's literature. In the 18th it had been both a common theme of the penny chapbooks hawked around the country by travelling salesmen, and a society art form in which participants of all social classes could mingle in disguise at masquerade balls. A century before that the world upside down had emerged as a ballad, published in 1646 as a protest against Parliament's decision to ban traditional Christmas festivities, and pointedly sung to a royalist tune. Popular throughout the turmoil of the Civil War years, it is said to have been played by the defeated British Army in the American War of Independence, and a song of the

---

11 Images in the Ormesby, Macclesfield and Luttrell Psalters. See Frederica Law-Turner, *The Ormesby Psalter* (Bodleian Library, 2017), p. 7. Illustrations from the original manuscripts are available online.

same name features today in the 2015 Broadway musical *Hamilton*. The pub on the Old Kent Road closed its doors for the last time in 2009, but the question remains: what do you do when things are no longer as you have always known and expected them to be?

It turns out that this is a supremely biblical question. The source of the phrase is found not in the topsy-turvy world of the English Civil War, but in the New Testament, and more specifically in the shockwaves which had begun to ripple across the Roman empire following the life, death, and resurrection of Jesus. In AD50, or thereabouts, Paul and his companion Silas visited the Greek city of Thessalonica, where, as was their wont, they went to the Jewish synagogue and explained that the long-awaited Messiah had come, that his name was Jesus, and that he had been crucified and then raised from the dead in Jerusalem. Many of those who heard the news responded with enthusiasm – but the religious leaders did not. Recognising it for the revolutionary message that it was, they instigated a riot, seized Paul and Silas' hapless host Jason, and dragged him before the civil authorities. 'These people who have been turning the world upside down have come here also,' they protested, 'and Jason has entertained them as his guests!' And they spelt out the charge: 'They are all acting contrary to the decrees of the emperor, saying that there is another king named Jesus.'[12] Paul and Silas were forced to flee. In reality, of course, they had been attempting, in declaring that Jesus had been raised from the dead, to turn an already upside down world the right way up.

When something momentous happens which threatens the settled order, which unleashes the possibility that from now on things are going to be different, we have to ask ourselves which way up we want the world to be. Jesus had made it abundantly clear that something new was on offer, something which paid scant regard to established social conventions and political realities, something which would indeed, as the religious leaders of Thessalonica had instinctively realised, turn their way of doing things upside down. It wasn't just the extraordinary

---

12 Acts 17:6–7.

ways in which he behaved – making friends with women, shaking hands with lepers, eating with sinners and living like a vagabond. It was what he said. Jesus had taught not in the schoolroom manner of the rabbis, but in beatitude and parable, subversive in both form and intention. The beatitudes invite us into a topsy-turvy world in which received values are turned on their heads. The winners, said Jesus, are not the rich, the successful, the men of high status and worth. The winners in this new upside-down kingdom are the poor, the grieving, the overlooked, the victims of injustice, the persecuted. More often he taught in parable, weaving nonsensical stories out of common sights or situations, telling tales in which subversive conclusions burst like dynamite out of a coal bunker. We have been inclined to reduce both beatitude and parable to moral fables, teaching which will tidy us all up a bit and improve the way we do things. In fact they are early announcements of the bombshell which was to come: that through the resurrection of Jesus, death, mourning, crying and pain have been conquered, and we are invited to live now in a world which is in the process of being turned not upside down, but the right way up.[13]

When I was ordained, I was given a leather-bound copy of the New Testament and Psalms. It's such a familiar combination that I tucked it happily under my arm and thought no more about it. But the more I read the Psalms, the more I realise that psalms and gospels go together. It's not just that the Psalms speak of the coming of the Messiah in words which find direct fulfilment in the life of Jesus – although they do. And it's not just that Jesus himself prayed the Psalms and quoted from them – although he did. It's that in both form and content, the Psalms articulate the story of the gospel itself. With their three-part movement of orientation, disorientation and reorientation, the Psalms foreshadow the path taken by Jesus, the path through life, death and resurrection.[14] They invite us to see our own journey of faith not just in the wider context of the whole story of the people of God (which

---

13 See Matthew 5:1–9; Revelation 21:3–4. For the subversive nature of Jesus' teaching, see Alison Morgan, *The Wild Gospel* (Monarch, 2004), ch. 3.

14 Clearly expressed in, for example, Philippians 2:6–11, and reflected in our own baptism. See Brueggemann, *Spirituality of the Psalms*, pp. viii–x.

we notice follows the same movement from stability to exile to restoration) but in the story of Jesus himself. In so doing they open up a pathway for each one of us to navigate the triumphs and disasters of our own lives, lending us the words we so desperately need as we move from a place of oppression, through a process of liberation, to a final destination of redemption. They open a door through which we may walk, stumbling with raw emotion, no longer seeking to hide our hurts and flaws, into the presence of God himself. Imbued with the spiritual energy which tore through the temple curtain at the moment of Jesus' death, the Psalms burst into the broken reality of our lives and propel us into the upside-down world of the kingdom of heaven.

Over the past few years I have learned to relive my experiences through those of the psalmists. I have limped from the darkest places through to a newfound peace and security in the company of the Lord who is my shepherd; I have found that, when you are run over, the ambulance does come. I hope, as you read this book, that you will make the journey your own; and I promise that the psalmists will guide you gently, step by step, never asking more of you than you are able to give.

An anatomy of pain

I climbed to the crest,
And, fog-festooned,
The sun lay west
Like a crimson wound:

Like that wound of mine
Of which none knew,
For I'd given no sign
That it pierced me through.

'The Wound', Thomas Hardy (1840–1928)

It seems odd to think that we might find solace in times of trouble through a series of texts composed thousands of years ago by people far away, whose lives were very different from ours, who spoke in a language we do not understand and set their compositions to music of which we have no record. And yet perhaps it is their very antiquity which commends the Psalms to us. These are works which have stood the test of time. Forged in a furnace of suffering, they have been owned and sung by generation after generation.

Perhaps they have two characteristics which more than any other have ensured their portability. Firstly, the Psalms do not attempt to offer a theology of suffering. They insist on feeling the pain rather than questioning or analysing it, and in so doing they force us to face up to the emotional reality of what is going on inside us. Opening a door through our mental self-defences, the psalmists thrust us into the presence of God and insist that we say it as it is, and not as we would like it to be – you will, they announce firmly, have this difficult conversation, you will have it now, and you may find you feel differently as a result.

Secondly, the Psalms rarely explain the specific circumstances in which they were written and for which they seek help. We may know that the psalmist has been betrayed, that he cannot sleep at night, that he is facing all sorts of obstacles and threats – but we are not told who has betrayed him, or precisely what is going on inside his head as he tosses and turns on his bed, or what exactly is the outcome he most fears. The timeless genius of the psalmist is that he leaves blank spaces for us to populate with our own experiences. 'Yes,' I find myself crying as I read his complaints; 'Exactly so!' I exclaim as I pour my troubled feelings into his words. And so it is that the conversation I wasn't sure I was allowed to have heaves itself out of the recesses of my most secret places and into the broad daylight of an encounter with God. You have been betrayed by someone you thought you could trust, you are being bullied at work, someone you love has died? Perhaps, says God, you would like to talk about it.

Who, why, when and where

The Psalms had been sung for generations before they were eventually shaped into the collection we find in our Bibles today. Composed by a series of authors, they are most commonly ascribed to David, with a smaller number attributed to his son Solomon, to the priestly family of Korah who served under David, to songmasters Asaph, Heman and Ethan and their successors, and in one instance to Moses. David is thus not the author of the entire Psalter, but he stands as the founder and sponsor of the genre.[1] David is thought to have ruled as king of

---

1 Robert Alter observes that it is not clear that the authorial inscriptions necessarily refer to particular individuals or groups; the Hebrew particle 'of' can also be construed as meaning 'in the manner of'. See his essay 'Psalms' in Robert Alter and Frank Kermode (eds), *The Literary Guide to the Bible* (Fontana Press, 1989), p. 245. Jerome Creach points out that Psalm 72 concludes with the statement that 'the prayers of David son of Jesse are ended', which implies that psalms in the later collections were not written by David: 'Did David write the Psalms?', *Discovering the Psalms* (Eerdmans, 2020), ch. 3. In this book I will

Israel from about 1010 to about 970BC, which suggests that many of the psalms are more than 3,000 years old.

The general consensus is that the Psalms were collected into their current form some time after the enforced exile of the people from Judea to Babylon in the sixth century BC.[2] As the exiles began to return, the Psalms took their place as the hymnbook of the restored temple in Jerusalem, where they were still being sung in the time of Jesus. The original musical notation has not survived, but the Psalms have been set afresh to music by each succeeding generation, and we still sing them today, in the simple voice of thousand-year-old Gregorian chant, in the classical tradition of our cathedral choirs, and in the popular songs of contemporary worship.

The Psalms are grouped into five books, echoing the five books of the Pentateuch. The books are presented as five collections, rather than five separate works distinguished by type or content, and the psalms within them come in many different poetic forms. Nevertheless there is a gradual progression from book to book which echoes the movement within many of the psalms themselves: an early emphasis on lament gives way gradually to a renewed focus on praise. The ancient Hebrew title for the collection, *Tehillim*, simply means 'Praises' – which is in itself a pointer to the extraordinary realism of the psalmist's recognition that only when we have faced up to pain and suffering will we be able once again to give thanks to God. The strongest confirmation of this is found in those psalms which Jesus himself prayed, most notably Psalm 22 with its anguished opening, 'My God, my God, why have you forsaken me?' and its promised conclusion, 'Those who seek him shall praise the Lord.'

---

follow the attributions of authorship made by the editors of the final collection.

2 Most scholars assume that the Psalms were collected and shaped during the Babylonian exile (587–538 BC) – see Tom Wright, *Finding God in the Psalms* (SPCK, 2014), p. 9, and Creach, *Discovering the Psalms*, p. 5. But the Psalter may have reached its final form only during the following centuries – see Gordon Wenham, *The Psalter Reclaimed: Praying and praising with the Psalms* (Crossway, 2013), p. 78. The process was certainly complete by the second century BC, when the Psalter was translated into Greek.

Songs of suffering

The Psalms are not intended as texts for study – our modern title 'Book of Psalms' is not helpful in this regard – but as prayers to be sung.[3] Music is a powerful vehicle for expressing emotion; it has a way of bypassing the mind, opening up a direct channel into our hearts and preventing us from filtering, analysing, and sanitising the feelings that swirl around inside us. Nor can the Psalms be used prescriptively, as advised in the early Christian centuries by a Jewish work entitled *The Magical Use of the Psalms*, which recommended, among other things, Psalm 8 for crying children, Psalm 18 for vicious dogs, Psalm 124 for fording a river, Psalm 139 for awakening love, and Psalm 146 for sword wounds.[4] Today, we may helpfully remind ourselves that the Psalms are not simply reassuring litanies for comfortable repetition when all is going well, but pointers to a deeper communion with God when everything has fallen apart; the anticipated destination of trust and praise is often reached only by a very painful path. In the Psalms we find the desperate, heartfelt cries of individuals, spiked with the suffering experienced in their own lives or in the life of their community, reaching out for the security they know is to be found only in God. The Psalms are the tell-it-as-it-is prayer book of the Bible, and they descend to the most visceral, rugged parts of the human soul.

The starting point of many of these prayers is very basic: the psalmist is so distressed that he cannot sleep. 'Every night I drench my pillow and flood my bed with tears,' he laments, 'and my soul refuses comfort. I cry by night, but I find no rest.'[5] So great is the pain in his soul that he fears he is near to death: 'My strength fails because of my misery,' he wails, 'my heart is like wax, my tongue sticks to my jaws, my bones burn like a furnace; I sit in darkness like those long dead.'[6]

---

3 The Psalter is first referred to as the Book of Psalms, or Songs (*biblo psalmon*), by Peter, in Acts 1:20.

4 See Jonathan Magonet, *A Rabbi Reads the Psalms* (SCM Press, 1994), p. 6; and Kaufmann Kohler and M. Grunwald, 'Bibliomancy', **jewishencyclopedia.com/articles/3273-bibliomancy**.

5 Paraphrased from Psalms 6:6; 77:2; 22:2.

6 From Psalms 31:10; 22:14–15; 102:3; 143:3.

Sometimes this is caused, he acknowledges, by his own mistakes and shortcomings: 'My iniquities have overtaken me until I cannot see, and my heart fails me.' He accepts that God is rightly angry with him, but pleads for mercy: 'Your wrath has swept over me, your assaults destroy me.'[7] More often he pours out his despair at the cruel and vindictive treatment being meted out to him by others: 'They will tear me apart like a lion and drag me away,' he protests; 'my enemies surround me to take away my life, they have spoken against me with a lying tongue, they persecute me with falsehood and ask me about things I do not know.'[8] Even those to whom he was closest, for whom he has often prayed, have turned away: 'In return for my love, they set themselves against me.' Taking care to preserve an outward show of integrity, his oppressors 'speak peaceably with their neighbours while malice is in their hearts'. And he fears those who seem determined to strip him of his assets and to bring shame upon him: 'Must I now give back what I never stole?' he cries; 'let me never be put to shame!'[9] But the worst of it all – and here perhaps lies both the explanation for the depth of his pain and the chink in the door through which light will eventually shine – is that he feels that God himself does not care. 'There is no one to help me,' he begins circumspectly, before allowing his feelings to rise in an unrestrained crescendo of accusation and complaint: 'Why have you abandoned and forgotten me, cast me off and broken me; why have you given the soul of your turtle dove to wild beasts?'[10] He is, he points out, in desperate need of rescue: 'Listen to my prayer, don't ignore my plea; deliver my soul from death, hear my crying, deliver me from my enemies – for the waters are up to my neck. How long, O Lord, how long?'[11]

---

7   From Psalms 40:12; 88:16.
8   From Psalms 7:2; 17:9; 109:2; 35:11.
9   From Psalms 109:4; 28:3; 69:4; 71:1.
10 From Psalms 88:4; 22:1; 42:9; 43:2; 102:23; 74:19.
11 From Psalms 55:2; 56:13; 61:1; 142:6; 69:1; 13:1.

Then, and now

Life in 21st-century western society is very different from life in the Middle Eastern Iron Age. But while the life shocks we suffer may not be the same as those described by the psalmist, the emotions they engender are. Perhaps we are likely to be most deeply wounded in three areas of vulnerability: our relationships, our roles, and our reputations.

Firstly, we suffer relational shocks. The most universal, and the most poignant, is bereavement. It was the death of a friend which threw my confident student world into antacid, beta-blocking turmoil and led me to my first experience of God. More recently, a single year brought the death of my faithful father, the untimely demise of a close colleague, and the silent suicide of a young family member. What does it feel like when someone at the centre of your world suddenly slides off the edge? It's not only that someone has died, perhaps, but that part of us has died with them, for in a sense we *are* our relationships, part of a complex web in which a hole has suddenly been ripped. I understood this most powerfully when my husband, attempting to cross a busy road, was hit by a lorry and rushed into intensive care. The shock was immense: I was left muttering numbly to myself, unable to understand how it was that a previously smooth-running globe could be shuddering so violently on its axis, that he could be in hospital and I, being in some sense the same person, was not. Witless, I went from church to ward and sang Psalm 121 to him as he lay attached by tubes to beeping machines: 'I lift my eyes up to the mountains, where does my help come from?' Later someone brought him a collection of songs – again it was the Psalms, by Scottish musician Ian White. My pulse stayed on a three-month high – but his, as he listened to the Psalms, settled back to a stable 60 beats per minute.

If our identity is bound up in our relationships, it also resides in our roles: we are, we find, what we do. And when what we do changes, particularly through retirement, redundancy or dismissal, we are likely to be left struggling not just with sharply altered circumstances, but with a huge sense of loss. Journalist Christina Patterson writes powerfully of the impact of losing a job at which she had excelled: 'I was writing up an interview when I got the call. Five minutes later, I felt as if I was falling off a cliff. I walked out of an office knowing that I had lost the thing I had spent my whole life building up.' Her entire body went into spasm: 'It's actually quite hard to do anything when your heart is thumping in your chest like a mad prisoner trying to hammer a way out. You think that the shaking will surely soon stop. But your heart keeps hammering and your body keeps shaking and you still find it hard to swallow, while you're still gulping air and wondering why you seem to have forgotten how to breathe.'[12]

Threats to our reputation also strike at the root of who we are. Jack was falsely accused of abuse. 'I have never visited the GP so many times in my life,' he said. 'I suffered from depression, suicidal thoughts, self-harming, fear, immense anger against the police and my accuser, and anger at the lack of support from anyone in authority. I was very close to suicide on at least three occasions.'[13] Eventually Jack was fully exonerated; but it is all too easy, as the psalmists knew, to accuse others of things they have not done. Stories abound: the mother who complained at the way her daughter had been treated in hospital, only to find herself facing allegations that she herself had attempted to kill her; the village postmasters issued with faulty software and then charged with fraud; the Methodist couple whose children were taken into care on a flawed medical diagnosis of abuse.[14] In an increasingly connected and weaponised world, reputations can be shattered in a moment: the public exposure of private lives; the shaming inflicted no longer through the village stocks but now through the worldwide web; the scorn poured out through Twitter, aptly described by one journalist as 'a force for recreational cruelty'.[15]

---

12 *The Art of Not Falling Apart* (Atlantic, 2018), pp. 1–9.
13 From a 2016 study by Oxford University's Centre for Criminology, 'The impact of being wrongly accused of abuse in occupations of trust: victims' voices', pp. 35–36. Published online at **law.ox.ac.uk**.
14 BBC, 15 December 2019; *The Guardian*, 7 January 2020; *The Daily Mail*, 24 February 2007.
15 Polly Verdon, *The Times*, 16 February 2020.

Shocks to our relationships, roles and reputations are likely to go beyond the events themselves, striking us where we are most vulnerable, wounding our sense of identity and placing in jeopardy the fragile self-esteem which comes from knowing who we are. Sometimes we may recognise, as David did in Psalm 51, that the fault is our own, arising from things we ourselves have done or said, things of which we feel deeply ashamed. But sometimes it will come from the discovery that we have been deceived, cheated or abused by those in whom we had placed our trust. Over the years I have walked alongside many people as they have struggled to come to terms with experiences of this kind. The elderly friend who made the life-shattering discovery that the main beneficiary of her husband's will was another wife in another land. The stranger sitting on a clifftop turning over her tarot cards, lamenting: 'I'm sad today. This one is the problem; it tells me there's a knife in my back.' The woman whose three marriages had been poisoned by the unresolved pain of her first husband's betrayal; the man whose business partner had stolen his assets. And a whole succession of people who had in one way or another been abused, most of whom feared it was their own fault and all of whom were overwhelmed with shame.

The reality is that we live in a world where all too often the sunny promises of a trouble-free life recede into a distant mirage as a maelstrom of pain sweeps in from the horizon. We may prefer to pretend it is not so, at least until it happens to us – but when it does, it is good to remember that there is nothing new under the sun, and that the tools of survival are found not only in the consolation of those who stand by us despite it all, but in the ancient poetry of the Psalms.

A diagnostic framework: Psalm 107

One of the least personal but most realistic psalms of pain is Psalm 107. Rather than focus on the traumatic suffering of an individual in a specific place and time, the psalm locates itself within the broad sweep of history and reflects the experience of an entire community. Intended for use in a liturgical setting, it looks back to the historical tipping point of collective exile, reflects on the deliverance provided by God, and points forward to the eucharistic celebration made possible by the death of Jesus. Opening and closing with thanks, it offers four case studies, each of which describes a painful condition from which an entire group of people cry out for rescue. In so doing, the psalm provides an overview of some of the things that can go wrong in our lives, and invites us to accept that God is here, that he understands these things, and that he can be relied on to bring us through them, should we care to turn to him for help.

The psalm begins with a reminder that the Lord is gracious, that his love endures forever, that he rescues his people, and that the appropriate response is thanks. Having thus pointed the compass firmly towards his intended destination, the psalmist heads into the storm.

The first group in need of rescue find themselves lost in a desert. The desert is both geographical (recalling the experience of those who suffered exile in Egypt) and spiritual (representing the experience of those who find themselves limping through a parched landscape of inner turmoil). As we enter in our imaginations into the physical scene described, we are invited to reflect on its spiritual reality within our own souls – are we, too, lost in a desert? For me, the thirst of a day in the burning salt wastes of the East African Rift Valley – the only place I have been where I knew that without assistance I would not survive – represents the spiritual crisis I experienced when a friend's cancer diagnosis swept away the self-constructed meaning of a life without God. The desert picture remains vivid today, acted out physically in the lives of those exiled from their homes and forced to seek refuge in lands far away, and experienced inwardly by millions for whom the signposts which pointed so confidently to happiness and fulfilment have instead led to a place of isolation and disillusionment. The weakening bonds of faith and community leave us in increasing despair, measured on the one hand by the suicides of reality TV stars and on the other by the 20 per cent who struggle quietly with loneliness at home.[16] And yet,

---

16 See gov.uk/government/news/pm-launches-governments-first-loneliness-strategy.

says the psalmist, there is hope, for those who were lost cried to the Lord, and he delivered them from their distress.

The second group languish in darkness, bound fast 'in misery and in irons'. The scene shifts from a desert to a prison: the problem is not that these sufferers have found themselves far from God, but that they have deliberately walked away from him. It's a vivid picture, as real now as it was then, and it comes with a promise of release – to be delivered with a strength which brooks no opposition, as the Lord forcibly breaks down the prison doors.[17] Three thousand years later, we continue to suffer from the consequences of our own desire to live outside the parameters set for us by God. And yet, astonishingly, the psalmist insists that God is still ready to meet us even when this strategy leads us into very dark places. I have met people convicted of violence, fraud and theft who had found God in prison and walked free to a new life; I have prayed with people who had engaged in various occult practices and found themselves oppressed by emotional and spiritual torment as a result; I have sought spiritual solace for people tormented by past mistakes small and large. Sometimes I have been tormented by my own. It is never too late, says the psalmist, to put things right.

The third group of sufferers are struggling with life-threatening illness: their foolish refusal to live within the guidelines provided by God is now reflected in the sickness of their bodies, and they face the prospect of death. We know of course that death is built into the way things are, part of the estrangement the whole world feels from God, and the psalmist will talk eloquently about that too. But here he is referring not to the sickness and death which is the legacy of living in a fallen world, but to that which runs faster than the tides of time, and comes as a result of our own sinful behaviour. We may make what a young man who was HIV positive delicately described to me as a 'lifestyle mistake'; we may grow used to drowning our sorrows in alcohol or

---

17 Echoed in Isaiah 45:2–3: 'I will break in pieces the doors of bronze and cut through the bars of iron, I will give you the treasures of darkness and riches hidden in secret places, so that you may know that it is I, the Lord, who call you by your name.'

overcoming them through the use of addictive drugs; we may nurse a tightly guarded resentment which erupts in headaches or ulcers. Our souls and bodies are intimately connected. And yet the psalmist insists that even when we bring misfortune on ourselves, God is ready to bring healing to our troubled lives.

Finally we come to those caught up in storms at sea: businessmen, adventurers, people whose ambition has led them to pursue wealth or status, and who find their best-laid plans swept up in a storm of disaster. It's an alarming image, as those reading of the perils of trade in the age of sail will know, or even those who, like me at the age of eight, embark on a tumultuous journey from a small Welsh island back to the mainland, with waves as high as mountains, and nothing more than a few oars to fend them off with. What happens to those who set sail in pursuit of wealth? A storm lifts up the waves of the sea, the psalmist says. The hapless businessmen reel and stagger on the deck as the ship is flung skywards and tossed back down between sheer walls of water. It's a picture of complete and utter loss of control, for people used to being in control but who now find themselves helpless as drunkards, forced to their knees by the recognition that they have reached the end of their own resources. This is the longest of the four case studies, and it describes a situation which has repeated itself throughout history and erupts all too often on the pages of our newspapers today, as we experience the devastating consequences of financial scandals, business failures and economic recessions. Here too help is at hand.

These, then, are the stanzas of the song. Each echoes with the cries of the afflicted for release, and each is followed by the insistence that they give due thanks to the Lord who has both heard and responded. This central message is carried and reinforced by the carefully designed, rhythmical structure within which it is contained. Each case unfolds through a four-part pattern, moving from suffering through despair to release and thanks. But while the circumstances and the nature of God's response vary, the core message does not, for like any good song, the psalm has a chorus – or, more technically, a liturgical refrain – and it is the chorus which we are to take to heart: 'Then they cried to the Lord in their trouble, and he delivered them from their distress; let them give thanks to the Lord for his steadfast love, for his wonderful works to humankind.' This repeated refrain serves to link each stanza to the opening and closing framework of the psalm, and emphasises the life-saving theme: this is a song not of disaster but of deliverance.

The psalmist concludes his song with a thankful celebration of God's mercy. He invites the hearer to reflect carefully on the wisdom of living within the parameters which God sets for his people and within which they can expect to enjoy his favour, and reminds us that God will always act to protect and save those who turn to him, even as they suffer the consequences of their own mistakes and failures. And so in this psalm we find the gospel itself, its message echoed by the prophets and summarised a thousand years later in the startling statement with which Jesus began his earthly ministry: 'The Spirit of the Lord is upon me, because he has anointed me to bring good news to the poor. He has sent me to proclaim release to the captives and recovery of sight to the blind, to let the oppressed go free, to proclaim the year of the Lord's favour.'[18]

Treasures of darkness

Psalm 107 makes it abundantly clear that some of our suffering is directly caused by our own actions and behaviours. But the psalmist knows too that some of it arises simply from our human fragility: our days are like grass, and the wind passes over us, and we are gone.[19] It is also the case, and here the psalmist will express his deepest anguish, that much of our suffering stems directly from the ungodly behaviour of others. We learn this slowly and painfully. 'It's not fair,' I would complain regularly to my father as I began to grapple with the daily injustices of childhood. 'Life isn't fair,' was his consistent but realistic

---

18 See Isaiah 61:1–3; Luke 4:18–19.
19 See Psalm 103:15–16; also Psalm 39:5–6.

reply, preparing me for the inevitable discovery that the injustices might unfold into ever deeper places as I grew older.

We may baulk at this, for one of our most cherished convictions is that life should indeed be fair. But perhaps my father was right, and the first step to dealing with pain is to face up to the certainty that it will be part of our experience. And perhaps the second is to accept that God knows this, and that indeed this is what our faith is all about. Many religions and philosophies offer a reasoned discussion of the problem of pain, but the Christian faith is the only one which actually rolls up its sleeves and joins in. Suffering, we learn, is not the end of the story, for treasure lurks in the darkness, and pain is a springboard for growth.

The problem of pain is one which has exercised the minds of the faithful for centuries. But from the day when Jesus echoed the despairing cry of Psalm 22 as his life dripped in agony from the cross, it has been recognised that suffering is something we should not only expect, but positively welcome. 'Do not be surprised at the fiery ordeal that has come on you to test you, as though something strange were happening to you,' wrote Peter; 'but rejoice inasmuch as you participate in the sufferings of Christ.' In fact, advised James, you should 'consider it pure joy whenever you face trials of many kinds, because you know that the testing of your faith produces perseverance.' Paul welcomed suffering even more emphatically: 'We also boast in our sufferings, knowing that suffering produces endurance, and endurance produces character, and character produces hope,' he declared.[20]

One of the greatest spiritual writers to explore the benefits of suffering was a 16th-century Carmelite friar known as St John of the Cross, whose work *Dark Night of the Soul* remains a classic today. John explains how in the early stages of faith God nurtures the soul just as a mother nurtures her child, feeding and caressing it, and helping it to grow through various spiritual exercises. But just as the child must eventually stand alone to face the reality of the world, so God draws

---

20 1 Peter 4:12–13 (NIV); James 1:2–3 (NIV); Romans 5:3–4.

believers into a place where they must face the dark fire of suffering which alone will free them from their earthly attachments and inner imperfections. The agony of this process is well documented, he reminds us, in the Psalms. The soul which has been through this experience of profound darkness and desolation becomes 'like one that has come forth from a rigorous imprisonment; it goes about the things of God with much greater freedom and satisfaction and with more abundant and inward delight than it did at the beginning'. This process, John says, is a kind of purgation, an experience from which we emerge stronger, more realistic about ourselves, better able to resist the troubles which assail us, and willing to surrender ourselves to God with a sense of freedom and joy.[21]

The Christian life has long been seen as a journey, and in recent years theologians have used the insights gained through the study of developmental psychology to explore the stages we may pass through as our faith matures. Janet Hagburg and Robert Guelich outline six stages of spiritual development in which we move from a simple faith commitment towards the union with God described so eloquently by St John of the Cross: we believe; we learn; we serve; we reflect; we surrender; we love. Not all of us make it through to the end of this process, but for those that do there is a hurdle which must be surmounted if we are to progress from reflection to surrender. The hurdle is known as the 'wall', and we may expect to experience it as we move from stage four to stage five of our faith journey. The wall is the dark night of the soul; different for each one of us, it is a place of profound vulnerability, a test which requires us to face our struggles head on and so come gradually to a position of forgiveness, surrender and healing.[22] The wall is the elephant which we may choose to welcome or to ignore, the elephant whose trumpeting echoes through the Psalms. It is said that most organised religion operates entirely on this side of the wall;

---

21 'The Dark Night of the Spirit', *Dark Night of the Soul*, trans. E. Allison Peers (Dover Publications, 2003), Bk 2, ch. 1.

22 Janet O. Hagberg and Robert A. Guelich, *The Critical Journey: Stages in the life of faith*, second edition (Sheffield Publishing Company, 2005); for a summary, see Alison Morgan, 'Stages of faith in our journey to God', **alisonmorgan.co.uk/Articles.htm**.

led by those who have not themselves experienced it, even the most vibrant churches may have nothing to offer those who find themselves overwhelmed by its dark impregnability.

This stage of our spiritual journey is alarmingly summarised by Franciscan priest Richard Rohr:

> Sooner or later, if you are on any classic 'spiritual schedule', some event, person, death, idea, or relationship will enter your life that you simply cannot deal with, using your present skill set, your acquired knowledge, or your strong willpower. Spiritually speaking, you will be, you must be, led to the edge of your own private resources. Normally a job, fortune, or reputation has to be lost, a death has to be suffered, a house has to be flooded, or a disease has to be endured.

This is the only way, Rohr suggests, that God can persuade us to change, let go of our egocentric preoccupations, and go on the further and larger journey.[23]

This has been my experience. I set out wanting happiness, and at first I thought I'd found it. But in between undoubtedly sunny times I have found myself walking through increasingly rugged landscapes. In our 40 years together, Roger and I have much to be thankful for, but there have been some difficult times too; we have experienced some of the circumstances and all of the emotions laid out in the darkest of the psalms. Over the years our lives have intermeshed with the lives of thousands of others. Most have been deeply fulfilling encounters, but some have not, and some of the most acute pain has come unexpectedly from fellow believers. Looking back now, some of those painful times have been of our own making, some have come simply because that is the way things are, and some have come from the deliberate actions of others. But each period of suffering has opened the door to a deeper relationship with God and a greater appreciation of his

---

23 *Falling Upward: A spirituality for the two halves of life* (Jossey-Bass, 2011), pp. 65, xix.

faithfulness. Pain is like fire; it can burn or it can refine, and which it does is up to us. Afterwards, I have been left with a curious sensation of having been scoured out on the inside; sadder, perhaps, but also more peaceful. Disaster comes not when we experience pain, but when we deny it.

C.S. Lewis has said that pain is God's megaphone; it is through pain that we discover who we are and who he is, that we are set free from the things we think we need, and that we find the resources which will enable us to help others.[24] Life may bring suffering, but suffering also brings life.

How bad does it get? Psalm 88

We do not know who wrote Psalm 107, but it is clear that the intention is to remind us that notwithstanding the desperate situations into which our flaws and failures may have led us, God is nonetheless ready and willing to put things right. Carefully arranged within a measured structure of lament and refrain, the very orderliness of the psalm reassures us that whilst the world may have gone awry, the underlying God-given stability we crave is sure to be restored.

This is not the perspective of Heman the Ezrahite, author of Psalm 88. Heman was one of David's singers, once appointed to play bronze cymbals during the procession of the ark to Jerusalem.[25] Perhaps the cymbals were Heman's special instrument, for we can imagine him crashing them together in fury as he howls his way through this psalm. Psalm 88 is the psalm of the wall par excellence. Sometimes those with whom I have been angry have told me that if I insist on expressing my feelings in such extreme and emotive language, they cannot possibly be expected to listen to them. Perhaps that is how God feels as Heman launches into his tirade of complaint and recrimination – for answer

---

24 *The Problem of Pain*, C.S. Lewis Signature Classics edition (Collins, 2012), p. 91.
25 1 Chronicles 15:6–22.

An anatomy of pain 43

comes there none, and eventually Heman subsides into silence. No ending, no statutory expression of thanks for deliverance present or future, no expression of trust, nothing. He just runs out of steam.

As ever, we have no idea what the problem is. But Heman is unstinting in his efforts to make us understand how upset he feels. However bad we may be feeling, Heman feels worse. Fully half the psalm is devoted to making this clear in the most graphic terms. I have cried out to you, he laments, by day and by night; indeed it is the first thing I do each morning, and I repeat it daily. The situation is now dire. I feel I am about to die; my strength is gone and my sight is failing. It's been going on for years; the grave beckons to me, and I am trapped in prison – or, no, wait – I am surrounded by the rising floodwaters of impending doom!

It seems that God greets this outpouring with silence. So Heman does what we have all done; he turns from his own woes to focus instead on God's inadequacies, and launches into a full-scale complaint. It's not just that he's in a pit, it's that God has put him there. It's not just that he feels lonely and abandoned, it's that God has deliberately alienated all his friends. And it's not just that the floodwaters are rising, it's that God has sent them. Heman turns to blame.

And yet God remains silent. His anger turning to fury, Heman ramps it up yet another notch, and flings out a barrage of sarcastic questions – six of them, in rapid fire. Look, he shouts. Do your great works save the dead? Do the dead sing your praises? Do the dead recall your love? Are they able to speak of your faithfulness? Are your miracles celebrated beyond the grave? What happens to the memory of your deeds in a place where everything is forgotten? Eh? Well? I thought not! So come on, then, God, Heman urges; this lack of action is not going to do your reputation any good – what use will I be to you if I die? You cannot afford to ignore me!

This is followed by a reiteration of his suffering and a reminder that it's all God's fault. And then he stops. Did he mean to complete it in the usual thankful way, but couldn't find the words? Or was it that the pain was so overwhelming that he was unable to see through his tears? Whatever it was, Heman has left us the most anguished psalm in the entire collection. And with it, he leaves us permission to feel the same way, to speak in the same intemperate language, to give full vent to our suffering, our despair and our anger – even when we feel angry with God himself. As for God, I find myself wondering whether perhaps God's silence is not the silence of a Father who doesn't care, but rather the patience of one who waits for the storm to subside and the real conversation to begin. We may not yet be ready to have that conversation; but bit by bit the psalmist will help us to rebuild our trust, to get in touch with our feelings, and to tremble with hope in the presence of God.

3

Who am I?

> God is everywhere, so you can find him everywhere. But in the desert, in the pure clean atmosphere, in the silence – there you can find yourself. And unless you begin to know yourself, how can you even begin to search for God?
> Fr Dioscuros, Monastery of St Antony, Egypt[1]

A journey through the Psalms

However golden our lives may seem to be, sooner or later we are liable to find a dark stain creeping over the polished surface of our daily experience. Perhaps we find ourselves plunged into the reality of Psalm 107 and feel lost, trapped, ill or afraid. Or perhaps we are immersed in the agony of Psalm 88, lashing out in anger and despair. When life has lost its shine, how do we get it back? How do we find a way out of this new and frightening darkness? Where do we start?

One of our major tasks as adults is to carve out a stable identity for ourselves, to shape a self-image from our relationships, our roles and our experiences. But identity is not fixed; it is a complex and nebulous thing which shifts in the sands of time and follows the changing scenery of our lives. Identity is not moulded in stone, set in our genes, determined by the kind of start we had in life or by the image we have chosen to project. It's fluid. It flows in and out like the tide, eddying around the flotsam of our talents, qualifications, relationships, roles and experiences. Change any one of those things, and we are forced to re-evaluate who we are. Many of the changes are positive – becoming a parent,

---

1 In conversation with William Dalrymple, *From the Holy Mountain* (Flamingo, 1998), p. 410.

or starting a new job, hobby or friendship. But often they are not. Who am I, when my partner or my child has died, or after my divorce? Who am I, when I have made a catastrophic mistake? When I have been disabled through accident? When I have been bullied, abused, or humiliated? When I have lost my job or when I retire, when chronic illness strikes, or death menaces? Such changes strike at the heart of our self-understanding. The earthquake which rumbles beneath our feet will pass; the one it unleashes in our soul may reverberate for years.

It is at this point that the Psalms come to our rescue. The Psalms are not primarily about the great themes of law, history, prophecy and wisdom which sweep through the Old Testament. Nor yet are they about the coming of the Messiah, the Holy Spirit or the church, the major preoccupations of the New Testament – although all these things are present within them. The Psalms are primarily, and quite unashamedly, about the life of the psalmist. They are about what it feels like to be human, in the context of all the things, good and bad, that happen to us in the course of our lives. More specifically, they are about how to find a place for all those things within the framework of a relationship with God. The Psalms are fundamentally about identity – yours, mine, ours.

The great gift of the Psalms is that when everything is collapsing all around us, they provide us with a sense of perspective. As we read them together, they will invite us to acknowledge our pain, and then to set it in a much wider context. They will help us, step by step, to refresh our spiritual lives, to draw closer to the God who made us and who knows everything about us. They will encourage us to reconnect with God through contemplation of the created world and in the presence of the life which flourishes all around us. They will invite us to consider the wider sweep of human history, and to reflect on the experiences of other peoples in other places. And then, when we are ready, the Psalms will suggest that perhaps it is time to examine our own souls, to talk with God about our failings and about the injustices and losses we have experienced, and to entrust these things to his care. Finally, they will bring us to understand that even when things go wrong it is possible to give thanks and praise to a God who has not only walked beside us but who promises that he will never leave us.

These are the stages we shall follow, chapter by chapter, as we seek to integrate the Psalms with our own experience. It is not an easy journey, but it's the best way I know of responding authentically to the rollercoaster of human life.

The Psalms as poetry: a user's guide

The Bible is a collection of books written at different times, in different forms, for different purposes. Most of these books come to us as prose texts: they are constructed as a series of sentences which flow in an orderly fashion one from another, much as they do in ordinary speech. The style may vary – we do not expect laws to be written in the same way as histories or prophecies, for example – but prose follows a structure which we are used to. We think, read and write in prose every day of our lives.

The Psalms, however, are conceived as poetry. This means first of all that they have a different shape. Gone are the measured, logical sentences rolling steadily across the page; the psalms have short lines, rhythmical and structural patterns, echoes and jolts, and frequent switches in tone and mood. This indicates that they expect us to engage with them in a completely different way from the way we read newspapers and novels. Their style and shape reflect their purpose: a poem makes no attempt to offer information or invite discussion; it is intuitive, evocative, suggestive. Instead of ushering us soberly and carefully from room to room in a linear way, a poem uses metaphor, ornament and pattern to confound our expectations and burst open the shutters of our hearts. These are not texts for thinking about; they demand to be felt.

Each psalm, then, draws us into the feelings of the psalmist in a particular situation. Nonetheless a question may occur to us. The psalmist himself is long dead, and the situation long past. Writing the psalm clearly helped him – but why should it help us? Here lies the most important characteristic of a poem: as we read the poem, the poem comes to life in us. A poem connects with feelings we too have had, and helps us to express and accept them. It is, to use the technical term, cathartic. To give a simple example, I have – ahem – at times found anger exploding inside my head in elemental, furious words. The psalmist does it so much better. He lends me his words – and as I replace my street vocabulary with his eloquence, I find myself not only strangely cheered but even chuckling aloud. This too is odd, because of course nothing has actually happened. Perhaps it's just because he seems to understand; and so he enables me to let go. The power of poetry is extraordinary.

Who am I? Psalm 139

We start our journey with the most basic question of all, the question of our own identity. Now that this has happened to me, who am I? How do I respond? Who will help me? These are the questions asked, and answered, by David in Psalm 139.

Psalm 139 is one of the best-known psalms. For 18 verses David reflects that God is so close to him that he knows his every thought and action; that wherever he goes, God goes with him; that God formed him in his mother's womb; that God knows every day of his life, not only those that have passed but also those that are still to come. This, says David, is extraordinary. These are comforting thoughts, and we have grown used to reassuring ourselves with them.

But then something unexpected happens. David follows these 18 verses of happy reflection with a violent outburst of anger. There are people he hates! They are malicious and wicked! They are his enemies! He wants them killed! His inner tension released by the force of the blast, David utters a plea: 'You have searched me and known me,' he had said as he began his prayer; search me again now, he begs as he comes to the end. Examine my heart, test my thoughts – tell me it's not me!

All this anger comes as bit of a shock. The psalmist appears to have lost his temper. The psalm isn't quite so nice any more, and our comfortable understanding is placed in jeopardy. How should we respond? Most commonly we simply pretend that these intemperate verses are not there. This just isn't the way we do things, we tell ourselves; this is another of those Old Testament anger trips demanding the death and destruction of invisible enemies, and we know better now – after all, Jesus taught us to love our enemies. So we smile and skate over these verses in some embarrassment. In the three-year cycle of the Anglican lectionary, Psalm 139 is prescribed reading six times. Verses 19 to 22 are excluded on every single occasion. The final plea of verses 23 and 24 appears just once.

And yet it seems to me that it is precisely in this unexpected outburst that the key to the psalm is to be found. There is clearly a startling inconsistency between the long, happy reflection on God's providence and the bitter outburst which follows it. But we may helpfully remind ourselves that if we allow the text to speak for itself, it becomes much more powerful than if we try to fit it into our own preconceptions. So it is here, with the inconsistency, that we must begin.

One of the best-known definitions of poetry is that given by Wordsworth: 'Poetry is the spontaneous overflow of powerful feelings: it takes its origin from emotion recollected in tranquillity.'[2] It is during this more peaceful time of recollection, Wordsworth says, that the poet is able to get back in touch with the depth of his earlier feelings and to express them – preferably not in exalted language but in the everyday speech of the ordinary person for whom he is writing. Poetry permits this much more powerfully than prose, he adds; a poetic account will be read a hundred times for every single reading of a prose one. If Wordsworth

---

2 'Preface to... the Lyrical Ballads' in Thomas Hutchinson (ed.), *Wordsworth: Poetical works* (Oxford University Press, 1975), p. 740.

is right, we should expect to find two things in a poem: one is strong emotion; the other is subsequent reflection. And that is exactly what we find in this psalm. The strong emotion is to be found in verses 19–24, and the reflection which paves the way for its expression in verses 1–18.

Let's start with the emotion, which we must now accept is not a disconcerting addition to the body of David's poem, but the well from which it springs. Having calmed himself by reflecting on God's care and compassion, David is now able to express his pain. He realises how angry he is. He feels himself to be surrounded by wicked and bloodthirsty people. Malicious, slanderous and evil-scheming, they oppose both God and the people of God, and David feels threatened and outraged. Reminding himself that God is with him, he articulates his feelings without making any attempt to dress them up. He screams his loathing, anguish and despair at God.

Understood like this, our perception of the psalm changes. Perhaps this psalm is not about how to thank God for the good things he has given us after all; it's about how to pray when disaster strikes. It isn't about you and God when things are going well, it's about you and God when everything is falling apart. It's about how to handle your anger, and how to come to God when your feelings overwhelm you. As ever in the Psalms, David does not tell us what has happened; he leaves the blanks for us to fill with our own experience, hoping that once we have entrusted ourselves to God's care, we too will be able to articulate, and thus overcome, our anger. He is giving us somewhere to go.

Finding our identity in God

David realises that before he can face his own feelings, he must calm down. Perhaps he walks in the garden, or plays soothing music on his harp. Perhaps he just settles into a chair by the window and looks back over his life, finding things to be thankful for. And as he prepares his heart, he considers three questions. These are not questions to do with the situation that is troubling him, but questions to do with God, and with David's identity as a person in relationship with God.

David's first priority is to ask who God is, and how does God's existence affect David? God, he reminds himself, is the one who truly knows him. He knows when David sits and when he stands, when he goes out and when he lies down. He knows David's thoughts before he has formed them, and his words before he has uttered them. He hems David in behind and before; he places his hand on David's shoulder.

At first sight this may seem a little restrictive. Is God a sort of supreme surveillance system, an ever-present speed camera, an all-knowing chief of the thought police? David doesn't think so; he trusts that God is motivated by the desire to protect him. God does not control; he knows. He hems you in behind – he knows your past, where you are coming from, and he understands it. He hems you in before – he knows your future, where you are going, and he will protect you in it. The verb David uses here simply means enclose or surround; whichever way David turns, God is there protecting him. David feels the touch of God's all-knowing hand on his life, and he reflects that this is a wonderful thing.

I think we all want to be known; and yet we are afraid of it too. We crave intimacy and understanding, but we are only too aware of our own imperfections. We fear that others will discover the flaws we try so hard to hide; that they will judge and reject us.

One half-term I took the children to London to stay with my parents. We went to the park, where the donkeys were out giving rides. As the man beside us in the queue settled his daughter onto the next available donkey, I glanced at his wife, only to hear her exclaim 'Good grief, it's Alison Keymer!' And I found myself face to face with Stella. I had not seen Stella for years. But she is one of the few people whose knowledge of me stretches back to my childhood – far beyond the time when I learned to edit my own identity. It was with Stella that

I entered into the battleground of life at the age of five; primary school was lived with Stella. As Stella gazed at me in astonishment, my different identities collided, and I felt a little tremor of uncertainty. Was she pleased to see me?

At eleven Stella and I were sent to different schools, and her place was taken by Pauline. It has to be said that my friendships with Stella and with Pauline were not always plain sailing; they know things about me which none of my adult acquaintances know – not terrible things, but things which are perhaps less impressive than those I choose to present to those I connect with today. God, on the other hand, does know them, for God witnessed them. God was there when Stella didn't want to be my friend, and when we played hide and seek and they couldn't find me because I was in the dustbin. He was there when I fought Pauline in the cloakroom, and when we compared our exam results. He knows that these experiences have contributed to the person I am now. Not only does he know, and accept, every day of my past, David reminds me; God knows and understands the days which are yet to come. And yet still he walks with me. Stella and I arranged to meet up the next day.

'The secret of my identity,' writes Thomas Merton, 'is hidden in the love and mercy of God. Therefore there is only one problem on which all my existence, my peace and my happiness depend: to discover myself in discovering God. If I find Him I will find myself and if I find my true self, I will find Him.'[3] So with David: David is finding God, so that in God he may once again find himself.

Affirming our trust in God

Having assured himself that God knows every day of his past and every day of his future, David turns his attention to the present and asks his second question. Where is God, he asks himself, now that things are

---

3 From *New Seeds of Contemplation* (New Directions, 1972), pp. 35–6 (abbreviated).

so difficult? Have I perhaps stepped outside the boundaries of God's protection, so that God is no longer with me? Where is God when my enemies blatantly ignore his existence, and seem willing to stop at nothing to secure my destruction?

At this point David's imagination grows wings. He imagines himself floating over land and sea, travelling from dawn to dusk, sweeping across the globe from light to darkness and back again. Now it is David who is the protagonist. He rises to the heights of heaven and plunges to the depths of the earth; he flies over the ocean at dawn and settles in the darkness of distant lands. Where is God now, he asks? The answer, of course, is that God is still with him; God is in all these places. God's presence does not depend upon our actions, and it does not depend upon our location.

Sooner or later it's a question we all ask. I remember my daughter at the age of three. 'God is everywhere, isn't he, Mummy?' she stated confidently one day. 'Yes,' I said, reassuringly. 'But you can't see him, can you, Mummy?' she continued. 'No,' I agreed, placidly. She paused, considering the problem of God's apparent absence. 'That's because he's hiding.'

David, of course, knows that God is not hiding. And so he turns the question on its head: if God does not hide from me, is it possible for me to hide from God, for me to find myself somewhere where he is not? David concludes that it is not. God is everywhere, and yet we can't see him. If I go up into the heavens he's there, and if I go down into the earth he's there. If I go east he's there, and if I go west he's there – as Jonah would discover some five centuries later. God is there in the dark, and he's there in the light. When I feel close to him in prayer, he's there. When I feel suicidal and distant, he's still there. When I feel like fleeing from my enemies, he's there. Wherever you go, whatever your circumstances, God is there.

This was brought home to me vividly some years ago. We were about to move from the city where we had lived for nearly 20 years to a small town in a distant part of the country – a place that would be completely new to us. It meant leaving behind all those to whom we had grown close – people who had loved us in difficult times, people to whom we had tried to be faithful when they faced struggles of their own. A month before our move I was due to spend two weeks in Zambia with Rooted in Jesus, the discipleship programme we support in Africa. I hadn't wanted to go; it felt like one transition too many. The trip involved long bus journeys through remote areas; I found myself dozing. And as I slept it seemed to me that God was asking me, 'Why have you so often not believed that I am always with you, that I will protect you, that I truly want to bless you? For I do.' I woke up surprised, and thought, yes, here I am 5,000 miles from home, travelling down dirt roads in a rattling vehicle with a fuel tank which keeps falling off, and facing the loss of everything that is familiar when I get back. And it occurred to me, as we stopped once more to tie the tank back on with string, that God really meant it. Wherever I go, he goes with me.

God is the one who made me

So God knows David; God is with David. David is now ready to move on to his third question, and ask what does God do? The next stanza is probably the best-known part of the whole poem. God is so intimately involved in David's life because it was God who made him in the first place. 'It was you,' David reflects, 'who formed my inward parts; you knit me together in my mother's womb. My frame was not hidden from you when I was being made in secret; your eyes beheld my unformed substance.' From the moment of his conception, God had been there, not just watching David but actually creating him.

Pregnancy is an extraordinary thing. You become increasingly aware that not something, but someone, is growing inside you, and you wonder at the miracle that is life. This first happened to me as I awaited the arrival of our son Edward: when he was born I gazed at him and thought it quite extraordinary that a whole new person had been created seemingly out of nothing. But it was my second pregnancy that really astonished me. This time I was expecting twins. David's frame may have been hidden from all but God as he grew in the womb, but today this is not so. I first saw Bethy and Katy on an ultrasound scan just four weeks after their conception: two tiny sacs, and in one of them a little pulse, going throb, throb, throb. They scan you all the time with twins, and as the weeks went by I saw them turn into blobs, then arcs, then things like fish, then minute babies. I felt them move and I saw them put their thumbs in their mouths. I saw they were girls. We chose their names, and I knew which was which, because their personalities were quite different from the moment of their creation. When you are expecting just one baby, you feel it move and you think, yes, baby, that's what they do. But if you are expecting two, you discover they behave in completely different ways – even if they are the same sex and the same size. Bethy hardly moved, staying curled up down at the bottom. Katy on the other hand wriggled and kicked and punched under my ribs. When they were born, Roger asked me which was Bethy, and I said this one, the first one, the still one. And which was Katy: the second one, the wriggly one. And so they proved to be: Bethy turned into a placid, easy-going toddler, while Katy responded to every stimulus. Same process: two outcomes.

David's wonder at the miracle of his own creation is not surprising. We now know that we are made from very little: a human being can be constructed, according to the Royal Society of Chemistry, from just 59 elements, most of which are needed only in microscopic traces. To all intents and purposes we consist of oxygen, carbon and hydrogen. Now an adult, Edward finds these elements have combined within him to form over 37 trillion cells, containing some seven billion billion billion atoms. To these have been added about 40,000 species of microbe, which together make up another 30–50 trillion cells.[4] God, with a little cooperation from me, had knit Edward together from startlingly basic ingredients.

---

4 A readable summary is given by Bill Bryson, *The Body: A guide for occupants* (Doubleday, 2019), chs 1, 3.

This is in itself remarkable; but there is more to it even than that. God's interest in and commitment to us is not purely physical, for we are more than a collection of organic and inorganic components bundled together in a bag. It is helpful to remind ourselves that our identities are reflected in, but not formed by, our bodies: every seven years our body completely renews itself, following the instructions of 25,000 randomly inherited genes; none of the cells I now have are those I was born with. We know too that our identities are expressed by, but not contained in, our thoughts, for these are no more than fleeting electrical impulses crossing minute synaptic gaps in our brains. 'I think, therefore I am,' Descartes concluded four centuries ago – but we still don't know what a thought actually is. The same applies to our feelings – we know that an emotion is a biological state brought on by some kind of neurophysical event, but we aren't able to define it any more precisely than that. In fact we have no agreed definition of life itself: there are apparently over 300 scientific theories which seek to explain it.[5] I have a personal one: remembering the wind from God that swept over the deep at the beginning of time, I reflect that life is the presence of the Spirit of God within something. I am alive because the Spirit of God is within me – the same Spirit who knitted me together in my mother's womb.

As David ponders the mystery of his own creation, he is filled again with wonder. How vast are the thoughts of God, and how numerous; more than the grains of sand on earth, he says – all seven quintillion and five hundred quadrillion of them, according to researchers at the University of Hawai'i. And this God not only reads David's thoughts, he is able to see every day of David's life before any of them has come to pass. I may have a problem, David concludes, but it is clear that I also have a God who is not only bigger than my problem, but is completely committed to me. David begins to feel better.

---

[5] Bryson, *The Body*, ch. 23. For our brains see Danah Zohar, *The Quantum Self* (Flamingo, 1991); for our genes see Francis Collins, *The Language of God* (Simon and Schuster, 2007).

Getting to the heart of the matter

David has now asked and answered three questions in his search for God. He has reminded himself that God knows him, that God is with him, and that God made him. What seemed like an all-encompassing crisis has been placed in the wider context of his relationship with the creator of the universe; David is beginning to regain his perspective. Having reassured himself that he is not alone, he is able now to put his anguished feelings into words, and express them to God in prayer. As his anger mounts, it spills out in hatred – a hatred so vehement that David repeats it four times, his articulacy temporarily deserting him. 'I hate those who hate you' (indeed I loathe them); 'I hate them with *perfect* hatred.' Hatred, he says, does not get any more intense than mine.

Despite his insistence that he is concerned entirely for God and God's reputation, we may infer that it is rather more personal than that, and that David himself feels deeply threatened. We may conclude that this volcanic eruption of anger is the inevitable consequence of a rising tide of fear, as David recognises the bloodthirsty intentions of those who surround him – for it is after all not God's blood for which they thirst, but David's. But David has reminded himself that God is with him, and knows all this. He will appeal to the Lord himself. And so he does, pouring out his anger and his fear, smarting at the injustice of it all, demanding action on God's part: 'O that you would kill the wicked,' he implores.

But then, just as at last he has got his feelings out into the open, a terrible thought occurs to David. Could it be that his enemies are justified in their treatment of him, that their allegations have some basis in fact, that God has permitted and sanctified their actions? Can he be completely sure that he is not to some extent to blame for his own misfortunes? He turns again to God. 'Search me, O God, and know my heart; test me and know my thoughts,' he pleads, echoing the words with which he began; 'See if there is any wicked way in *me*, and lead me in the way everlasting.'

This simple question opens up a dialogue that will recur throughout the Psalms. 'Clear me from hidden faults,' David pleads in Psalm 19. 'Prove me, O Lord, and try me; test my heart and mind,' he cries in Psalm 26, when again he finds himself up against people of evil schemes and plentiful bribes; for I do not keep company with the wicked, my hands are innocent, my love is constant and my integrity unblemished – please, please vindicate me! The same thoughts rattle round inside him in Psalm 40, when he seeks to reassure himself that he has always spoken freely of God's love and faithfulness, and in Psalm 143, when he pleads with God to protect him lest he become like those who oppress him, and implores God not to leave him defenceless against their schemes. David knows that none of us can stand before God purely on the strength of our own merits, however hard we may have tried to honour God in our thoughts and behaviour – and sometimes, as we shall see, he is painfully aware that he has fallen a long way short even of his own standards.

When I first read Psalm 139 I decided to pray David's prayer. 'Search me, O God, and know my heart; test me and know my thoughts. See if there is any wicked way in me,' I said, cautiously. 'Seeing as you mention it,' said God, 'we could start with just one thing' – and he showed me a destructive pattern in my own relationships, a misplacement of anger which was damaging both me and the person towards whom I was directing it. To seek to understand ourselves is instructive; to do so in the conscious presence of God is transforming.

Most of us will at some point in our lives find ourselves on the receiving end of rough treatment from others, crying out to God in disbelief and fear as people we had thought we could trust turn out to be the very opposite of trustworthy. Sometimes our heartfelt pleas will be followed by David's agony of self-doubt – could it be that we ourselves are to blame, that the situation is in fact primarily our fault? Perhaps it is in that question that the real pain lies, for it strikes at the very heart of our own self-understanding. Fear laps around our heart as we tremble at the power of our enemies, finds its release in an outpouring of anger – but then returns again, creeping within as we wonder whether, given our own undoubted imperfections, God might not in fact be on our side. And that is why David needed to go back to the beginning, to reassure himself that God has always been there for him, and always will be. We do not need to be perfect; we do not need to be afraid.

Know yourself

Philosophers and theologians have always insisted that learning to know oneself is the key to life. 'Have you ever been to Delphi?' Euthydemus asked Socrates at about the time the Psalms were being collected together; 'and did you notice an inscription on the temple: *Know Yourself*?' The oracle at Delphi had existed since prehistoric times as a place where people could go to seek guidance from the priestess of Apollo, and the inscription recurs throughout classical literature. Socrates had indeed noticed it, and his teaching echoes it. 'Know yourself,' he urged, 'for a life unexamined is not worth living.' If you do not know yourself, he explained to Euthydemus, you will be vulnerable to all sorts of disasters. You would not think, he says, of buying a horse but then making no attempt to assess its character, for without that understanding you will not be able to put it to work. The same is true of your own character: you must learn to understand yourself if you are to navigate the pitfalls of life, for this will provide you not only with wisdom for your own conduct but with a gauge by which to understand the behaviour of others.[6]

Self-knowledge is an introspective process, and introspection is not encouraged by our hasty, extrovert society; we are, in our attempts to understand ourselves, left largely to our own devices. When did I start to examine my own existence, to record it, consider it? I suppose when I was about eight years old, on the day my father took us to his office in Whitehall so that we could watch the jingling, historic procession of horseguards and carriages as the Queen passed by on her way to the state opening of Parliament. Leaning wide-eyed out of the window

---

6   Socrates' dialogues are recorded in Xenophon's *Memorabilia*, Bk IV ii.

I wrote it all down, in green and yellow felt-tip pen, in a little spiral-bound notebook which I still have – the green parts legible, the yellow parts now faint and faded. It was my first conscious voluntary piece of writing, my first expressed desire to capture life in print. The habit grew, until I was filling exercise books bought on holiday in French supermarkets, then page-a-day desk diaries, long typewritten letters and eventually folders full of Word documents. It was through reflecting on my daily experience that I learned to write, and through writing that I acquired the capacity to think. Perhaps even now my most real world is the one which lives in my fingertips, skittering over the keys and helping me to understand who I am and what I am for.

And yet David knows that introspection alone is not enough. We need a point of reference outside ourselves; and the only real point of reference is God. It is striking how in Psalm 139 the word which echoes from the beginning to the end is the verb 'know'.[7] God knows me, he knows when I sit and stand, he knows the words on my tongue; this knowledge is wonderful, David thinks. I know God's works, he continues, and they too are to be wondered at. So please, search me and know me now, he urges; know my heart, know my thoughts. Seven times it comes: 'Know, know, know,' David sings. The precipitating events behind the composition of the psalm may be the threats of David's enemies; but the way forward is to be found not in action but in knowledge – knowledge of our own selves, and the knowledge that we are known by God.

Far away in ancient Greece, those who visited the priestess in the subterranean cavern at Delphi did so because they had realised that we need help in navigating the complexities of life. Today, little has changed: all too often we find ourselves overwhelmed by the circumstances in which we find ourselves, and every year millions of us seek professional help as we struggle to cope with the powerful and destructive feelings we experience as a result. David offers another path; turning to God in

---

[7] For David's emphasis on knowledge see J.C. McCann Jr, 'Book of Psalms', in L.E. Keck et al. (eds), *The New Interpreter's Bible Commentary*, vol. 4 (Abingdon Press, 1996), p. 1235.

prayer, David discovered that we can in fact discuss our troubles with God in the privacy of our own room, and that this is indeed the only way forward when everything seems to be out of our control. Without God's help we will remain at the mercy of our own feelings – feelings which may well be generated by the actions of others, but which grow tall and strong in the fertile soil of our own fragile sense of identity.

David had understood what everyone who seeks honestly to know himself or herself sooner or later finds out: that we are complicated, and that half the time even our own hearts and minds are a mystery to us. This, perhaps, is the key to the Christian life, and the starting point for our journey. The aim is not simply to know yourself, but to know that except in the context of a relationship with God no such knowledge is fully possible; to know that it is as you travel with God, as David did, that you will both come to terms with yourself and at the same time grow into the person that God made you to be. This does not mean, of course, that David's enemies were in the clear with God, but he receives no guarantee that God will spring into action on his behalf. The same is true for us: we cannot control the behaviour of others, but we can allow their behaviour to deepen and refine our own sense of identity, secure in the knowledge that God is with us and that he promises to complete the work he began at our conception and lead us into the way everlasting after our death. What matters in the long run is not the presence or absence of pain but whether we are depending on ourselves, on others or on God for our self-understanding, for our direction, and for our ultimate destination.

As we travel through the Psalms, we will find that they help us to handle the emotions which surge up within us as we navigate through the days that are written for us in God's book. They will guide us as we experience not only fear, anger and shame, but also gratitude, wonder and joy. They will make it possible for us to seek security not through the validation of others or through our own experiences and achievements, but through the enduring stability of our relationship with God – which after all will last for much longer than the passing attention of our enemies. Indeed, those who threaten, criticise and undermine us may even be helping us as we seek to know ourselves and to know God. 'God,' said a friend unexpectedly to me in a moment of crisis, 'must love you very much, Alison, if he is allowing you to go through this.' At the time this seemed singularly unhelpful; but as I have travelled slowly through the Psalms, I have come to see that perhaps she was right.

So my first task, when things have got on top of me and my head and heart are spinning with anguish and anxiety, is to remind myself that I do not face this battle alone. God is with me – God knows me, protects me, and indeed made me in the first place; God can be relied upon to guide and rescue me. My continued existence, peace and happiness depend not on my ability to stave off disaster, but on my willingness to locate my identity first and foremost in him. 'There is but one point in the universe where God communicates with us,' wrote Bishop William Ullathorne two centuries ago, 'and that is the centre of our own soul. There He waits for us; there He meets us; there He speaks to us. To seek Him, therefore, we must enter into our own interior.'[8] It is the only possible starting point.

We have completed stage one of our journey: reminding ourselves that we are not alone in our struggles, we have recentred ourselves in God. What then can we expect of this God? What do we know about him, and what kind of help is he likely to provide? These are the questions the psalmists will help us with next.

---

8   *The Little Book of Humility and Patience* (Burns and Oates, 1860), III vi.

4

Who is God?

Ever since the creation of the world his eternal power and divine nature, invisible though they are, have been understood and seen through the things he has made.
ROMANS 1:20

I have now embarked upon my conversation with God. I have, with the help of the psalmist, calmed myself down. I have reminded myself that God made me and that God is with me. I have begun to recentre myself in him, and my problem seems a little less all-consuming. But of course it hasn't gone away; it is still there, raging about like an elephant inside me. You are with me, I say now to God; what then should I do with this elephant? Take it outside, where it belongs, says God. You have remembered who you are; now you need to remember who I am. Go for a walk; start by looking at the things I have made, at the world which is all about you – for through it, you may begin to hear my voice. Asaph will point you in the right direction.

So I turn to Asaph. Asaph was one of the songmasters appointed by David to lead worship in the temple. Twelve of the psalms which have come down to us bear his name; we do not know whether they were composed by Asaph himself, or by the 'sons of Asaph', the guild of musicians who continued his legacy long after his death.[1] The first of these psalms is Psalm 50; the rest are grouped together in Book Three of the Psalter, where they are numbered 73 to 83. Of these, Psalm 74 is particularly helpful.

---

[1] Asaph's role in the consecration of the temple under Solomon is described in 2 Chronicles 5:12; for his appointment and duties under David see 1 Chronicles 6:39 and 1 Chronicles 16. The 'sons of Asaph' were appointed by David to work under Asaph (1 Chronicles 25:1–2) and the 'descendants of Asaph' are listed among those who returned from Babylon after the exile (Ezra 2:41).

The power of God: Psalm 74

Asaph begins where David ended in Psalm 139: with the problem. Like David, Asaph is overwhelmed by the destructive power and malicious intent of those who oppose God and the people of God. He begins his psalm with a cry of anguish. 'Why do you cast us off?' he wails. Are you angry with us, have you forgotten us? Have you not noticed what is happening? To make sure that God is up to speed with the situation, Asaph spells it out. Not only has the temple been destroyed by axe and by fire, but every meeting place in the land has been burned to the ground. The symbol and heart of the people's faith is gone; no longer able to gather, their very identity is under threat. The prophets have fallen silent, the future is uncertain. Go take a look, Asaph urges God; inspect the ruins for yourself – are you really going to sit back and do nothing?

We do not know which historical event has triggered this psalm, but most commentators assume that the reference is to the destruction of the temple in 586BC by the forces of King Nebuchadnezzar of Babylon.[2] But, as ever, the precise event does not matter, for this is a pattern which has been repeated throughout history. Here in England we may recall the destruction wrought as Vikings plundered churches and monasteries in the ninth century, or the angst caused by the Puritan destruction of the symbols of faith in the 17th. In recent times the drama has been played out in countries from Africa to the Middle East, with churches looted and burned, villages destroyed and communities of faith forced into exile. Elsewhere, those who do have access to a church have found themselves prevented from worshipping together by the threatening spread of a viral pandemic, or by the divisive actions of denominational leaders who force secularising doctrinal changes on orthodox believers. For all of us, as for Asaph, the future seems uncertain. At such times, the spiritual crisis of a community is sharpened to

---

2 'Nebuzaradan, the captain of the bodyguard, a servant of the king of Babylon, came to Jerusalem. He burned the house of the Lord, the king's house, and all the houses of Jerusalem; every great house he burned down' (2 Kings 25:8–9). The temple was rebuilt later that century, but desecrated by the Syrians in 168BC and destroyed again by the Romans in AD70 – this time with the sack of the whole city.

a point in the life of every individual; unable to help one another, we cry out to God for succour.

At this point Asaph remembers something: God may be more powerful than we think. Looking up from the smoking ruins of the temple, he realises that God is not found only within the worshipping community. God does not dwell primarily in Zion, in the temple or the church, even if that is where the people have grown used to meeting with him; God has been at work in the world since the beginning of time, and his presence and power extend not just over human affairs but over the whole created universe. Reminding himself how God had once parted the sea to release his people from captivity in Egypt, Asaph reflects that God's authority over the cosmos is not only absolute, but evident to us every morning as we rise – this is the God who made fresh water flow from the hills and who dried up the land, who created day and night, sun and moon, summer and winter. God is not confined to the temple; God is to be found out of doors, and the whole world bears witness to his ability to conquer the powers of darkness. So Asaph invites us to lift our eyes from the horizon of our own troubles, and focus on God. God, he says, is big. And God has been working salvation in the earth since the beginning of time.

Asaph begins his reflection by directing our attention to the sea. He does so in a way which is very particular, for he draws not only on the familiar creation stories of Genesis, where God brings order out of chaos to create life, but also on the creation myths of the surrounding peoples. Our English word 'sea' is a Germanic word of unknown origin; it just means sea, the salty stuff which sloshes about in the world's oceans. In Hebrew, however, the word 'sea' is derived from the name of Yam, a malevolent sea god portrayed in local Caananite myth as the water dragon defeated by the god Baal.[3] Asaph reminds us that it was God (and not Baal) who broke the heads of the dragons in the waters

---

3   For the Canaanite myths see Karel van der Toorn et al., 'Dragon', *Dictionary of Deities and Demons in the Bible* (Eerdmans, 1999). See also Walter Brueggemann and William H. Bellinger, *Psalms*, New Cambridge Bible Commentary (Cambridge University Press, 2014), p. 322.

and crushed the sea monster Leviathan; he uses this ancient story to affirm God's sovereign power over every other god and every force of evil – not just at the beginning of time as the cosmos came into being, but in the ongoing storms which continue to afflict us in this fallen world. We fear the sea; the sea, as we remember from Psalm 107, has always represented a danger which we cannot overcome. But perhaps it is in the sea, Asaph says, that the answer is to be found.

Roger and I once spent a couple of weeks on the Isle of Lewis, an ancient land lying far off the north-western shore of Scotland. It was at a difficult time for me, and each day I rose early to walk off my angst in the most remote and beautiful areas of the island, determined to get the pain out of my head and into the open air. One morning my walk took me across a wide sandy bay. It had been a stormy night, and the winds were striking the shore at over 30 miles an hour. I stood on the beach facing into the gale, watching huge, distant waves break and crash one on top of another, and thinking of the psalmist's dragons. Gannets and fulmars surfed the currents, skimming the surface just behind the breakers – they seemed to ride out the storm so much more easily than me. Suddenly I became aware that the sea was sliding rapidly, silently over the sand towards me. I stepped back, caught off balance. It raced on. I turned, ran, tripped, half landed, bounced back up, tried again, fell again. The water caught me; I escaped it; it caught me again. It's a trick the sea has here, I discovered later; it sneaks up and grabs you, covering huge distances in the blink of an eye, only to retreat again at speed, dragging every obstacle into its stormy waters. Regaining my feet as the wave finally raced back out to sea, I was left with my legs dripping, my boots full of seawater, rough sand grains clinging to my chapped hands. I set off damply up the beach, thinking how suddenly things can change, how unsuspected dangers can spring from nowhere, how quickly violent waves can overcome you while you are going perfectly innocently about your daily business.

Retreating from the distant tide, I walked across the shimmering sand for the length of the beach, and followed a grassy sheep track back through the dunes. Below me, the waves continued to assault the shore; but here in the soft morning light the grass was a riot of colour, speckled with daisies, bird's-foot trefoil and the delicate lilac petals of wild thyme. The wind dried my trousers, a skylark rose into the sky and showered me with song, and I reflected that life can probably be expected to throw up nasty surprises – but perhaps they will go as suddenly as they came; perhaps the storm does not, after all, have the last word. Asaph hopes so too: for after the storm, he continues, God dried up the waters, fixed the bounds of the earth, created the sun and seasons – will he not do so again today?[4]

Having reminded himself of the power of God, Asaph moves into the third and final section of his psalm. Assured now of God's ability to act, he stops complaining and simply asks for help. Deliver us from the forces which threaten us, do not let us be put to shame, he pleads; restore us and help us to rebuild our relationship with you. It's a prayer he will echo more personally in Psalm 77, as again he recalls God's power over the violent storms of a threatening sea; and one which his colleague Ethan will offer in Psalm 89 as he too reminds himself in troubled times that the Lord rules the raging of the sea, that the heavens and the earth are his, the world and all that is in it. Get yourself out of doors, God says through Asaph, and look for me in the places where my eternal power and divine nature, invisible though they are, can be understood and seen through the things I have made.[5] It's the same answer God gave to Job, whose story of undeserved suffering was written at about the same time as this psalm. Battered by bereavement, illness and personal ruin, Job had accused God of indifference and cruelty. God takes him outside. Where were you when I laid the foundations of the earth? he asks. Who shut in the sea with doors, and prescribed bounds for it, and said 'Thus far shall you come, and no further'? Who was it who defeated Leviathan?[6] It's a consistent message: don't focus on your sea of troubles, on the monsters who rise up to threaten you – focus

---

4 Psalm 18 is conceived in a similar way: David finds himself threatened by the surging waves of an inimical sea, hears the voice of God speaking through the storm, and is brought safely into a spacious place.

5 Romans 1:20.

6 Paraphrased from Job 38:4, 8–11; 41:1.

on the Lord, the maker of heaven and earth, who alone has the power to deal with these things.

Hundreds of years later the storm story of God's supremacy over the powers of evil will be re-enacted on the Sea of Galilee, as Jesus rebukes another tempest and the disciples wonder at this man who seems, like God himself, to have the power to command even the winds and the waves.[7] 'Thus far, and no further,' I whispered to myself. Stop thinking about the storm; start thinking about God. That day, on the Isle of Lewis, I managed to do it.

Trusting in God: Psalm 29

Psalm 74 urges us to lift our eyes from the troubles which threaten to overwhelm us and to focus instead on God, for in God we find not only someone who understands and cares for us, as David reminds us in Psalm 139, but someone in whom we can place our trust, knowing that our problems are both trivial and transient in comparison with those he has already overcome. It is time now to go back to David, and sharpen that focus by looking at Psalm 29, one of the most graphic of all the psalms.

Psalm 29 takes us straight into a thunderstorm. Who is God, David asks. Imagine a great storm, he says; it starts out at sea, sweeps inland over Lebanon and tears south towards the Egyptian desert. Follow the storm: listen to God's voice in the thunder, in the thrashing branches of the storm-tossed trees, in the raging sound of a forest fire; hear him in the roar of an earthquake, in the flying leaves of a wood stripped of its foliage. Imagine the greatest havoc with which the world can be shaken – and then look up, for God sits enthroned above it all in a place of strength and peace; and not only is he in control of all these forces, he is actually speaking through them! Storms are not to be feared. They are not manifestations of the power of evil (for this psalm

---

[7] Luke 8:22–25.

too glances back at Canaanite tradition, which believed Baal to be the force present in a thunderstorm); they lie fully within God's sovereignty.

As so often, the message of this psalm is embedded within a carefully chosen poetic structure. The psalm is divided into three parts: the opening and closing sections are set in the throne room of God, providing an eternal framework for the middle section, which deals with events on earth. This circular structure enables the psalm to flow in a tripartite movement, from heaven to earth, eternity to time, and back again; from God as he is to human experience and back again. The psalm intends to rescue us from the confusion of a ruffed-up world, and take us on a journey into the eternal order which lies beyond it. Pray that he will bring us to that place of peace, David says.

That is what we might call the outer structure. But the psalm has an inner structure too, formed by the careful repetition of key words and phrases. There is no doubt that the emphasis here is on God, for the word 'Lord' echoes from beginning to end of the poem. In the introduction David repeats 'Lord' four times, once in each of the four phrases; and this is echoed in the conclusion. The same word 'Lord' comes ten more times in the middle section of the psalm, and within this section the phrase 'the voice of the Lord' is repeated seven times in seven verses. In a culture where harmonious numerical patterns were regarded as having special significance, this careful repetition has a specific job to do. Not only does it keep our attention firmly fixed on God, but it invites us to recognise that the order of the psalm reflects the order inherent in the universe itself – an eternal order into which one day we too will be fully and finally drawn.

There remains, of course, a slight conundrum. We are used to thinking about God as a kindly figure, someone who leads us into green pastures and invites us to lie down by still waters. For us God is more daffodils and lambs, perhaps, than hurricanes and forest fires. And yet this psalm says quite clearly that hurricanes and fires are also an expression of the voice of God. It's a challenging thought but, if we follow our principle of digging in the difficult places, perhaps a creative one. We now know that life on earth depends on the daily movements of continents, tectonic plates, ocean currents and wind patterns. Volcanoes spew out new land even as seas and rivers erode it. The moon tugs not just at the tides but at the land itself, which bulges and subsides daily beneath our feet. Trees photosynthesise sunlight into oxygen and food, and fires sweep through them to make space for more. Winds blow dust from the desert containing minerals and bacteria which bring life to far off places. Even viruses, it seems, are scraps of genetic material which play an essential role within every ecosystem.[8] The power which lies behind all life is the power of God himself, and it is neither tame nor predictable. God cannot be squeezed into a daffodil any more than he can be confined within a church or temple; he will, and must, speak with boundless and alarming force.

This leads me to the thought that perhaps this is true not just in the physical world, but also in the spiritual one. I may sometimes find myself swept up in stormy relationships or enveloped by frightening situations; I may give in to the selfish instincts which lie within me, and so bring trouble on myself. But maybe, just like the physical storms which sweep the world trailing life in their wake, maybe these spiritual tempests are in some way necessary to my life too. While God may not prevent storms from afflicting me, perhaps his voice can be heard within them; and through it all, David reminds me, I must remember that he can be trusted to give me strength, to bless me with peace. There is, after all, a certain security in knowing that God is not afraid to speak violently and act decisively. We may call to mind Psalm 97, which speaks in similar language of God's power over the earth: clouds and darkness are all around him, fire goes before him, his lightning makes the earth tremble and the mountains melt like wax. We do well to remember, says the psalmist, that the Lord is enthroned not only as king but also as judge – a judge who will deal as forcefully with those

---

8 See Lewis Dartnell, *Origins: How the Earth made us* (Bodley Head, 2018), and the fascinating 2019 BBC documentary *A Day in the Life of Earth*, presented by Hannah Fry. For viruses see John Lennox, *Where is God in a Coronavirus World?* (Good Book Company, 2020), p. 33, and **weforum.org/agenda/2015/11/are-viruses-actually-vital-for-our-existence**.

who wound his people as he does with the forces of evil embodied in Asaph's sea.

These stormy psalms take me back to my childhood wish to be happy. I haven't always been happy; in fact at times I've been extremely unhappy. There have been storms in my life – big black ones, ones which left me reeling, asking why me, why this? But into each of those storms God has spoken, often with great power; and through each one of them he has brought me peace. It hasn't been the peace of daffodils and lambs, the fluffy pain-free existence we so often crave for our children. Nor has it been peace while the storm was going on; I'm sure some people can manage to be peaceful in a storm, but I'm not one of them. My peace has mostly been the peace after the storm, the peace that comes when the rains have stopped, the clouds have been banished, and the sun shines on the wet streets. It's the peace that comes when the sparrows once again chirp in the bushes and human voices rise in song from the balconies. It's the peace which comes not from having successfully avoided the storms, which might yet at any time rear up their heads and engulf me, but from having weathered them, come through them, and found that the power which spoke into the chaos of creation has spoken in the same way into the chaos of my life. This, the Psalms tell us, is what we should be expecting.

Listening to God: the world as word

For too long, remarks theologian Brian McLaren, we have done theology indoors, our environment the city, our habitat the office, our tools the book and the screen. Working this way does not require us to know that flowing rivers, vast oceans, or swirling galaxies exist – but they do, and however helpful our urban insights, they must at best be incomplete. Is it not time, he asks, to get our theology out of doors, to imagine a wilder theology that arises under the stars and planets, a theology that resonates with the turning seasons and rhythmic tides of the natural world?[9]

The psalmists agree with him. 'The heavens are telling the glory of God; and the firmament proclaims his handiwork,' declares Psalm 19. 'You make the gateways of the morning and the evening shout for joy,' adds Psalm 65. 'In his hand are the depths of the earth; the heights of the mountains are his also, and we are the people of his pasture,' explains Psalm 95. 'You have established the earth, and it stands fast – all things are your servants,' announces Psalm 119.[10]

Emboldened by these thoughts, I strengthen my resolve to look for God out of doors. I reflect that the created world has always been seen in some sense as a language; if the voice of the Lord speaks the storm in Psalm 29, so the Word of the Lord had spoken the world in the first place: 'In the beginning was the Word, and the Word was with God, and the Word was God,' St John says, adding a new dimension to what we had always known – that each chapter of the creation story of Genesis begins with the magical words 'And God said'.[11] The world, it seems, is God's language, spoken into the unfolding pages of the universe: 'By the word of the Lord the heavens were made,' Psalm 33 reminds us. I know from my long study of literature that every human author speaks in a voice which is unique, leaving their own markers in the pattern of their syntax, in the particular balance of the various parts of speech in their sentences – so much so that it is possible to identify the author of an anonymous piece simply by analysing the component parts of the style in which it is written. It makes sense, then, that we should try to get to know God by paying equally careful attention to the world he has spoken. A word, we realise, is to be understood not simply as a shape on the page or a sound in the air, but as a unit of communication, of revelation – in whatever form it comes.

As the centuries wore on, people adopted other metaphors to convey

---

9   *God Unbound: Theology in the wild* (Canterbury Press, 2019), pp. xiii–xv.

10   Psalms 19:1; 65:8; 95:4, 7; 119:90–91.

11   John 1:1.

the belief that the invisible God may be sought in the visible world he has made. In the twelfth century, Alan of Lille likened the world to a mirror, not a spoken expression but a visible reflection of the thoughts of God; in the 13th, scholar Vincent of Beauvais titled the opening volume of his great encyclopaedia *The Mirror of Nature*, structuring it as an extended commentary on the biblical account of the creation. Leaves and flowers crept onto the capitals and carvings of cathedrals, and symbolic meanings were attributed to birds and animals in art and literature. As the centuries passed, art moved increasingly out of doors, and artists sought to express the presence of God in their landscapes, representing the attributes of the Creator through very different styles of painting. John Constable painted gentle, ordered scenes, depicting the ripe cornfields and tranquil rivers which flow from the benevolent provision of God, while his more rugged contemporary William Turner sought to reflect God's mastery of the elements in the savage grandeur of storm and flood.[12] Each artist captures different aspects of the presence of God in creation – each revealing not only the character of God in his art, but also his own: an artist, human or divine, is always reflected in his work.

Theologians have taken things still further, suggesting that the connection between the material world and its creator is more profound than that of the work to its author or the mirror to the source. There is, they point out, not just a likeness but a deep spiritual affinity between visible and invisible reality, for the world we can see is woven on the same loom as the world we cannot, and the physical order of the universe is itself a representation of the divine realities which underpin it. 'Why is it not rational to suppose that the corporeal and visible world should be designedly made and constituted in analogy to the more spiritual, noble, and real world?' asked Jonathan Edwards in the 18th century.[13] 'There is no mere analogy, but an inward affinity, between the natural order and the spiritual order,' explained C.H. Dodd in his discussion of the parables of Jesus; he suggests that Jesus was using

---

12 See the discussion by Graham Usher, *The Places of Enchantment: Meeting God in landscapes* (SPCK, 2012), p. 20.

13 *Images or Shadows of Divine Things*, ed. P. Miller (Yale University Press, 1948), p. 44.

illustrations from the natural world not simply because they made convenient teaching aids, but because they pointed to fundamental spiritual realities.[14] Physical and spiritual reality blend into one, as God speaks to us through the world he has made.

With these thoughts filling my mind, I hasten outside. I have, if the truth be told, spent much of my life hastening outside, following the sentiments of pioneering 19th-century conservationist John Muir, who once confessed 'I only went out for a walk, and finally concluded to stay out till sundown, for going out, I found, was really going in.' Get up into the mountains and get close to God, Muir advised, observing that 'this glorious valley might well be called a church'. For Muir, God was definitely to be found out of doors: 'The glory of the Lord is upon all his works; it is written plainly upon all the fields of every clime, and upon every sky,' he reflected from the Yosemite valley; 'but here in this place of surpassing glory the Lord has written in capitals.'[15]

I too once found myself in a place where the Lord had written in capitals. I was 18, standing on a clear sunny morning with my father on the Point of Stoer in Sutherland, north-west Scotland. It was, I thought, the most beautiful view I had ever seen – and over 40 years later I think it still is. A whole world was scattered at our feet – the sparkling blue sea, the intricate indentation of the coastline, the distant peaks of ancient mountains smoothed and rounded over millennia. The Hebridean islands lay in an arc beyond the sea, so clear that we could make out the houses on the cliff tops: from Cape Wrath in the north down to the Uists in the south, the panorama stretched pin sharp for more than 100 miles. Within me rose a feeling I have had many times since, but never more intensely: the feeling of being visually drunk, overwhelmed with a beauty so intense that even as it poured in through my eyes it took my breath away. Where did all this beauty come from, I wondered;

---

14 *Parables of the Kingdom* (Nisbet, 1935), p. 21.

15 *John of the Mountains: The unpublished journals of John Muir*, ed. L.M. Wolfe (University of Wisconsin Press, 1979), p. 439; *John Muir: Spiritual writings*, ed. Tim Flinders (Orbis Books, 2013), p. 1; letter to his brother, 20 March 1870, in W.F. Badè, *The Life and Letters of John Muir* (Houghton Mifflin, 1924), p. 204.

who thought of this astonishing landscape? Over the next few years that feeling would lead me to a growing awareness of God, a God who would whisper gently across fields of ripe barley and invite me to soar with the circling buzzard, so that I too could begin to look with his eyes at the world he had made.

I do of course live and think indoors: my thoughts are stimulated by books and articulated with the aid of a computer. But these are my tools, not my home, and it is not through them that I most readily connect with God, for the most important characteristic of my study is its huge windows, the lime tree that pulses with life beyond them and the hills that roll into the distance behind; and the most important moments always come when I am out of doors. Sometimes God speaks through storms; but at other times it seems as if I can wrap the world around me, like a cloak generously woven for my delight and protection. Perhaps it is time to forget about the storms and thank the Lord for his goodness. Out of doors, I find that I can.

Seeing God: Psalm 8

Of all the Psalms, perhaps Psalm 8 is the one which draws our attention most firmly away from our own troubles, inviting us to focus instead on the God who created the world and provides for us through it. In Psalm 19, David does this by considering the sun; here in Psalm 8, it is the night sky which claims his attention. 'O Lord,' David gasps, 'how majestic is your name in all the earth! When I look at your heavens, the work of your fingers, the moon and the stars that you have established, what are human beings that you are mindful of them, mortals that you care for them? You have given them dominion over the works of your hands; you have put all things under their feet, all sheep and oxen, and also the beasts of the field, the birds of the air, and the fish of the sea, whatever passes along the paths of the seas. O Lord, how majestic is your name in all the earth!'

Twenty years after the drunken moment on the Point of Stoer, I found myself standing beneath the night sky in the village of Yaeda Chini, a tiny settlement of sticks and straw deep in the Tanzanian Rift Valley. Perhaps my senses were sharpened by the bit about the dominion over the beasts of the field, for we had been told that a lion had eaten a toddler only the night before, and we were to sleep under nothing more robust than a nylon tent; but the stars were extraordinary. Used to picking out the single points of Orion or the Plough at home, I found myself staring at whole galaxies, each one a mass of stars clustered together as densely as grains frozen in a celestial sandstorm. There are, I read later, three hundred thousand million stars in the Milky Way, and that night it seemed to me that I could see them all, stretched out above me in a stupendous, dusty ribbon of light. Many before me have been overwhelmed by the intensity of the sight and the immensity of the God who created it. 'One might think,' reflected Ralph Waldo Emerson in 1836, that 'the atmosphere was made transparent with this design, to give man, in the heavenly bodies, the perpetual presence of the sublime.' God's presence was not lost on Richard Holmes, writing a century later from rural France: 'I slept out under an outcrop of pines. Only once, waking, I drank two ice-cold mouthfuls of water from my can and, leaning back, saw the Milky Way astonishingly bright through the pine tops, and felt something indescribable – like falling upwards into someone's arms.'[16]

How does this work, I wondered. Islands and stars are, after all, made of nothing more than rock and gas; they have, in themselves, no power to move us. And yet as words spoken by God, as expressions of his thoughts and reflections of his being, they open up a conversation in which he becomes as immediate and real to us as any human interlocutor – indeed, in which he can reveal himself to us in the most unexpected and startling of ways. Perhaps this is what the ancients meant when they talked about the gods throwing thunderbolts; it is certainly what theologians mean when they speak of theophanies, biblical moments

---

16 Ralph Waldo Emerson, *Nature* (Penguin, 2008), p. 3; Richard Holmes, *Footsteps: Adventures of a romantic biographer* (Viking Press, 1985), p. 22.

in which God appears in sudden and tangible form – a burning bush, a moment of silence after a gale, the spring blossom of the almond.

'What is this force which causes me to see in a way in which I have not seen?' muses Bishop John Taylor. 'What makes a landscape or a person or an idea come to life for me and become a presence towards which I surrender myself? – for it surely was not initiated by me.' It is as if in every such encounter, he says, 'there has been an anonymous third party who makes the introduction, acts as a go-between, makes two beings aware of each other, sets up a current of communication between them.' This current of communication, this invisible go-between, Taylor suggests, is none other than the Holy Spirit, the Spirit of God – the same Spirit who hovered over the waters at the beginning of time as the world came into being.[17] The Spirit of God is the invisible thread which joins us, the world and God together. 'God is everywhere, isn't he, Mummy,' said my little daughter, accurately.

Finding a new rhythm: pilgrimage and the poetics of walking

Go for a walk, God had said. That wasn't difficult; I was brought up to walk. 'Time spent in reconnaissance is time never wasted,' my father would proclaim as he ordered himself up and down the mountains of central Italy during the war, wearing the same signature army boots and baggy shorts which would later become the hallmark of our family holidays. When I was six he led me to the summit of Cader Idris in Wales; my childhood was written not in the London suburbs where we lived, but in the watery marshes of Suffolk and the trackless paths of the Scottish Highlands.

As I look back now, I realise that walking is more than a leisure activity: walking is what people do, and have always done. Walking is our

---

17 *The Go-Between God: The Holy Spirit and Christian mission* (SCM Press, 1972), ch. 1.

natural rhythm, the rhythm created for us by God himself, who walked in the garden of Eden each day at the time of the evening breeze. And so I too must walk. I walk as our ancestors once walked out of Africa and made their home in distant lands; I walk as the Israelites walked from captivity to the Promised Land; I walk as Jesus walked from village to village in Palestine. I walk as the people of Africa still walk today, with a slow, flowing, two-mile-an-hour motion along the paths and tracks which take them about their daily business. Just once, I walked along one of the ancient dreamtracks of the Brinja-Yuin people of Australia. As I ponder the Psalms, each morning I write, and each afternoon I walk – behind the house and up into the Mendips, or a few miles down the road and out onto the Somerset Levels. As I walk, I think; as I think, I pray; and often it seems to me that God walks beside me.

Walking is not just the natural rhythm of people, but also of poetry. It's said that Wordsworth could compose only as he walked, the rhythm of his steps creating the regularity of his verse. Writing in iambic pentameter, the alternation of stressed and unstressed syllables falling into the five 'feet' which make up each line, the feet of the poet would pace out the feet of the verse. Returning one sunny September day from a walk along the River Itchen, his contemporary Keats wrote an ode to autumn in the same iambic pentameter. I tried matching it to my own step as I walked – 'Season of mists and mellow fruitfulness, close-bosom friend of the maturing sun,' I proclaimed as I marched. It fitted perfectly. Thomas De Quincey calculated that Wordsworth, famous for his walking, had by the age of 65 covered up to 180,000 miles – many of them here in Somerset alongside his sister Dorothy and fellow poet Samuel Coleridge. He was, as it happens, the first to use the word 'pedestrian'.[18]

As I delve further into the Psalms, I find that some of them were composed to be sung whilst walking. Titled 'Songs of Ascent' (the word 'ascent' also meaning 'steps'), they are known today as the Pilgrim

---

18 David Wright (ed.), *Recollections of the Lake Poets* (Penguin, 1970), p. 135. See also Merlin Coverley, *The Art of Wandering: The writer as walker* (Oldcastle Books, 2012), p. 102.

Psalms, and numbered 120 to 134 in the Psalter. Thought to have been sung by pilgrims as they travelled towards Jerusalem each year to attend the major feasts of the religious calendar, these psalms are short, memorable and often joyful in their anticipation of the blessings to come. They have the rhythmic structure characteristic of all the psalms, and we hear the beat of the pilgrims' feet echoing not from word to word as in English poetry, but from line to line. Designed to be repeated antiphonally, we can imagine a small group dividing into two, some singing the first line of each pair, others echoing with the words of its partner. At least once, Jesus was among them, as he walked with his parents towards Jerusalem, aged twelve, for the Passover feast.[19]

Today these Pilgrim Psalms take their place in our pattern of daily prayer. Listening to them once on retreat, it seemed to me that the rhythm of walking is built not just into the Psalms but into life itself. The regularity of our feet follows the regularity of our breathing, and our breathing follows the alternating pattern of night and day, winter and summer, rain and sun. It's not unlike the rhythm of the sea, I thought; it feels as if I were back on the Suffolk beach of my childhood, hearing the waves beating onto the shore, withdrawing with a sigh over the pebbles, only then to surge forward again. As we recited the Psalms morning and evening, the words came and went; too many to take in properly, but adding up to a kind of bathing, a kind of sea-ness, immersion, and the feeling that life is about big things rising up, and pain leaching away. Perhaps this is why we walk: away from ourselves and into a pattern which is bigger than we are, reassuring in its repetitions, carrying us step by step towards God with the same certainty with which the sea breathes in and out upon the shore, and breath rises and falls within our own bodies. The Psalms, says philosopher Frédéric Gros, are the scanned realisation of faith in the body's movement.[20]

---

19 Luke 2:41–51. The Pilgrim Psalms are also known as Gradual Psalms (taken from the Latin title *canticum graduum*, degree or step).
20 Frédéric Gros, *A Philosophy of Walking* (Verso, 2015), p. 212.

Walking towards God: Psalm 125

'Those who trust in the Lord are like Mount Zion, which cannot be moved, but abides forever. As the mountains surround Jerusalem, so the Lord surrounds his people,' Psalm 125 begins. 'It is good sometimes to take the Psalter out of doors,' says poet Malcolm Guite, 'away from home and church, and recite it on a journey, in the midst of an open landscape.'[21] Having begun my day with the psalm and its commentary, I decided to take his advice. Spending a few summer days in a little town in the Cotswolds, I caught the train to Kingham and walked back along the Oxfordshire Way, some eleven miles through fields and woods, past streams and churches and old abbeys, over bridges and railway lines, beneath skylarks pouring their trembling song from the distant sky and fan-tailed kites quartering the meadows in search of food, past goldfinches jingling in the hedgerows. I ate my lunch beside the River Evenlode, beneath a great old oak tree and just beyond a row of whispering white poplars. As the sun warmed my body I thought about Mount Zion and the hills which surround Jerusalem, and imagined myself walking towards them. What would it have been like to walk as a pilgrim to Mount Zion, the highest point in the ancient city of Jerusalem and the hill on which the temple was built, I wondered – knowing that when you got there you would join a throng of others in a great festival of thanksgiving? And what would it have been like to cross the hill ranges which surround the city on every side, and then to walk down into the city itself, cradled safely among them?

And then I thought, what about the promises which cheer the pilgrims as they walk? 'The sceptre of wickedness shall not rest,' chant the first group of pilgrims; 'on the land allotted to the righteous,' echo the second. 'Do good, O Lord, to those who are good,' sing the first group; 'and to those who are upright in their hearts,' respond the second. 'Peace be upon Israel,' they conclude together as they bring their short song to a close. Is this promise not for me too, I asked myself; the promise

---

21 Commentary on Psalm 125, *Reflections on the Psalms* (Church House Publishing, Aimer Media, 2015).

of protection which the Lord offers to his people, and which is so vivid and tangible in this image of a resting place on a single hill which is itself surrounded by other hills? I began to imagine myself encircled by mountains as I continued my journey across the fields and paths of England; and I too became just a little bit of a mountain, a mountain which cannot be moved, a mountain enclosed by a protective ring of other mountains.

A couple of years ago I met Helen. Bolder than me, Helen had decided to follow one of the oldest Christian pilgrimage routes, walking 600 miles over the Pyrenees to Compostela. She had a particular reason: recently widowed, she had lost both her savings and her home. Her husband had collapsed one day and died; he had not got round to updating his will, and it turned out that everything he and Helen had built up in their 20 years together now belonged to someone else – who intended to take it. After two years struggling with grief, ill with resentment and anger, Helen decided to follow the ancient pilgrim path. Walking alone from wayside cross to cross, accepting hospitality from strangers on the way, she gathered a stone at each one and left it at the next, stopping beside every cross to pray. She returned home with a new sense of freedom; it felt, she said, as if she had physically deposited her burdens with the stones at the foot of those little crosses.

The Pilgrim Psalms are composed specifically to be sung as they are walked. But in a sense walking is the dominant theme of the entire Psalter. The Psalms take us on a journey; and they take us on foot. Twenty-three of them speak of walking: I walk before God, I walk in his truth, I walk with integrity, I walk in his ways, and yet I walk too through dark valleys, I walk in the midst of trouble. In 19 more the psalmist talks about his feet: although his feet stumble, they have not slipped, for thanks to the Lord his feet are like the feet of the deer; his feet are set upon a rock. In eleven psalms he speaks of the steps he takes along the way, and in 16 he refers to the path he takes on his journey through life. The whole Psalter is conceived as a journey undertaken on foot, a map of the difficulties and the joys which we encounter as we make our way towards God – and this is the most frequent image of all, for no fewer than 37 of the Psalms talk about the need to find the right way.[22] 'Suddenly it [all] comes to life,' continues Malcolm Guite; 'and one realizes how deeply the sights and sounds that meet the wayfarer inform the psalms, as all those prayers for the right path, the firm footing, the lamp for our feet, come into their own.'[23]

Walking through history: Psalm 136

Watching ocean waves crash onto the shore, feeling the power of a hurricane, gazing at distant stars and mountains – these are all experiences on which we can draw as we try to get our heads round the power and provision of the God who hovers behind them. But it is as we walk across the land that God has created for us that our conversation with him moves on to a deeper level, for the whole of human history is embedded in the landscape through which we pass. When Jesus walked with his family to Jerusalem to remember the people's deliverance from Egypt at the Passover, he was walking through a landscape which was not just geographical, but profoundly historical. Throughout the Old Testament, land is conceived not simply as an entity in itself, but as the locus for an ongoing conversation between a people and their God. God's relationship with his people begins in a garden, continues with expulsion, migration and enslavement, evolves through a long desert journey into a new country, and reaches a crescendo as the pattern of exile, restoration and loss is repeated there too. Land remains the promise of the future: one day, as Psalm 102 suggests and the New Testament describes, God will create a new city in a new heaven and a new earth, where those who remain faithful to him will find a permanent home. So for the psalmists, land is not just scenery or environment, as it so often is for us. Land is not what's

---

[22] 'Walking' psalms (NRSV): 15, 23, 26, 37, 42, 43, 48, 55, 56, 68, 78, 81, 82, 84, 86, 89, 101, 115, 116, 119, 128, 138, 142. 'Feet' psalms: 2, 8, 17, 18, 22, 25, 31, 40, 47, 56, 58, 66, 68, 73, 105, 115, 116, 119, 122. 'Step' psalms: 17, 18, 37, 40, 44, 56, 57, 73, 74, 85, 119. 'Path' psalms: 1, 8, 16, 17, 23, 25, 27, 57, 77, 78, 85, 110, 119, 139, 142, 143. 'Way' psalms: 1, 2, 5, 10, 17, 18, 25, 27, 32, 35, 36, 37, 39, 44, 50, 51, 67, 68, 73, 77, 80, 81, 86, 91, 95, 101, 103, 107, 119, 125, 128, 138, 139, 142, 143, 145, 146.

[23] *Reflections on the Psalms*.

coincidentally under the pilgrims' feet as they walk towards God; it's what their relationship with him is actually about, embedded in the covenant promise God had given to Abraham at the beginning of their history.[24] If we are to do full justice to the Psalms, we must learn to walk in a different way.

Like Psalms 74, 29 and 8, Psalm 136 sets the scene for our prayers by placing our relationship with God firmly in the context of the creation of the earth at the beginning of time. But unlike his predecessors, this psalmist continues the story, adding human beings into the landscape God has created, and remembering the way he has walked with them through it, fashioning it according to their needs. He begins his recital by celebrating God's work in creation: God made the heavens, spread the earth on the waters, created sun, moon and stars, he sings. He then moves on to thank God for his continued presence in the life of the people throughout history – a history written in the valleys, deserts and fields of the places through which they have passed. He tells how God brought his people out from Egypt, leading them across the Red Sea, through the wilderness, and out into a new land which became their own, striking down kings and defeating pagan peoples in order to release it to them.[25] This recital of God's work in creation and through time is introduced and concluded by an outpouring of thanks echoed after every new point: 'for his steadfast love endures forever; his steadfast love endures forever; his steadfast love endures forever…'

We aren't used to thinking like this. Our sense of collective identity is weak, our grasp of history is poor, and relatively few of us still have a direct relationship with the land on which we live. Our trips to the countryside are motivated by the desire to seek relaxation in places known for their beauty; we go as visitors, seeing only what is there today, unaware of what is past. And yet the more I read the Psalms, the more I realise that every landscape is a carrier of human history – and

---

24 For the new heaven and new earth see Isaiah 65:17; 2 Peter 3:13; Revelation 21:1; for the promise to Abraham see Genesis 15:18.

25 See also Psalm 68, where David offers a powerful reminder of how it was through his authority over the created world that God was able to make this provision for them.

therefore of the gospel spoken into that history. And so I find myself prompted to engage more closely with the landscape around me, wanting to restore the continuity I have lost, wanting to connect not just with the God who made the land on which I live, but with the people who have walked here before me and whose stories are written into its contours. For the people of the Old Testament, as Walter Brueggemann observes, land *is* history.[26]

Fifteen years ago we moved to Somerset. Having lived most of my life in cities, I found myself for the first time in a landscape whose history stretches visibly back far beyond that of its buildings. As I began to walk in this new country, it was borne in on me that even here, far from the Holy Land, God did not create and then remain silent; that this landscape, just like theirs, carries embedded within it the record of a conversation that stretches back over millennia. How would the psalmist have celebrated God's creative presence in the ancient limestone hills of the Mendips, I wondered? For this too is an ancient landscape, created over hundreds of millions of years through volcanic eruptions, river depositions and the slow settling of marine sediments, all folded together by the shifting of the continents into the hills which now rise behind our house. To the south the scene is quite different; the peats and clays of the Somerset Levels offer a rolling panorama of field and marsh, created millions of years later by the rise and fall of the sea, the settling of muds and sands, and the growth and decay of vegetation. It's punctured still by the scattered hills and tors which stand like islands in a green valley – one of which, pleasingly, was chosen as the symbol of England and Englishness in the opening ceremony of the 2012 Olympic Games.

And how would the psalmist have chosen to recall the people who have walked through this landscape, adapting their lives to its provisions, learning to shape it in an ongoing conversation with the one

---

[26] 'Land is history with Yahweh. It is never contextless space. It is always a place where memories of slavery and manna are recalled and where hopes of fidelity and well-being are articulated. Land is always where Israel must come to terms with the Lord of memories and hopes.' *The Land: Place as gift, promise, and challenge in biblical faith* (Fortress Press, 2002), p. 55.

who made it? Often I have carried my own troubles up into these hills, hoping to walk and talk with God; often I have been comforted by the overwhelming sense that whole communities have walked here before me. Modern humans have lived in Somerset since the end of the last Ice Age, and you can still clamber down into Britain's oldest burial chamber, created 10,000 years ago in a cave known as Aveline's Hole, deep in a limestone gorge in the heart of the Mendips. Four thousand years later a new wave of settlers arrived from the east, bringing with them strange ritual practices which have left their traces high on the hills in the form of Neolithic burial chambers, henge monuments and standing stones. If you scramble up the ancient path which climbs from Aveline's Hole onto the plateau above, you find yourself emerging a few thousand years later still into a large rectangular Bronze Age enclosure, whose walls can still be seen humped beneath the bracken, and whose people lie beneath the round barrows scattered in mysterious lines and clusters across the hills to either side.

Walking on through history, I wander from the plateau onto summits and promontories, over earthen ramparts into the grassy centres of Iron Age hillforts created in the last millennium of the pre-Christian era, and still there today – over 70 of them in Somerset alone, and three within walking distance of our house. Down on the Levels these same people created lake villages, building wooden houses and crafting oak canoes to replace the ancient wooden trackways – again the oldest we have – which had served their forebears until submerged by the rising waters. These peoples too had their own religious practices, glimpsed in the evidence of cremations and the discovery of sunken votive offerings. These, I reflect, were Somerset's Canaanites, peoples who lived here, worshipping unknown gods, long before the gospel first came to this land.

As the centuries rolled on, other peoples and cultures came and went, each leaving their own marks on the land. Some of them brought the Christian faith, and by the seventh century Somerset was part of the Christian kingdom of Wessex under the Saxon King Ine. Villages grew up in the shadow of the hills where the water which runs through the porous rock emerges in natural springs, and in the eighth century a church was built beside the wells which gave our town its name, and which still pour out four million gallons of fresh water daily. But then trouble came, of a kind which would have been only too familiar to the psalmists: a violent invasion by a hostile pagan people. In 798 the Vikings landed on the coast of Northumberland and began a century of pillage, destroying churches, looting monasteries, and reducing the people by now known as English to servitude. In 871 a Danish army swept down into the west, threatening to overwhelm Christian Wessex.

Many of my walks take me down onto the Somerset Levels, and a few years ago I discovered the little island of Athelney, now surrounded by farmland, but restored to its island state whenever the rushing waters of winter spill over the river banks and flood the fields. It was here that King Alfred took refuge from the advancing Danes, and from here that he led his forces to victory, baptising their leader Guthrum afterwards in the little church at Aller, where a Saxon font stands to this day. To secure the fragile peace thus obtained, Alfred ordered small fortified towns to be built and established a palace for himself at Cheddar, beside what is now the Kings of Wessex secondary school. Convinced that the heathen invasion was a sign of God's anger, and realising that the well-being of the people would depend on a renewed commitment to live in accordance with the will of God, Alfred embarked on a programme of Christian education, personally overseeing the translation into English of key parts of the Old Testament, including the Psalms, and organising the copying and distribution of texts such as Bede's *Ecclesiastical History of the English People*, which sets out the divine purpose in history in much the same way as the chronicles of the Old Testament.[27] As prosperity grew, abbeys were founded on the fertile floodplain, farms established with their tithe barns and fish houses, and village churches constructed from stone quarried in the hills. Alfred, a man of deep faith, had laid the foundation for what was to become England, securing its future as a Christian country.

---

27 The story of the conquest is told by Alfred's contemporary and biographer Asser in his *Life of Alfred*. See also **britannica.com/biography/Alfred-king-of-Wessex**.

The people of Somerset have been forced to their knees many times since then, and the evidence of natural disasters, bloody battles and threatened invasions is written just as clearly into the landscape in the centuries which separate us from Alfred. But for me it's these two periods in particular which stand out: the prehistoric societies of the Mendip hills, and the early Christian kingdom of the Somerset Levels – as if in the marks they left I find translated not simply the words of the Psalms, but also the experiences of which they sing. Who is God, I ask myself, this God to whom the psalmists invite us to pour out our pain and our praise? Surely he is the one who created this landscape of hills and moors, far though it is from Jerusalem; surely he is the one who, here as there, has watched a succession of peoples find their place within it; surely he too is the one who gave it to a determined king who honoured him and whose people thanked him through the building of towers and the casting of bells, and whose help they have sought ever since in times of natural disaster and enemy threat. Perhaps the psalmists speak not just for their own times and their own people, but for all of us; perhaps they trace the universal themes of divine creation, human struggle, and the need to depend upon God which are to be found in every culture and every place, and which I find written into the landscape of Somerset. Landscape, Anne Whiston Spirn has pointed out, 'is a literature of lived life', the sum of countless dialogues; if I am to engage fully with the Psalms I must learn to read their story in the language of my own place.[28]

As I allow the psalmist to draw my attention towards the historical landscape in which I live, I find that my perspective changes. I begin to draw closer to the God who reveals himself to me through the world he has created, sometimes in whispers and reflections, sometimes in capital letters; I begin to think about those who have lived here before me, and I learn to listen to their voices too. I discover that there is something deeply restorative about gazing at a distant galaxy, or standing in the middle of a Bronze Age enclosure, or contemplating a small Saxon font. It occurs to me that my own rather fleeting desires and fears may

---

28 *The Language of Landscape* (Yale University Press, 1998), pp. 40, 81.

be more of a lens than a reality; that there is a wider perspective to be sought. Having acknowledged my pain and committed myself afresh to God, I find that I have now begun to listen to his voice, knowing that the conversation which he has sustained with his people throughout history continues today in me. As I do these things, I am reminded of the words once spoken by St Paul to the Athenians:

> The God who made the world and everything in it, he who is Lord of heaven and earth, does not live in shrines made by human hands, nor is he served by human hands, as though he needed anything, since he himself gives to all mortals life and breath and all things. From one ancestor he made all nations to inhabit the whole earth, and he allotted the times of their existence and the boundaries of the places where they would live, so that they would search for God, and perhaps grope for him and find him – though indeed he is not far from each one of us.[29]

God, as the psalmists knew, is to be found out of doors.

---

29 Acts 17:24–27.

5

Connecting with God

God gave Solomon very great wisdom, discernment, and breadth of understanding as vast as the sand on the seashore... He composed three thousand proverbs, and his songs numbered a thousand and five. He would speak of trees, from the cedar that is in the Lebanon to the hyssop that grows in the wall; he would speak of animals, and birds, and reptiles, and fish. People came from all the nations to hear the wisdom of Solomon.

1 KINGS 4:29–34

King Solomon was the son and successor of David; it was during his reign that the great temple was built in Jerusalem, where many of the psalms that have come down to us were first composed and sung. Solomon was renowned as a poet and revered for his wisdom: the book of Proverbs, the Song of Solomon and Ecclesiastes are attributed to him, as are (less plausibly) the apocryphal book of Wisdom and two much later collections known as the Psalms of Solomon and the Odes of Solomon. Just two of the psalms in the Psalter bear his name, Psalms 72 and 127, but his legacy lives on in the references to plants, animals and birds which echo throughout the five books – for it was from the natural world, the historian of 1 Kings tells us, that Solomon first drew his wisdom. Even Jesus recalls him, urging his hearers to calm their anxieties by considering God's provision for the lilies of the field, more gloriously clothed, he pointed out, than the great Solomon himself.[1]

So it is with Solomon that we enter the next stage of our journey. We have lifted our eyes from the horizon of our own troubles and turned our attention to the God who created the world and whose longstanding

---

1 Matthew 6:25–30.

presence within it is reflected in the landscape which surrounds us. We have recognised him as a God of power and promise. We are ready now to draw closer.

The Psalter opens with a simple image: that of the tree. Think of a tree, Psalm 1 urges: a tree planted by streams of water, a tree whose leaves do not wither even in times of drought, a tree which bears fruit in the appointed season. Model your life on that of the tree, the psalmist advises; draw spiritual refreshment as you meditate on the law of the Lord – do not be like those who follow the path that sinners tread, for they are lifeless husks blown away by the winter winds. The message is clear: that tree is you; if you want to live wisely and well, root yourself in God, and he will sustain you. This single image sets the tone for the entire Psalter, and will determine how we respond to everything that follows.

The image of the tree returns in Psalm 52, where David compares himself to a green olive tree standing in the temple; and again in Psalm 92, which likens the righteous to the palms and cedars which flourish in the house of the Lord. But it is Psalm 65 which sweeps us from the focus on a single tree into a broader vision of an entire world sustained by God. We know now that a tree does not stand alone: linked to its neighbours by a complex network of roots, partnered with fungi and bacteria and dependent on its relationship with insects and birds, every tree is part of an entire ecosystem – an ecosystem first described in the book of Genesis, where God creates light and darkness, sky and sea and land, plants and fish and birds and animals – and only then, man and woman. This is the world I have made for you, God says; this is the web of life created to sustain you; this is the context within which you will know me.[2]

---

2   For the interdependence of trees see Peter Wohlleben, *The Hidden Life of Trees* (William Collins, 2017).

The landscape comes to life: Psalm 65

Psalm 65 is attributed to David. Locating himself in the temple, David opens with praise: happy are those, he says to the Lord, whom you bring to live in your courts, for in you we find forgiveness, deliverance and salvation. But David does not stay in the temple. Sweeping outwards from the temple precincts to the earth itself, he affirms his trust in God, honouring him as the creator who established the mountains and silenced the roaring of the seas, and whose presence is marked each day by the rising and setting of the sun. Then David turns his attention to the land on which he lives, celebrating the fact that God actively and constantly sustains both the land itself and everything which inhabits it. This is not a God, David reminds himself, who created heaven and earth only then to withdraw, job done; this is a God who remains fully engaged with the life he has brought into being – a God who visits the earth and enriches it, softening it with showers and blessing its growth; a God who clothes the meadows with flocks of sheep, decks the valleys with grain and crowns the year with bounty. Finally, with a great leap of poetic insight, David notes that as God blesses the landscape, so it comes to life. Responding to him with cries of thanks, the gateways of the morning and the evening rejoice, the hills gird themselves with gladness, and the meadows and valleys shout and sing for joy.

And so David invites us to take another step forward. You know that God is the all-powerful creator of heaven and earth, he says, and you know that he has shaped the landscape on which you stand; but remember too that he is present in every running stream, in every flock of sheep, in every ear of wheat. The world is alive, and you are part of it: it is time to join in the conversation, for God is with you. This psalm may have begun as a conventional song of praise in the temple, but by the end David has been caught up into a magical flight of fancy over a land which responds with its own chorus of voices. This is not just a temple rite, a dutiful song of praise for its own sake; it is pure, imaginative poetry.

Can we too learn to see the world this way, as a magical, living landscape in which we are no more than a small part of a much larger reality? Perhaps we need to stop being so practical and grown up when we step outside, and embrace the vision of the poet. Children make good teachers, I discovered one autumn as I walked along a narrow path on an overcast day, my seven-year-old daughter padding along beside me. For me, the path was a path. For her, it was an enchanted track through a living forest, where glistening silver birches dropped leaves of liquid amber, red fungal treasure glowed in the shadows and snakes hissed in the waters of mountain streams. 'This is a good walk, Mum,' she said happily; 'you get to pretend it's a jungle.' Perhaps, I thought, every walk is a good walk, if only we have ears to hear and eyes to see.

Reading what God has written

Solomon had become wise, the Bible tells us, through paying attention to the living world. Born before most of the Hebrew scriptures had been composed or written down, he had learned, to use a later metaphor, to read the book of nature. 'Let your book be the divine page to which you listen; let your book be the universe that you observe,' advised Augustine in the fifth century as he commented on the Psalms. 'Only those who know how to read and write can read the pages of Scripture, while everyone can read from the book of the universe.'[3]

It was an image which gained wide currency. 'The whole physical world is a kind of book written by the finger of God,' declared Hugh of St Victor in the twelfth century; 'each particular creature is like an image which reveals the invisible things of God's wisdom.'[4] Solomon had known that 'through the grandeur and beauty of the creatures we may, by analogy, contemplate their Author', as the book of Wisdom

---

3 *Enarrationes in Psalmos*, commentary on Psalm 45. Reading was done aloud at this time – so when Augustine says listen, he means it.
4 *Eruditionis Didasalicae*, Bk VII ch. iv, from Migne PL 176 col 814, original abbreviated.

puts it.[5] The psalmists had understood this instinctively, for they fill their poems with plants, animals, birds, reptiles and fish. Sixty-eight psalms, nearly half the total, offer over 130 references to the creatures of the living world, with more than 50 distinct species mentioned.[6] The images serve different functions: some are there simply as indications of the diversity of God's creation, while others offer living testimony to his provision. Some help us to understand God's concerns, others enable us to express our own. Some serve as models for our guidance; others as a stimulus to praise. So common are these images and metaphors that they become a kind of thought language of their own – the psalmists do not simply illustrate through creation; they *understand* through creation. And so the natural world becomes both a tangible channel for God's voice, and a metaphorical one for our response.

The person best known for drawing the creatures of the living world into his prayers was St Francis. Looking not to the power and pomp of the church but to flowers and birds for the basis of his spirituality, Francis would enter each day into animated conversation with God. 'Who could tell the sweetness which he enjoyed in contemplating in his creatures the wisdom, power and goodness of the Creator?' wrote his biographer Thomas of Celano; 'he discerned the hidden things of creation with the eye of the heart.'[7] Within a generation, Franciscan theologian Bonaventure had written a treatise called *The Soul's Journey into God*. If you wish to learn to pray, he advised, you should follow the example of St Francis and start by meditating upon the creatures of the world, for they are signs set before us that we might know God.[8] Many have followed his guidance. In the 14th century Mother Julian

---

[5] Wisdom 13:5 (NJB).

[6] The formal classification of species came only with Carl Linnaeus in the 18th century, and the precise species referred to is sometimes difficult to determine. Others are named generically – e.g. fruit trees.

[7] *The Lives of St Francis of Assisi by Brother Thomas of Celano*, trans. A. G. Ferrers Howell (Methuen, 1908), First Life, ch. 29, para 80–81.

[8] 'All the creatures of the sense world lead the mind of the contemplative and wise man to the eternal God. For these creatures are shadows, echoes and pictures of that first, most powerful, most wise and most perfect Principle… vestiges, representations, spectacles proposed to us and signs divinely given' – *The Soul's Journey into God*, trans. E. Cousins (Paulist Press, 1978), p. 78.

famously meditated on a hazelnut, finding that it spoke to her of God as creator, protector and lover. The disciples of Ignatius of Loyola noted in the 16th century that 'even the smallest things could make his spirit soar upwards to God. At the sight of a little plant, a leaf, a flower or a fruit, an insignificant worm or a tiny animal, Ignatius could soar free above the heaven and reach through into things which lie beyond the senses.' A hundred years later, Sir Thomas Browne wondered why it is that we look so carelessly at the hieroglyphics of nature, 'and disdain to suck divinity from the flowers'. In the 19th century, naturalist Richard Jefferies not only listened to God speaking in this way, but adopted the language as his own: 'Through every grass-blade in the thousand, thousand grasses; through the million leaves, veined and edge-cut, on bush and tree; through the song-notes and the marked feathers of the birds; through the insects' hum and the colour of the butterflies; through the soft, warm air, the flecks of clouds dissolving – I used them all for prayer.'[9]

This has been my experience too. I was brought up not in the church but out of doors – not just on our family holidays, but in the long, semi-wild suburban garden which was my primary locus of being as a child. Intrigued by worms, terrified by stag beetles, stung by bees, armed with bows and arrows made of golden rod and calmed by perfume created from rose petals, for me the garden was a place of adventure. I received no religious instruction either at home or at school, but my wonder at the natural world fostered the growing feeling that there must be more to life than met the eye. My suspicions were confirmed in the wilder landscapes of Scotland. There, with my parents and my brother, I tramped through bogs, pausing to examine the sundew and listening to the wild whistling of redshank and golden plover; I walked along paths above cliffs of screaming seabirds and watched white gannets plunge cigar-shaped into a blue sea where puffins swam with their pyjama-striped beaks; I gazed into caves made of hexagonal

---

[9] Mother Julian of Norwich, *Revelations of Divine Love*, eds H. Backhouse and R. Pipe (Hodder and Stoughton, 2009), p. 48; Ignatius of Loyola, quoted in Hugo Rahner, *Ignatius the Theologian*, trans. Michael Barry (Geoffrey Chapman, 1968), p. 23; Richard Jefferies, *The Story of My Heart: My autobiography*, eds B. Williams and T.T. Williams (Torrey House Press, 2014), p. 37.

basalt columns and marvelled at the green iridescent plumage of shags; I climbed mountains, collected raptor pellets, bird skulls, deer horns. On holiday in Suffolk I found a giant puffball the size of a rugby ball, and followed flocks of bearded tits pinging their way across beds of golden reed. At 16 I took up bird ringing, wondering at the red eyebrows of long-tailed tits with their football rattle calls, and gazing deep into the tawny eyes of owls. I spent nights with the mosquitoes in the fens and caught skylarks at dawn in the fields.

As the years rolled by, my suspicions shaped themselves gradually into a conversation. It was through a soaring buzzard that I first became aware that God was speaking directly to me; so clear was the message that I responded with the first prayer of my own. Later on I set about colouring my Bible green, carefully marking all the references to the natural world in an attempt to assemble the disparate pieces of my experience into a single jigsaw. I am not sure whether, like Solomon, this has made me wise; but it has undoubtedly been as I have gazed in astonishment at the living world that I have felt closest to God, most nearly able to hear his voice and to talk with him.

A new vocabulary of prayer

The psalmists use this natural language in a whole variety of ways. The faithful look to trees for guidance, and in them we find models of sustenance, fruitfulness and praise – whereas the wicked who overwhelm us are, spiritually speaking, like chaff dispersing on the wind, thorns burning in a fire, weeds withering on a rooftop. Our dependence on God is traced through a trail of ripe wheat, lush grass and heavily laden vines, our human fragility represented by the short-lived flowers of the field, our divinely appointed rulers anointed with the fragrance of aloe and cassia. We experience our enemies as raging lions, marauding dogs, sharp-horned wild oxen, ravaging boars, stinging bees and venomous snakes – but learn to regard them, spiritually speaking, as snails whose legacy is nothing more substantial than a trail of slime, and ourselves as nimble-footed deer guided over rocky terrain by the

Lord himself. The accuracy and realism of the psalmists' observations of plants and animals is made all the more striking by their distinct lack of expertise when it comes to fish. Willing to remind themselves that there are 'creeping innumerable things' in the sea, their land-locked experience offers them only the shapeless threats of mythical dragons and unknown sea monsters.[10]

If the Psalms open with the image of a tree, they even more frequently adopt that of a bird: doves, sparrows, swallows, owls, eagles, storks and ravens flock to the psalmist. They help him express his feelings to God: I am like an owl in the wilderness, a lonely bird on a rooftop, he laments as he tosses his way through a sleepless night; shelter me in the shadow of your wings, he pleads repeatedly – do not deliver the soul of your dove to the wild animals. As his prayers are answered, it is again to birds that he turns to convey his relief: 'We have escaped like a bird from the snare of the fowlers,' he gasps. His confidence growing, he invites us to consider that as the Lord strengthens his birds, so he will strengthen us: 'Your youth is renewed like the eagle's,' David reminds himself as he praises God for his mercies.[11]

Sometimes birds leave the realm of metaphor and take up residence among us as visible signs of God's goodness. For the author of Psalm 84, God's provision of nesting places for sparrows and swallows is a sign of his care. The psalm came unexpectedly to life for me in Zambia, where I was part of a small team teaching in an enormous, barn-like church. The first day had been hard going, but as we prayed together on the second morning we found ourselves reading from Psalm 84: 'My soul longs for the living God – even the sparrow finds a home, and the swallow a nest for herself at your altars. Happy are those who live in your house, ever singing your praise.'[12] As we walked into the church, a lesser striped swallow swooped over our heads. It had done what

---

10 Trees (Psalms 1, 52, 92, 96, 104, 128, 148); chaff (1, 35, 83), thorns (118), weeds (129); wheat (65, 72, 81, 147), grass (104, 147), vines (107, 128); flowers (103), fragrance (45). Lions (7, 17, 22, 35, 57, 58, 91), dogs (22, 59), wild oxen (22, 68), boar (80), bees (118), snakes (58, 91, 140), snails (58), deer (18). Sea creatures (74, 96, 104, 148).

11 Psalms 102 (owl); 17, 36, 57, 61, 91 (wings); 74 (dove); 124 (fowlers); 103 (eagle).

12 Summarised from Psalm 84:2–4.

the psalmist said – built its nest inside the building. It spent the whole day flying high above the rafters, from nest to altar and back again. We received it as a sign of God's presence, a promise of the blessing which unfolded more and more powerfully as the day wore on. Recognising that the swallow came as a message from God, I have learned now to ask for the bird, to accept the unexpected appearance of striped swallows, singing starlings and iridescent kingfishers as reassurance that God is indeed close at hand.

For many years now I have tried to follow the psalmist's lead and allow the living creatures of God's world to inform my prayers. Often I walk on the hills above the ancient limestone gorge of Cheddar. Up here I have witnessed the scything flight of hunting peregrines, and watched wild goats settling their head-butting disputes on the rocky crags which overlook the valley far below. There are rare wildflowers here, protected by the cliffs of the gorge: Cheddar pinks, and a unique species of yellow hawksbeard. Despite its beauty, this can be a tough environment. Walking there on a particularly torrid August day in the hottest summer for 40 years, I found myself in a landscape drained of colour, scorched autumn-brown, arid as the thoughts which had been rattling insistently inside my head since the arrival of the morning post. And yet even in this heat there were signs of life. Two green woodpeckers emerged from a hawthorn bush and flew with rapid wing beats into the stunted birches ahead; a pair of bullfinches flitted softly from tree to tree, their white rumps and shy calls giving them away; a jay looped across the path to drink at a newly restored dewpond. An uncomfortable letter, an unresolved conflict: how small these things seemed as I stood surrounded by the birds which have found sustenance in these ancient hills for generations. Never mind about the letter, I thought; I was enjoying, I suddenly realised, the sunlit peace of a late summer's day, in the presence of a God who provides for me in the most unpromising of circumstances. No wonder the swallows and sparrows of Psalm 84 twitter their songs of praise.

When things catch fire

'We are living in a world that is absolutely transparent, and God is shining through it all the time,' wrote Cistercian monk Thomas Merton. Poets, of course, have always known this. 'The world is charged with the grandeur of God,' observed Gerard Manley Hopkins; 'it will flame out, like shining from shook foil.' 'I have seen the sun break through to illuminate a small field,' mused R.S. Thomas; 'life is the turning aside to the eternity that awaits you.' 'Everything beckons to us to perceive it,' said Rainer Maria Rilke.[13]

Sometimes we whisper; sometimes we shout. It seems that God does too. Just as words can leap off a page, so trees and birds can thrust themselves upon us, bursting uninvited into our consciousness and demanding our attention. God has always spoken to prophets and poets in this way; pouring the results into their work, they have struggled to define their experience in words. There is a 'thisness' in things which connects them to God, said theologian Duns Scotus in the 13th century; an 'eachness', said W.H. Auden; a 'quiddity', said C.S. Lewis. Hopkins invented the word 'inscape', by which he meant 'God's utterance of himself outside himself'; James Joyce talked about an epiphany, and J.V. Taylor an annunciation.[14] Whatever you call it, it's when things catch fire, and God appears in a mighty cedar, or a soaring eagle, or a deer on the hills – and says something. 'Sometimes,' reflects Annie Dillard,

> God moves loudly, as if spinning to another place like ball lightning. God is, oddly, personal; this God knows. Sometimes en route, dazzlingly or dimly, he shows an edge of himself to souls who seek him, and the people who bear those souls, marvelling, know it, and see the skies carousing around them, and watch

---

[13] 'A life free from care' in C.M. Bochen (ed.), *Thomas Merton: Essential writings* (Orbis, 2000), p. 70; Gerard Manley Hopkins, 'God's Grandeur'; R.S. Thomas, 'The Bright Field'; Rainer Maria Rilke, 'Everything Beckons To Us' – all available online.

[14] See Michael Mayne, 'Hopkins and the inscape of things', *This Sunrise of Wonder* (Darton, Longman and Todd, 2008), ch. 17; James Joyce, *Stephen Hero* (Jonathan Cape, 1956), p. 218; J.V. Taylor, *The Go-Between God* (SCM Press, 1972), p. 12. The original concept comes from a phrase of Aristotle, via Thomas Aquinas, who translated it into Latin as *quidditas*.

cells stream and multiply in green leaves. He does not give as the world gives; he leads invisibly over many years, or he wallops for thirty seconds at a time.[15]

The Psalms encourage us to expect that he may wallop us too. Often I have found that he does.

Once, God spoke to me through a rising sun at dawn, and changed the course of my life; a few years later he spoke again through the twisting flight of a red kite, dancing above my head and asking a question. More recently, a few weeks after my father died, I was driving along a country lane near my home. As I rounded a corner I was greeted by a burning tree – not burning with flames, but burning, as the bush for Moses, with the presence of God – or so in that moment it seemed to me.[16] Like Moses, I screeched to a halt, reversed and got out for a better look. It was a birch tree, glowing with the deepest oranges and reds I had ever seen; God flaming out, like shining from shook foil. Look, I can still do this, he said: I am. Your father is with me.

At other times, God seems to speak just because he is, and that is what he does – as he spoke the world in the beginning, so he speaks it each day; and sometimes we get caught up in the conversation, as a reminder, perhaps, not to take things for granted. Two years ago, on holiday in Shetland, we woke one morning to find the land bathed in bright sunlight, the loch sparkling, the valley green. We drove to Lerwick, and boarded a boat which took us round the island of Bressay and out beneath the steep sea cliffs of Noss. Razorbills and guillemots stood precariously in rows high on the cliff face; gannets crowded white onto the ledges below, and puffins bobbed on the waves. We anchored beneath the cliffs, ate our sandwiches, and suddenly found ourselves in the middle of a feeding frenzy as the birds joined us for lunch. The air filled with gannets, plunging and diving for mackerel, folding themselves up and shooting pencil-like into the deep water,

---

15 *For the Time Being* (Vintage Books, 2000), pp. 167–68.
16 Exodus 3:1–6.

disappearing into a white mist of bubbles only to shoot back up seconds later, bursting through the surface, shaking their feathers, flying away from us and then back up, and round, and down again with the same explosive force. It was breathtaking; the most glorious five minutes, I think, of my entire life. All around us the cliffs were folded into ancient layers, the islands scattered like afterthoughts into the pounding waves, and the sea heaped itself up behind us as all too soon we sailed away, skuas gliding effortlessly behind us. The world is huge and beautiful and glorious, I thought breathlessly, stars still wheeling about my head: so much bigger than me, so magnificently astonishing that I am as nothing, just a small part of a reality I can scarce comprehend – and yet here it is, all displayed before me. The psalmist does not pretend that life is without its troubles; even here, the skuas harry the gannets to steal their catch, and the mackerel, perhaps, enjoyed the occasion less than I did. But it was the gannets that filled me with wonder that day, the gannets which live in some of the harshest conditions on earth, and yet are perfectly designed to flourish there. I am, said God, quite good at this – what was it that you wanted to say?

Psalm 104

The psalmists' evocation of the natural world reaches a climax in Psalm 104, one of the great creation texts of the Bible. The book of Genesis expresses the creation story as a myth, and the gospel of John will explore it as a philosophy; here the psalmist transforms it into a huge, soaring hymn of praise.

The psalm opens with an extended poetic meditation on the creation of the world by God: closely following the text of the first chapter of Genesis, the psalmist sings his way through the six days of creation – not simply recording the events, but bringing them one by one to life. In Genesis, the focus is on God: God speaks, things take shape, God is pleased. Here, the focus is on the things themselves, springing one by one to life like dead toys in a night nursery; the activity is theirs, carried

Connecting with God 101

in a stream of verbs which cascade from line to line as a whole world comes into being. 'Bless the Lord, O my soul,' the psalmist begins, getting into his stride with a flurry of metaphors. Here, God does not simply create the heavens and the earth: God is clothed with honour and majesty, wrapped in a garment of light; he stretches out the heavens like a tent, makes the clouds his chariot, rides on the wings of the wind.

Genesis records God's next task as the separation of sky from sea and sea from land. The psalmist renders this much more dynamically: God does not simply create the oceans, he covers the earth with a garment. He does not merely gather the sea, he issues a stream of instructions to the chaotic waters, which respond with a burst of compliant activity: they flee, rush away, rise up the mountains, run down to the valleys. Genesis tells us that God then made vegetation grow on the earth. The psalmist brings this together with the creation of birds and animals, and calls up the whole variety of nature in a series of vivid word pictures: the newly tamed waters gush out from the hills and flow in streams through the valleys, where wild asses quench their thirst and birds raise their voices in song. Cedars and firs grow strong and tall, and storks nest in their branches; goats and hyraxes find shelter in the mountains, cattle graze in the meadows, and wheat, olives and vines provide food and wine to strengthen human beings and gladden their hearts.

Returning to the fourth day of creation, the psalmist celebrates God's provision of sun and moon: the sun warms the earth by day, permitting people to labour in the fields, and the moon ushers in the cool of the night, when forest animals and lions emerge to seek their prey. Finally the psalmist turns his attention to the distant sea, where there are living things both small and great, and Leviathan (now tamed) plays in the waves. This is a conversation coming to life, the celebration of a whole natural system in which we are invited to rejoice for its own sake – noting that human beings do not make their appearance in this idyll until almost halfway through, when we take our place as just one small part of this bounteous, living landscape.

The most remarkable part of the psalm, though, is still to come. In case the profusion of verbs has not given it away, our attention is now drawn to the fact, as in Psalm 65, that all this activity is not confined to the past – it's not simply that God is the owner of the patent or the holder of the copyright for this world he has made, but that he is intimately present and active within it at every moment, sustaining what he has created, breathing it afresh each day as he breathed it at the beginning of time. The psalmist spells it out: all these creatures look to you, Lord, for their food – you open your hand, and they are filled with good things; you hide your face, and they are dismayed; you renew the face of the ground. The conversation is two-way, the relationship between Creator and created ongoing and reciprocal. 'God is creating the entire universe fully and totally in this present now,' concluded Meister Eckhart in the 14th century. 'The act of creation did not take place only in the beginning. It occurs at every moment,' affirms modern theologian Walter Pannenberg.[17]

But even that is not quite the end of the story. 'I will sing to the Lord as long as I live,' declares the poet as he draws to a close; 'may my meditation be pleasing to him.' Before he signs off, though, he has a request to make. Coming after such a sustained outpouring of thanks and praise, it is unexpectedly direct: 'Let sinners be consumed from the earth, and let the wicked be no more,' he prays. Pain is receding into the background, perhaps: but, as in Psalm 139, it is still there, and the psalmist takes the opportunity to remind God gently that we rely on him to provide us not just with bread and wine, but also with justice – for destructive intention resides not only in the unruly waters of the sea, but also in the depths of the human heart.

Returning to Genesis, we find that once God had finished the work of creation, he called Adam in for a chat – for one thing still remained. Presenting him in turn with every animal and every bird, God waited to see what Adam would call them; 'and whatever the man called every living creature, that was its name.'[18] Perhaps, for this God who spoke a

---

17 For Eckhart see Matthew Fox, *Creation Spirituality* (HarperSanFrancisco, 1991), p. 8; Walter Pannenberg, *Toward a Theology of Nature* (Westminster John Knox Press, 1993), p. 34.
18 Genesis 2:19.

world into being, a thing cannot truly exist until it has a name. Perhaps God simply wished to draw Adam's attention to the living creatures which surrounded him, and for which he was now responsible. In either event, close attention is what was required; the kind of attention that we find in the Psalms, and that one day will characterise the teaching of Jesus.

Allowing for some uncertainty in identification, between them the psalmists invite us to consider eight named species of bird, 13 species of animal, at least four of 'creeping things' (snakes, frogs, snails), and five of insects.[19] But the greatest attention is paid to plants, with no fewer than 21 kinds of tree, shrub, grass and flower pressed into service. Each one is chosen for its particular properties – strength, fragility, beauty, fragrance, cleansing, fruitfulness, or simply the shape of its foliage. Each one testifies to the abundant creativity of God; each one speaks to the psalmist and informs his prayers.

For much of my life, plants have been mostly nameless; my major preoccupation has been with birds. But a few years ago I put a wildflower app on my phone, blocked out some time for a retreat, and set off in the record-breaking heat of an English summer into the fields of Oxfordshire. Oxfordshire didn't seem to mind the heat: the limestone tracks shone white as they wound their way through fields of ripening barley and rye, the forest glades were clothed in cooling shade, and wayside flowers dotted the field edges. I began to look them up, and a whole new world opened up before me. In sunlit fields I found starry clusters of lady's bedstraw, once used for filling pillows and mattresses, and purple petalled mallow, and fragile spikes of spotted orchid. In shady lanes I came across clumps of green alkanet, small and hairy and blue flowered, introduced 300 years ago and used to make red dye; and white-laced hedge bedstraw, and delicate blue field scabious. I discovered plants traditionally used for healing: St John's wort, its golden petals bristling with tiny stamens, purple-headed

---

19 Five distinct Hebrew words are used for snakes, of which at least two are clearly generic. A helpful guide for plants is Michael Zohary's *Plants of the Bible: A complete handbook* (Cambridge University Press, 1982).

hedge woundwort, and stubby blue self-heal. I admired the long stalks of meadow cranesbill, its pointed seed heads earning its name; and rejoiced in red-splashed poppies, tall spikes of yellow agrimony, sturdy clumps of Russian comfrey, fragile clusters of common fumitory and a gloriously ragged knapweed; and creeping cinquefoil and bird's-foot trefoil, hemp agrimony and white campion. All just dotted about the place; flowers I had never previously noticed, all springing magically into being under my gaze – as if, by naming them, I had in some sense brought them to life.

For the rest, I could have been walking through the landscape of Psalm 104. A hare ran black-eared into the sunlight; a beautiful demoiselle damselfly hovered beside the river, its dark green wings cloaking a thin metallic body; a swan drifted into view and then disappeared. Sparrows chattered in the villages, house martins flitted between houses as they always have, and a red kite floated overhead, flicking its tail occasionally, the sun catching the white markings on the underside of its wings. Leaving the fields, I followed a path through the scattered remnants of the old Wychwood forest, where blackbirds and robins sang and nuthatches whistled as they flitted between the trees. The path through the forest was long and magnificent, dappled with sunlight and deserted except for a startled deer which sprang out of the undergrowth as I passed. Whitethroats jumbled their notes in the hedges, a beech tree exploded with rooks and jackdaws, flights of woodpigeons and stock doves clapped their wings in the fields, and three baby swallows perched on an arm of a stag-head oak, waiting noisily for their parents to fly past with a food parcel. I ate my lunch sitting on a dead tree stump, and thought how restorative the different shades and shapes of green are, how cheering the profusion of the flowers; it was immensely peaceful. It's good, I thought, to be part of this timeless bustle of life, to know that however fast some things seem to change, others never do, because they are all held together by something, or someone, who knows what he is doing.

As I respond to the psalmist's suggestion that I shift my attention to the living landscape of the world around me, my own inner landscape changes too. My understanding of God is enlarged, and my ability to enter into conversation with him enhanced – as if I am learning a whole new vocabulary in which he may speak to me, and in which I may respond to him. When I look for the first time at the lady's bedstraw, I receive it as a word which he has spoken, and which I embrace by learning its name – a simple name, but one which carries a reminder of the provision God has made for us through the abundance of his creation. My spirits rise; here is one tiny reason, surrounded by a myriad others, to give thanks to God. 'I am no botanist,' confessed novelist George Gissing in 1903, 'but I love to come upon a plant which is unknown to me, to identify it with the help of my book, to greet it by name when next it shines beside my path. No word in human language can express the marvel and the loveliness even of what we call the vulgarest weed, but these are fashioned under the gaze of every passer-by. Even in my gladness I am awed.'[20]

This, though, is not all, for I find that as these new words crowd into my brain, so others, less helpful, are forced into the background. The pressing concerns of life fade from my mind, and something altogether more wholesome takes their place. I am not, I discover, the first to find peace through the contemplation of plants. 'My aim is to find a simple and pleasant pastime which I can enjoy without effort and which will distract me from my misfortunes,' wrote the hapless Rousseau; 'it costs me neither money nor care to roam nonchalantly from plant to plant and flower to flower, examining them, comparing their different characteristics, discovering the reason and purpose of their varied structures, and to give myself up to the pleasure of grateful admiration of the hand that allows me to enjoy all this.'[21]

And so I learn to live in the present. I discover that I, and my interests, are not the focus and point of reality; I accept the psalmist's reminder that if God himself took pleasure in the world that he had created,

---

20 *The Private Papers of Henry Ryecroft* (CreateSpace, 2016), p. 8.
21 *Reveries of the Solitary Walker*, trans. Peter France (Penguin, 1979), Walk 7, p. 115.

so should I. It seems a long time ago that I was floundering my way through the despairing cries of Psalm 88.

Medicine for our souls

Ever since Solomon encouraged his subjects to pay attention to the natural world, people have sought relief from their troubles out of doors. 'I think that I cannot preserve my health and spirits, unless I spend four hours a day at least sauntering through the woods and over the hills and fields,' confessed Henry Thoreau. 'I have two doctors, my left leg and my right,' explained G.M. Trevelyan; 'my thoughts start out with me like blood-stained mutineers debauching themselves on board the ship they have captured, but I bring them home at nightfall, larking and tumbling over each other like happy little boy scouts at play.'[22]

Others have been more specific; it seems there is no existential pain which cannot be assuaged through paying attention to the natural world. Isabel Hardman sought relief from post-traumatic stress by seeking out wildflowers; locating a rare lady's slipper orchid, she realised she'd forgotten how bad she was feeling for a whole 20 minutes. Many flowers later, Isabel paid tribute to the healing power of nature in a book called *The Natural Health Service*. Rosamund Richardson dealt with betrayal by taking up birdwatching, welcoming birds as 'a kind of divine intervention' and concluding that 'waiting for birds and watching birds, I'd picked myself up and realised how interconnected and part of a continuum we all are, and how beautiful and mysterious life is.' Brokenness, she said, had led to unanticipated resources.[23] And John Lewis-Stempel tells how the soldiers of World War I found strength and consolation in birdsong: 'It was like a great sanctuary into which we could go and find refuge,' wrote Sir Edward Grey. 'There

---

[22] The essays by Henry Thoreau, 'Walking' (1862) and G.M. Trevelyan, 'Walking' (1913), are included in the anthology by E.V. Mitchell, *The Pleasures of Walking* (Vanguard Press, 1979); see pp. 132 and 57.

[23] *The Natural Health Service* (Atlantic Books, 2020); Rosamond Richardson, *Waiting for the Albino Dunnock: How birds can change your life* (Weidenfeld and Nicolson, 2017), pp. 2, 319.

is something so extraordinary hanging in the air,' stammered Lance Corporal Alfred Vivian as he listened to a skylark, 'that I feel the thing I would most enjoy would be to visit a church.' The same was true in World War II, where British POWs kept up their morale by birdwatching and planting gardens, and came home to found bird observatories, national parks and conservation organisations.[24]

The wisdom of the psalmists in directing our attention to God's creation is confirmed not only by countless individuals, but also by contemporary scientific research. A whole host of studies conducted by universities, institutes and charities confirms that the more time we spend out of doors, the healthier, both physically and emotionally, we become.[25]

'Ornitheology'

For the last twelve years I have been helping with the common crane reintroduction project here in Somerset. This has involved not only regular monitoring of the released birds, but many hours spent lying in the marshes, waiting to catch their young in order to fit them with the coloured rings and radio tags which will enable us to monitor them after they fledge. During these years the usually stable pattern of my life has been interrupted by periods of intense personal pain – bereavements, family illnesses, unexpected crises at work. But each summer, as we creep onto the moor at three in the morning to wait in the long vegetation until the cranes lead their chicks out into the hayfields to feed, something happens inside me. Often I have arrived upset, haunted by troubles which seemed bigger than me. But never have I left feeling like that. There is something extraordinarily therapeutic about waking

---

24 *Where Poppies Blow: The British soldier, nature, the Great War* (Weidenfeld and Nicolson, 2017), pp. 15, 49. For World War II see Derek Niemann, *Birds in a Cage* (Short Books, 2012).

25 Research studies into the benefits of nature have been published by the universities of Exeter, Sheffield and Derby, Stanford, Duke and Michigan; reported in scientific journals and summarised in the popular media; and widely cited by organisations which focus on conservation, ecology and mental health. See for example *Health and the Natural Environment* (University of Exeter, 2018), **beyondgreenspace.net/2018/09/07/defra_health_review**.

amongst the damp grasses of an ancient grazing marsh, lying at the edge of hayfields surrounded by deep drainage ditches, listening to reed warblers churring and watching clouds of rooks and jackdaws gust overhead on their way from their woodland roosts. Life, at ground level, is astonishing in its living, breathing richness: shiny black wetland slugs march up the wet grasses, tiny hidden quail ring out their whip-whip calls, and snipe spread their stiff tail feathers and drum their way back down to earth, filling the air with vibrations. As the cranes emerge cautiously into the hayfield, we spring out of our ditches, surround the chick, ring, tag and release it. It's over in minutes; the purple vetch closes its head protectively over the ginger-headed bird, the circling parents return, and we are able to follow its movements and protect it as it fledges, joins the winter flock and, if all goes well, lives to rear its own family in four or five years' time. Now the Somerset Levels echo once more, as they did for centuries until hunting drove the cranes to extinction, with the bugling cries of these huge, graceful birds – birds celebrated in the poetry of Homer and hailed in the prophecies of Isaiah and Jeremiah; birds which have left their mark on village place names and plant species across the English landscape; birds whose history is older than the words with which we label them. Pinned to the kitchen wall in the old farmhouse which houses the reserve office, a notice suggests that if you find yourself feeling depressed, you should seek out someone to talk to. The notice is helpful; but the real healing is to be found out on the moor.

Sometimes people laugh at me for being so passionate about birds. But, as poet Emily Dickinson once said, 'Hope is the thing with feathers.' I am told that my first word was 'duck'; the word I use now is 'ornitheology', borrowed from the great birdwatching preacher John Stott.[26] I have learned to welcome birds as living components of my ongoing conversation with God. I have one sitting on my shoulder as I write.

---

26 *Poems by Emily Dickinson: Second Series* (Roberts Brothers, 1891), p. 27. John Stott, *The Birds our Teachers: Essays in orni-theology* (Angus Hudson, 1999), p. 10.

Rediscovering thankfulness: Psalms 147 and 148

Perhaps the closing prayer for protection in Psalm 104 has been answered, for in Psalm 147 the poet once again thanks God for his provision – but only after he has praised him for his willingness to gather the outcast, to heal the broken-hearted and bind up their wounds. Only then does he launch into the familiar celebration of the way God creates the stars and names them, covers the heavens with clouds and brings rain, provides food for animals and responds to the cry of young ravens. And, in case we are tempted to think that blessing can be found only in the warm greenery of summer, the psalmist sings a song of winter. The Lord gives snow like wool, scatters frost like ashes, hurls down hail like crumbs – and then, just as the cold begins to bite, he sends out his word, and melts it all. Here is a wintry version of Psalm 104, a reminder of the childhood joy of snowballs and sledges, the seasonal wonder of icicles and whitened fairy landscapes. Snow really can seem like wool, we discovered in Norway as we shed some of our over-cautious layers of clothing and joined the local church outside for a winter barbecue. And frost and ice can look like ashes, I thought one February as I cycled along the frozen shore of the Severn estuary, passing waves of ice curled into the shape of a retreating tide, a sea made solid and left behind by its own waters. The waves became shards, and then crinkled heaps of ice, frothed into immobility, moments frozen in time. It looked like ash; it looked like foam – but it was solid, a strip of ice stranded in a sea of sand.

Hail can pour down like crumbs, too. Several years ago I was leading a retreat in the Yorkshire Dales; it was April, but one afternoon God did indeed cover the heavens with clouds: clouds which gathered in great black frowns, sweeping over the landscape and disappearing into the horizon, then reforming themselves in the blue-and-white sky and doing it all over again before driving a tidal wave of hail through the valley. The emerald pastures turned to grey, lambs shivered beside the hedges, and the ragged fleeces of the ewes lifted in the passing wind – and then God sent out his word, and made his wind blow, and the waters flow. The hail turned to rain, and once again the daffodils nodded in the sunshine between hedges of star-spangled blackthorn. It was a remarkable display – the more so for being quite unexpected.

We've come a long way; but we have one final step to take in this part of our journey. Often the psalmist has sung God's praises; sometimes the hills and meadows have joined their voices to his. But in Psalm 148, the creatures of the earth take centre stage, and the song is theirs alone. Starting with the Lord himself and working from angels downwards, the whole of creation joins in an oratorio of praise: angels, sun and moon, mountains and hills, wild animals and flying birds, men and women – all of them praising the name of the Lord.

When I walk through this God-given landscape of life, I too find myself pausing to listen to the chorus of voices: the whispering of trees, the buzzing of bees, the baaing of sheep. But it is the birdsong which most often stops me in my tracks. Why is it that birds sing, I have often wondered. There are, of course, scientific answers – to attract mates, to protect territories. But, as one scientist has pointed out, the birds sing far more than Darwin allows them to.[27] The songs themselves are astonishing – a tiny wren sings 740 notes per minute, a rattling jumble of sound to us, but when we slow it down a complex, melodic tune emerges.[28] I have listened to whole orchestras of birds performing in a spring dawn, wondering at the glorious mosaic of sound being woven in the morning air.

In winter too, birds sing: every year I watch half a million starlings arrive to roost in a frozen reedbed, coming in like curtains sweeping across the marshes. More and more gather until suddenly as if by an unseen signal they detonate the sky, scattering a whirlwind of black shards through the still air, twisting it into swirling ribbons and tying the air in knots before plummeting like rockets into the silent reeds. And then they explode the silence, and a thousand songs crackle into the orange dusk, rising like mist from the swaying reeds. They come

---

[27] Dutch biologist and psychologist Frederik Buytendijk, quoted by Jean-Jacques Suurmond, *Word and Spirit at Play* (SCM, 1994), p. 41.

[28] Simon Barnes, *The Meaning of Birds* (Head of Zeus, 2018), pp. 56–57.

to pool their warmth in a communal roost – but why the song? You can hear them from half a mile away. Once, I watched a man who had brought his camera. As the birds plummeted into the reeds beside us and burst into song, his arms dropped, his camera forgotten: he just stood there, laughing.

'Is it possible,' asks biologist Roger Payne, 'that the universe sings? Is it possible that God is the song of the universe? The beautiful songs of life are older than our entire species, and they will continue long after all human music has dissolved. If the words of God are to be heard on Earth, there is no better place to find them than in the deep intricacies of incomprehensible bird song.'[29]

Living a life of moments

As I have prayed my way through these psalms of creation, I have come to the conclusion that to live life to the full it has to be divided into moments; moments which gain their validity not from the efficiency with which they lead into the next moment, but for the way in which they can be savoured as epiphanies, dynamic little parcels of time which interrupt, or perhaps encapsulate, the present. Perhaps the secret of life is to be found not just in the intentionality of days, but in the accumulation of moments; not just in the avoidance of pain, but in recognising which moments are the most valuable, and learning to savour them. What was the best thing for you today, my husband asked each child on holiday in Sardinia one year. They named fleeting moments – running over rocks, seeing a kitten, finding giant pine cones. And so it was for me too: observing the ripples in a pool of water; seeing the sun shining through the red petals of a skeletal poinsettia bush; watching a griffon vulture soar with effortless ease on a thermal. Such moments come not just on holiday, but on work days and chore days too: rounding a bend and finding river and field laid out in an unfolding view; pausing to take in the lights dancing in

---

29 Quoted by David Rothenberg, *Why Birds Sing* (Allen Lane, 2005), p. 218.

shop windows, the signposts hanging from old buildings, the autumn leaves glowing on trees; breathing in the smell of cut grass, listening to the sad autumn mirth of a singing robin. Life is full of moments: to live a life of moments is to live a life which reaches beyond the tyranny of the immediate; a life in which we can, in our ragged incompleteness, strain towards the bigger truth of a reality which stretches beyond us – something we did not create, something we did not earn or buy. It is not in the moments themselves that meaning lies. The moments merely offer an invitation – the chance to step aside, to look at life in a different way. To be open to moments is to be open to the chance to reflect on how we might weave the threads of our own lives into the cloth of the universe, to integrate our own stories into the bigger story of a life which is more complex, more painful but also more wonderful, than we had imagined. The Psalms are full of moments.

'There is no event so common-place,' says Frederick Buechner, 'but that God is present within it, always hidden, always leaving you room to recognize him or not to recognize him. Listen to your life,' he advises. 'See it for the fathomless mystery that it is. In the boredom and pain of it no less than in the excitement and gladness: touch, taste, smell your way to the heavenly and hidden heart of it because in the last analysis all moments are key moments, and life itself is grace.'[30]

---

30 *Now and Then* (Harper and Row, 1983), p. 87.

6

Travelling with God

Who can live and not see death, or who can escape the power of the grave?
PSALM 89 (NIV)

Much of this book has been planned sitting at the kitchen table of a little stone cottage far from my home. The cottage belongs to my brother and sister-in-law, who kindly allow me to use it as a writing retreat. Bought a few years ago after the death of my father and the admission of my mother to a nursing home, the cottage is full of memories. For over half a century our parents, Bill and Faith, had made their home in the same semi-detached house in south-east London. Both had lived through the war, and neither ever threw anything away; they had accumulated a lifetime of possessions. We had to clear the house, keeping what we could, selling or giving away what we couldn't. And so coming to this tiny stone cottage feels a bit like coming home. My father's handsome collection of books fills the shelves which nestle under the wooden stairs, alongside my mother's battered childhood set of French dolls, three big ones standing side by side like sentinels, the smaller ones inside them. The little square table where every weekend evening they ate their supper in the sitting room, discovered years before by my grandmother in an antique shop, sits in the corner; the engraved glasses from which they drank their wine are in the cupboard to the left of the fireplace. Two little side tables with drawers stand by the wall, one still lined with a copy of *The Times*, dated Saturday 1 May 1954, the other home to a set of patterned fish knives and forks, relics from our father's family home in Alderley Edge. Our great aunts are remembered here too, in the Wilton rug which lies beside the hearth, the ancient oak blanket chest positioned behind the sofa. On the landing my mother's walnut desk stands beneath four little framed engravings of Enfield bought by my grandmother who brought her family up there, and those too were part of my childhood. I am surrounded by comforting familiarity; but also by a pervasive sense of poignancy.

It is seven years now since my father died. Some months earlier I had asked him whether he ever thought about what would come next, whether he had ever tried talking to God. 'No,' he had said. Would you like to do that now, I had asked? 'Yes, I would,' had been the unexpected reply. He had once told me over the washing up that he had tried Christianity in his 20s, but found he could not live up to its expectations – the beatitudes had been the particular obstacle – and so had given up. We talked and prayed together that day, and then again at intervals over the next few months, and then one final time, as he lay dying in hospital. 'Dad, you aren't going to get better,' I had told him, for no one else seemed to want to tell this frail 93-year-old man that his time was up. One eyebrow shot up; he said nothing. We listened to Beethoven's Pastoral Symphony; later that evening he slept, and did not wake. I took my mother to visit. He was still lying in bed, pale, cold, his mouth open. A man who had fought for his country, devoted himself to his family, a man whom we had loved, reduced now to nothing more than skin and bone. We buried him two weeks later.

I watched my father die physically; now I am required to watch my mother dying mentally. She cannot remember the square table, or the family wine glasses, or the walnut bureau in which she kept everything – certificates, school reports, family photographs, writing things. Not only does she not know that these things are here, she does not even remember that they once existed. Life comes, and it goes, and it tears holes in our souls. We know that we must die, but death comes rudely, harshly, like an amputation which leaves us feeling that some part of our own being has been brutally and abruptly severed – for I am, in part, also the people I love, and they are me. In the 15th century huge wall paintings offered a daily reminder of the uncomfortable reality: Death, a skeleton, rides a bony horse across a brutal landscape of human devastation, people of all ages and classes succumbing in despair to his passing. Today we prefer to look in the other direction, celebrating life, hiding death away; but perhaps that makes it all the harder when it comes calling – which, one way or another, it will.

After my father died I took to the hills, determined to continue my journey the other side of this new barrier of pain, wanting to enter more deeply into the mystery which is God; resolved to make the most of the beautiful, singing world he has made, and with which he is surely still pleased; thanking him for it, finding him in it, blending my body with its contours and my ears with its song. Why am I alive and not dead, I thought as I climbed past drystone walls, walls which have stood there for centuries, built by hands which, as will mine, have both lived and died. Why am I alive and not dead, I thought as I gazed at the rippled hillside, the grassed-over signs of land sliding into a stream long ago, and listened to the piping of the curlew. Why am I alive and not dead, I thought, as I reflected on something my widowed cousin had said to me after her husband died prematurely and suddenly of a ruptured aorta. He had wanted to live forever, she said; for her part, she hopes she won't still be around at 87, 88, for she has nothing to do, nothing which matters; she'd be happy to go. And yet this is not depression, or self-pity, for my cousin lives life busily and cheerfully. Perhaps it's just how things are, once people close to you have died.

Many people have written movingly of the agony of bereavement. 'The memories are like heavy blocks of glass,' said Helen Macdonald after the sudden death of her father; 'for weeks I felt I was made of dully burning metal.' 'It was as if someone had slashed me across the face,' confessed Helen Brace as she struggled to bring up her three young children after the death of her husband. 'It felt scandalous to be alive,' wrote Gretel Ehrlich, 'obscene to experience pleasure or pain.'[1] Death keeps coming, not just to the old but also to the young: brain tumours, traffic accidents, miscarriages, suicides, terrorist attacks, even something as unexpected as trampling by bullocks on a country walk, or a new virus which shuts people away to die behind sealed doors, far

---

1 Helen Macdonald, *H is for Hawk* (Jonathan Cape, 2014), pp. 13, 15; Helen Brace, letter to *Country Walking*, Spring 2020, p. 19; Gretel Ehrlich, *The Solace of Open Spaces* (Daunt Books, 2019), p. 51.

from their loved ones. During the coronavirus pandemic I was not able to visit my mother for months on end – my mother who in the early stages of her dementia found being widowed so hard, so unlikely, that she repeatedly reported my father to the police as missing. Surely, he could not have gone; surely, he could not have left her?

Death, observed Canon Henry Holland, is inexplicable, ruthless, blundering; it comes as an ambush in which we are snared, breaching our gladness with careless and inhuman disregard for our feelings. Death, agrees Tom Wright, is a 'real and savage break,' a 'horrible denial of the goodness of human life'; we experience it, adds Henri Nouwen, 'neither as a release or an occasion for rest and peace, but as an absurd, ungodly, dark nothingness'.[2] There is something outrageous about death, something which just feels wrong. And so we struggle to talk about it; reshaping funerals as celebrations, we seem unable even to say that someone has died: they have passed away. My father did not pass away. He died.

Running away from our fears will not help, Denise Inge observed as she sought to come to terms with the reality of death in her moving reflection on the collections of human bones carefully, and sometimes startlingly, preserved in Europe's ancient charnel houses. 'Death is a crucial part of the human condition,' she wrote; 'when we avoid talking about death we avoid talking about life.'[3] As I think about this, I am forced to recognise that life itself is a constant process of loss, and that this is necessary, for new life and new experiences can come into being only in the space created as yesterday's present recedes inexorably into the past. I am no longer the girl standing beside my brother on the cobbled street of Clovelly, holding a small monkey, as in the photo which sits opposite my desk. I am no longer punting on the River Cam, or teaching a tame jackdaw called Gripper to talk. My beautiful, funny toddlers have vanished into the mists of time, and

---

[2] Henry Holland, sermon after the death of Edward VII, quoted by Tom Wright, *Surprised by Hope* (SPCK, 2007), p. 21; Henri Nouwen, 'A letter of consolation', in *Making All Things New and Other Classics* (HarperCollins, 2000), p. 220.

[3] *A Tour of Bones* (Bloomsbury, 2014), p. 13.

we will never again walk as a young family over the hills of Swaledale. Even my own body is fading; outwardly it still looks much as it always has, but every day it is dying and being reborn, until one day the dying will come to dominate, and I too will move on, making way for those who will come after me. I am compelled to accept that it is death which makes new life possible, a new life painted in the changing seasons and incarnate in a daily torrent of new moments. Death, I remind myself as I watch each Mendip winter give way to the outpouring of life which comes in spring, is not a full stop but a semi-colon.

Wondering what to do with all these feelings, I turned to the Psalms.

The psalmist faces death: Psalm 22

Perhaps it is only the poet who can write adequately about death, catching into verse powerful emotions which refuse to conform to the measured logic of orderly sentences. To this day we experience the horrifying slaughter of World War I not from dispatches sent from the front but through the anguished poetry written by those who fought and died there. Death leaves its scars in the deepest recesses of our hearts, and finds expression in its own genre of writing, the lament. Lament, both personal and collective, has been a consistent subject for poets from the time of Homer to the present day; and the Psalms provide us with one of the richest collections of lament ever written.

Of all the psalmists, it is David who writes most consistently and movingly about death. Whether threatened by his enemies or languishing on his sickbed, David expresses horror and revulsion at the prospect that his life may be about to end. A horrible dread has overwhelmed me, he cries; my heart is disquieted within me, my bones are out of joint and my tongue sticks to my mouth! If you do not hear me, he implores, I will become like those who go down to the Pit; the flood will sweep over me, the waters swallow me up.[4] He prays repeatedly and

---

4   Psalms 55:5–6; 22:14–15; 28:1; 69:15.

fervently that his body would be healed and his enemies confounded. David's anguish is echoed by his fellow psalmists. 'My soul is full of troubles, and my life draws near to death; I have lost my strength, and am numbered among the dead,' laments Heman; 'remember how short my time is, how frail you have made us,' entreats Ethan; 'you have covered us with the shadow of death,' complain the Korahites.[5] If one thing is clear from the Psalms, it is that the threat of death is real, and that to respond with fear and anguish is both natural and normal. In the Psalms we find no soft answers; the psalmists do not speak reassuringly of passing away, of finding peace or falling asleep – they speak of loss, despair, annihilation, horror and fear. For them, death is a trap and a pit, the forced exchange of a multicolour life on earth for a shadowy one elsewhere; death is not what they want, and it is not what they believe God intends.

These are the concerns which motivate David as he composes the best known of all the lament psalms, Psalm 22. This remarkable psalm can be read on several different levels. First and foremost, it stands as a personal outpouring from the psalmist as he faces the prospect of his own death. But it can also be read as a communal lament, giving voice to the cries of a people deeply threatened by their enemies and calling on God for deliverance. Finally, to modern ears it rings out as a prayer echoed by Jesus on the cross, as he expressed deep anguish in the words of the opening verse: 'My God, my God, why have you forsaken me?'

The psalm falls into three parts. It opens with what has become the most quoted cry of desolation in history. David, a rich and powerful king, has reached the end of his own resources; making it clear that humanly speaking he sees no way forward, he throws himself upon the mercy of God. David does not doubt that God is there, or that God is listening, for he has depended on God since the time of his birth. Having learned to trust God through the trust he had as an infant in his mother, he reminds himself that his ancestors too have found

---

5 Paraphrased from Psalms 88:3–4 and 89:47; 44:19 (KJV).

Travelling with God   119

God trustworthy. David knows who God is, and he knows who he is: he cannot understand why God is not responding. Humiliated by the scorn and mockery of everyone who sets eyes on him, bewildered and angry, David demands to know why God does not answer. Most modern translations suggest that in these opening verses David is groaning, calling out, crying to God – but the verb here means 'roaring' – roaring as a lion roars; roaring as his enemies will roar in verse 13. David is not cowed, not begging; he simply cannot believe that this is happening – if he is like a lion, it is a lion caged. He urges God to be true to himself, to once again prove himself trustworthy; and then sets out to describe the dire nature of his situation.

The second part of the psalm is dominated by a cascade of powerful metaphors as David relates not the factual details of his circumstances, but how he feels about them. He is at the end of his physical endurance: he feels as weak as water, his body disjointed, his organs turning to liquid; his mouth is as dry as a broken pot, his hands and feet are shrivelled, his bones stick out. Then, in an abrupt change of scene, David is swept from his deathbed to the centre of a circle of wild bulls, lions and dogs, the violence of his emotions matched by the violence of his surroundings. The bulls threaten with their horns, the lions prepare to tear him limb from limb with their teeth, and the dogs are waiting to scavenge his body and carry off even his clothing. If David's outer world is under threat, his inner world is now in complete disarray: deliver me from the sword, he cries in desperation; save me, O Lord, save me! This great man of faith does not want to lose his life.

And then suddenly it all changes. Does David wake from his nightmare? Is he looking back on his sufferings now that they have passed? He bursts into a prayer of thanks. You did listen, he cries; you did act! His dignity as king restored, David promises to proclaim God's faithfulness in the temple, to host a dinner for the poor, to invite all nations to come together in worship. Even future generations will hear of the deliverance that the Lord has provided, David says. And so the scope of the psalm widens to encompass the whole of life and death, not just for this particular psalmist, not just for the people he serves as king, but for everyone who makes this prayer their own. Both Mark and Matthew tell us that Jesus quoted the opening verse of this psalm from the cross. David's words are recognised to be prophetic, pointing forward to this very moment. Perhaps Jesus was not simply borrowing the first line but calling to mind the entire psalm, with its outcome of deliverance from death for all generations – deliverance which, in that moment, he was in the act of providing. The gospel writers certainly thought so.[6]

Many of the Psalms are written as laments. Lament is powerful and necessary, and in these poems we find the words we need to express our pain, and so open the door to its resolution. 'Lament keeps us turning toward trust by giving us language to step into the wilderness between our painful reality and our hopeful longings,' Mark Vroegop has said; lament occupies 'the space between brokenness and God's mercy.'[7] And so David teaches me that when I am in despair, when death or the threat of death shatters my world, I should not assume that my pain comes as a test or a punishment, or as yet another example of the suffering and injustice that life metes out; I should neither turn my anger inwards nor crumple into a heap, and I should certainly not pretend bravely that everything is fine, as if God had enrolled me in a school of Stoic philosophy. Confronted with death, the psalmist gives us permission to shake, howl, cry and plead – and in so doing, he enables us to find a new way forward. The gospel is tragedy, comedy and fairy tale, said Frederick Buechner; and all of those are in this psalm, for here is Good Friday, Easter Saturday and Easter Sunday all rolled into one, and yes, God can be trusted.[8] David promised to hold a celebratory feast of thanksgiving; 'Do this in remembrance of me,' said Jesus eucharistically as he prepared for the death which would invite us to enter into a new reality on the other side of the barrier of time. As he faced his own death, all these things became true for my father – as one day they will for me. 'Even though I walk through the

---

6 The gospel writers recall other elements of Psalm 22 in their account of the crucifixion of Jesus – the casting of lots for his clothing, the derision and taunting of onlookers, his thirst, and his final exclamation, 'It is finished!', echoing David's closing words, 'He has done it.' See Matthew 27; Mark 15; Luke 23; John 19.

7 *Dark Clouds, Deep Mercy: Discovering the grace of lament* (Crossway, 2019), pp. 77 and 28.

8 *Telling the Truth: The gospel as tragedy, comedy and fairy tale* (HarperOne, 1977).

valley of the shadow of death,' David was able to write in the very next psalm, 'I fear no evil; for you are with me.' Pain, and the resolution of pain, is written into the landscape.

A historical perspective

One of the notable things about Psalm 22 is that even in the midst of a life-threatening crisis, David does not confine himself to the present and the future for which he hopes: he looks back into the past, both his own and that of his ancestors. Perhaps it is natural, when facing our own death, to remember those who have gone before us. One of the unexpected benefits of my father's death is that I have been able to do this in a more detailed way than I had ever thought possible – a way that was instinctive for David, but is less usual for us.

Family had always been important to my father. From his own father he had inherited a strong sense of family history, embodied not just in the longstanding family cotton business but also in generations of service in the armed forces and within the community. From his mother came a tantalising muddle, a tale of such inconsistency that he doubted she herself remembered the facts she had so carefully managed for so long. After they died, he began to explore their histories, and when he retired he embarked on 25 years of painstaking genealogical research. He joined family history societies and spent hours in libraries and record offices, delving further and further not just into our direct family line but also into those which had flowed into it through marriage. After his death I found myself in possession of 61 manila folders stuffed with the fruits of his research – photocopies of wills, amused articles he'd written for family history journals, long letters to fellow family historians. Perhaps it was redemptive, a recovery of the ambitions he had lost when instead of completing his education and going on to university to read history, he'd found himself firstly in army uniform and subsequently creeping his way reluctantly up through the ranks of the civil service. 'You can be interested in anything,' he had said bravely as he dealt with ambulance strikes, changing county boundaries and hospital building projects. But what he was really interested in lies in those 61 folders. Two years after his death, finding myself surrounded by a growing crowd of forebears from all walks of life, I decided to do what he lamented he had not had time to do, and write it all up. It led me to some startling insights – insights which would contribute in unexpected ways to my reading of the Psalms.

The first thing I noticed was the sheer variety of circumstances and occupations represented in my history. On his father's side, my father found woollen drapers and glove-makers, merchants and haberdashers, innkeepers and farmers, booksellers, clergy and teachers; sea captains and shipwrights, dressmakers and milliners, coppersmiths and watchmakers; a knight of the realm, a couple of colonels, an admiral, and several lords of the manor. On his mother's side were labourers, mariners, farm managers, weavers and drapers, fading within a couple of generations into the undocumented history of rural Scotland – a history of which she was as proud as she was uncommunicative. All these people have become me, and their living and dying has influenced who I am and who I have become.

Secondly, I found that if parts of my own history have been painful, so had theirs. Watching their fortunes rise and fall, I became increasingly aware of the way pain is threaded through the tapestry of life. As my father made his way patiently back over 15 generations, he found both success and failure, prosperity and poverty, long life and sudden death. Of the 19 children born to Robert and Mary, five generations back from me, only four lived to have children of their own; of the twelve born to Robert and Dinah two generations before that, six died – and this was the normal pattern. A tiny church in Dorset is still dominated by a 17th-century monument of the Mary who died in childbirth, the baby beside her. In London our ancestors died of plague, and in Suffolk of smallpox.

For those who did reach adulthood, life remained precarious. Eight family members were declared bankrupt; one had seen his trade as a wine merchant decimated by the Napoleonic wars; another blamed prime minister Robert Peel for the failure of his textile business, attributed more plausibly by his father to wilful mismanagement. Accidents and disasters were common: watchmaker Mark saw his newly built and uninsured house go up in flames; Robert, thrown out of home at the age of twelve by his drunken father, took a job with the railways, only to be run over by a train and lose a leg. Agnes married a sea captain who died a few years later, leaving her to contest a forged will produced by a mutinous shipmate. Mary Ann was predeceased by her husband Walthall, a solicitor whose will described her as 'abandoned and false', accused her clergyman father of simony and perjury, wished part of his estate to be invested in a lottery, and appointed the Lord High Chancellor as guardian of his children. Custody was awarded to Mary Ann, who patiently brought them all up on her own. Four generations later my grandfather, whom I just remember, served in World War I; contracting dysentery at Gallipoli and subjected to mustard gas in France, he was left with permanent lung damage. On his return home he went back to work, only to see his business founder in the Great Depression which followed. Life is a dangerous and uncertain business.

And yet as I continued my journey through my father's papers, I found these painful stories matched by others, stories of hard-earned prosperity and social recognition, stories of bravery and philanthropy, of happy family life and faithful service to the community. Like me, my ancestors published books, ministered in the church, set up charitable institutions; they too married widowers, brought up their children and passed on their furniture. The process was restorative in itself, as if I were having a conversation with my father, sharing in all that had been important to him and connecting it with what is important to me. But it helped me also to place his death in a wider context, so that it became not a catastrophic single event, but part of a pattern – a pattern which finds an ending not in oblivion, but in God. One by one my ancestors reached the end of their lives, wrote wills commending their souls to their maker, and went to their graves.

In the course of all this I found out something else – something more surprising. Reflecting on the genealogical trees drawn up by my father, it occurred to me that the Bible too is full of family history, carefully preserved and passed down from generation to generation. The book of Genesis contains no fewer than seven genealogical summaries; there are further records in Numbers, where the people are reckoned by their ancestral houses; in 1 Chronicles, where we learn that all Israel was enrolled by genealogies; and in Ezra and Nehemiah.[9] Sometimes the genealogies are fired off rapidly as a series of names; sometimes mini-biographies of individuals and snapshots of events emerge in the midst of the names, for genealogy serves as a vehicle for the remembering of history. As the genealogies develop, it becomes clear that the identity of an individual was formed not primarily by their roles or relationships, but by their place in history – indeed, it was often people's ancestry which determined their occupations. Only those descended from Levi could serve as priests, and the branch of that family descended from Korah would become the Korahite psalmists, composers of 25 of the psalms which have come down to us.[10] Even Jesus – or perhaps above all Jesus – has a family history: both Matthew and Luke begin their accounts of his life with a genealogical summary, demonstrating that he is descended not only from David, the king whose earthly kingship pointed towards Jesus' heavenly kingship, but also from Abraham, to whom God promised that he would become the ancestor of many nations.[11]

According to Matthew, 14 generations lie between Abraham and David, 14 between David and the Exile, and 14 between the Exile and the Messiah. My father traced our ancestry back 15 generations, taking him with certainty to the mid-15th century. Beyond that, descent can be surmised but not proved, for surnames are rare and documentary records incomplete. But we can, in one particular family line, glimpse our origins as far back as the eleventh century – at which point the number of my father's ancestors would, should each of them appear

---

9 Genesis 5, 10, 11, 22, 25, 36, 46; Numbers 3, 26; 1 Chronicles 1—9; Ezra 7, Nehemiah 11—12.

10 For the Korahites see 1 Chronicles 6:18–47. Eleven Psalms are attributed to the Korahites in general and a further 14 to Korahites Ethan, Heman and Asaph.

11 For Jesus see Matthew 1, Luke 3; for Abraham, Genesis 17:5.

in our family tree only once, be four times as numerous as the then population of England.[12] In practice every marriage is between people who have common ancestors, which means that the further back we go, the higher the proportion of our ancestors within the general population becomes. Mathematicians and geneticists have demonstrated that *every* person living in England in the eleventh century who has a descendant alive today is in fact my ancestor.[13] On the same basis they calculate that once we get back to about 1400BC (the time of the Egyptian exile), every person living anywhere in the world is my ancestor. If this is so, I must conclude that my ancestors were also enslaved in Egypt, and that I too am descended from Abraham, not just in a spiritual sense, but physically. And so it becomes apparent that the biblical genealogies are not, as I had supposed, those of a remote people with whom I have no historical connection: they are my genealogies too.

The historical psalms

These unexpected insights lead me to look with fresh eyes at the psalms which tell, as Asaph is keen to point out, of the 'things that we have heard and known, that our ancestors have told us'.[14] There are historical references in many of the Psalms, but five in particular offer a long and detailed recital of the salient events of preceding centuries. Psalms 78, 106 and 136 begin with the experience of our ancestors during the Egyptian exile; Psalms 105 and 135 start with the promises made by God to our ancestors Abraham and Jacob. The psalmists have a twofold purpose: to ensure that we remain properly

---

12 Over 8 million ancestors, compared with the estimated total population of just under 2 million in England and Scotland. My mother of course would contribute an additional 8 million ancestors.

13 Statistical study by Joseph Chang, 'Recent common ancestors of all present-day individuals', Department of Statistics, Yale University, 1998; genetic study by Peter Ralph and Graham Coop, 'The geography of recent genetic ancestry across Europe', *PLOS Biology* 2013. Research summarised by Mark Rutherford, *A Brief History of Everyone Who Ever Lived* (Weidenfeld and Nicolson, 2016), ch. 3, and Carl Zimmer, 'Charlemagne's DNA and our universal royalty', *National Geographic*, 2013.

14 Psalm 78:3.

grateful to God for the way he has walked with us and protected us, and to emphasise our need to learn from past mistakes so that we may continue to enjoy his blessings.

First come the warnings. We must, says Asaph in Psalm 78, pass these stories on to our children, so that they will set their hope in God, remember his works and keep his commandments – as so often our ancestors failed to do. Exactly so, the psalmist echoes in Psalm 106; even after God had delivered our ancestors from Egypt they forgot his faithfulness to them, and their trust in his promises weakened. Time and again they provoked the Lord to anger with their deeds, repeatedly suffering the consequences of their own failure to obey his voice and keep his commandments. Many times the Lord rescued them, the psalmist points out as he turns directly to God in an appeal that he might do so again: will he deliver them now from their exile in Babylon as he had from their former enslavement in Egypt?

Then come the encouragements. Psalm 105 takes up the story. Give thanks to the Lord, the psalmist sings: remember the covenant he made with Abraham, repeated to Isaac, confirmed to Jacob – the promise of land, the consistency of protection; remember how he appointed Moses to lead our ancestors out of exile, how he inflicted plagues on their Egyptian captors, how he brought us into a land of our own and made us prosper – in order, ends the psalmist rather pointedly, that we might keep his statutes and observe his laws. Psalm 135 is equally upbeat. Praise the Lord, chants the psalmist: the Lord who chose Jacob for himself, who struck down the Egyptians, the Amorites, the kingdoms of Bashan and Canaan. Give thanks to the Lord, Psalm 136 continues, for he is good. Each line lists a saving action on God's part, and each concludes with a ringing reminder: 'his steadfast love endures forever.' Here there is no reprimand; perhaps the psalmist hopes that the constancy of praise will provide a better catalyst for heartfelt worship than the sorrow of rebuke – particularly now, as Asaph had pointed out, that God has provided a fresh start through the kingship of David and the building of the temple.

These psalms offer a lyrical recital of the historical records contained in the books of Exodus through to Chronicles, but they also follow the didactic theme launched in Psalm 1 and present throughout the Psalter. At every stage of history, the psalmists remind us, we have a choice: will we trust God and live within the parameters he sets for us, or will we be distracted by illusory alternatives? This choice must be made afresh in every generation, and the experience of our forebears is there to guide us. Is that so in my own family history, I wondered? Can that too be read as a series of lessons to be learned, thanks to be rendered? What does the experience of the various branches of my family teach me about those who walk in God's way, and those who do not?

At first sight, all is well. Our family history takes shape in the market towns of Suffolk, where Keymers, Haywards and Motts earned a solid living as woollen drapers, glovers and tallow chandlers. Prospering in business, they expressed their thanks to God through their roles as churchwardens and overseers of the poor, arranging apprenticeships for poor town boys, founding a hospital which would provide free treatment for those who lacked the ability to pay for it, and through wider contributions to worthy causes. At the heart of it all was my five-times-great grandfather Robert, who in 1775 wrote his own will, commending his soul into the hands of Almighty God and asking that all his sins be done away through the merits of his blessed Redeemer Jesus Christ. Two hundred and thirty-nine years later I found myself leading a day on prayer in St Mary's Hadleigh, his gravestone visible from the window. 'Stop, traveller, and read,' it commands; 'here lieth the body of Robert Keymer who, although necessarily engaged in much worldly Business in which he acquitted himself with great integrity, yet in the public and private duties of a Christian was strictly regular and punctual – not as a matter of ostentation, but of conscience.' And then, in Latin, 'Go, and do likewise.'

Robert's son Richard seems to have taken this seriously. Apprenticed at 16 to a manufacturer of small wares in the growing city of Manchester, Richard too was a man of faith; his subscriptions contributed to the building of five churches, and he was one of the pioneers of the new

Sunday School movement in the city. The business he established passed to his son Robert and in due course to his grandson John, who soon found himself employing over 1,000 people. John founded a Sunday School to provide a basic education and a medical subscription scheme for his workers, and built a church to provide for their spiritual needs. St Peter's closed its doors in 1975, long after the mills had gone and the workers moved away. But just two years ago I discovered that it has been fully restored; now the home to the Hallé Youth Orchestra, it stands at the heart of the regenerated area of Ancoats. I still have the leather-bound book in which John kept the trustee minutes, and his huge family Bible.

The writer of Psalms 105 and 135 would, I hope, have sung eloquently of Robert, Richard and John, celebrating the intertwining of divine blessing and godly service which flowed through their lives, encouraging me too to go and do likewise. Asaph, on the other hand, would surely have turned his attention to a branch of the family from whom different lessons can be learned.

Born two generations before Robert Keymer of Hadleigh, Abraham Houlditch also came from a family of merchants, this time in Totnes, Devon. His forebears were traders in grain and fish, which they shipped all over Europe, in the process becoming mayors, burgesses and MPs of Totnes – although already their record was not unsullied, for Abraham's great-grandfather Philip had been summonsed to answer a charge of profiteering during a time of famine by buying up grain in order to sell it at an inflated price. His merchant background took Abraham to London, where he joined first the Navy and then the Royal African Company, captaining ships and trading in gold and ivory. In 1671 he led the successful expedition to capture Cape Coast Castle, a Dutch trading fort on the coast of Ghana. Remaining as its governor, Abraham established it as a centre of trade not just in gold, but also in human beings. As the slave trade expanded, his son, also Abraham, made a fortune out of this increasingly brutal export – a fortune, that is, until a series of devastating losses at sea and distasteful court cases at home landed him in prison for bankruptcy; he spent the rest of his life begging for support from relatives. His sister Agnes, having lost her first husband at sea, had clearly had enough of this ungodly lifestyle. Although we have no record of how she felt, we do know what she did: mindful perhaps of Psalm 107, she turned her back on the pursuit of mercantile wealth, married a clergyman and settled into parish life in Middlesex, where she and her husband produced three generations of God-fearing clergy – and ultimately me, for Agnes was my seven-times-great-grandmother. Three hundred and forty-eight years after the capture of the castle, I found myself in Ghana, where I offered my apologies to the Anglican bishop. It is, suggests the psalmist, never too late.

The Psalms were composed a very long time ago. Vivid to those who first sang them, they sometimes stumble under the weight of their ancient words as we sing them now; they are all too easily lost, both verbally and culturally, in translation. But just as the psalmists' evocation of God's presence in landscape springs back to life once translated into the landscape in which I now live, so their record of his actions in history becomes vivid and relevant once I see my own family history as a continuation of theirs, subject to interpretation in exactly the same way. In 1797 Robert of Manchester was granted the right to bear the coat of arms of the oldest branch of the Keymer family, adding to it a new motto which summed up his understanding of the core commitment he wished to pass on: *Semper fidelis* – 'Always faithful.' Robert will have been familiar with the choice offered by Psalm 1 and given its fullest treatment in Psalm 119: to be the tree or the chaff, to walk in the way of the Lord or to pursue his own self-interest.

It is notable that the Psalms do not take a legal approach to this life of faithfulness, but a relational one; recognising our propensity to lose our way, the psalmists advocate a process of constant reflection and readjustment, both personal and collective. Walter Brueggemann notes that the Psalms are characterised by 'the insistence that an *agency of fidelity* is at the center of reality and that *responding fidelity* is the source of well-being, joy and liberty for all of human life.'[15] It is in this context that the historical psalms come into their own. They are there not to condemn us, but to teach us how to live.

Walking backwards into the future: Psalm 77

The historical psalms create a communal recital which celebrates God's faithfulness to his people through history, warning of the dangers of straying from the path he has set for us to follow, and calling on him afresh for help. What then of our own lives? Can we make use of this historical approach at times of more personal trial? Asaph suggests that we can. In Psalm 78 he took a collective approach; in Psalm 77 he looks back again at God's saving action in history, this time not as a warning to a people but as a reason for hope when his own life is in turmoil. 'I cry aloud to God,' he laments; 'in the day of my trouble I seek the Lord.' As he lies in bed unable to sleep, Asaph is tormented by the negative thoughts which so easily crowd into our minds at night. Will God turn away, or will he come through for him? Has God simply forgotten him, or is he angry? Will God honour his promises, or is his compassion a thing of the past?

We do not know what was causing Asaph such distress, though his fear that God is angry suggests that Asaph may be worried by his own shortcomings. Whatever it is that lies behind his anguish, Asaph responds by turning his mind to the past. He begins by pondering his own experience of God, remembering days gone by, times when he was able to sing God's praises. Then he reflects on God's record in history: 'I will call to mind the deeds of the Lord,' he says resolutely; 'I will meditate on all your work, and muse on your mighty deeds.' And off he goes, reminding himself how God took remarkable steps to rescue the descendants of Jacob and Joseph from captivity in Egypt, parting the sea and leading them out by the hand of Moses and Aaron. This, he says to himself, is the proper basis for my appeal: this is who God

---

15 *Psalms* (Cambridge University Press, 2014), p. 522.

is, this is how he responds when we are in need. He has not changed. And there Asaph stops. Perhaps it was time for breakfast; perhaps, his thoughts back on track, he simply fell asleep. At any rate, it is clear that he has, by the simple exercise of remembering, got himself back on an even keel.

Waking one morning in Ghana, I found that Psalm 77 was the reading set for the day. My visit there came at the end of another period of transition at home; in so many ways the future seemed uncertain. Would God still be there for us as we moved into the next phase of our lives, I wondered? Mindful of Asaph, I thought back not just to the history of my family, but to my own history with God. I remembered how I gave my life to God in the first place, and how the world had sprung into springtime colour. I remembered our first years in ministry, and how God met with us in completely unexpected ways through a faltering little prayer group which, mindful of the prophet Isaiah, we called Eagles. I remembered the trauma of Roger's road accident, and the cascade of visions, dreams and answered prayer which followed it; I thought back to financial difficulties, family difficulties, personal difficulties – and how God had been there in all of them. And as I continued my journey down memory lane, I realised that it wasn't simply that I had been forced to throw myself on the mercy of God at these difficult times, but that each time I had emerged a little stronger in my faith, a little better equipped to walk with compassion alongside others. We crave security, but in the counter-intuitive world of faith it is so often through adversity that we find it. 'My power,' said God to St Paul, 'is made perfect in weakness.' 'Therefore,' Paul explained, 'I am content with weaknesses, insults, hardships, persecutions, and calamities… for whenever I am weak, then I am strong.'[16] Pain serves to remind us of bigger realities.

Perhaps we should give the last word to our ancestor Moses, who has left us a single psalm, Psalm 90. In this song Moses contemplates the fragility of human life and the inevitability of death. God is everlasting and eternal, Moses reminds us; for him a thousand years are as a

---

16 2 Corinthians 12:9–10.

moment. We, on the other hand, are creatures of time: our lives are as fleeting as grass, renewed in the morning, withering and fading by the evening. Full of trouble and sorrow, our days end in a sigh, and even the most long-lived of us sink back into the dust from which we came. Moses, revered as the author of Genesis, knows that all this is to do with the way in which we insist on going our own way; our history, both collective and personal, is riddled with failure and rebellion, and we suffer the inevitable consequences of our alienation from God. And yet Moses knows too that God, creator of heaven and earth, has been our refuge for generations and always will be; that we have a future as well as a past. 'Teach us to count our days,' he pleads, 'that we may gain a wise heart'; 'satisfy us with your steadfast love, so that we may rejoice and be glad.' Moses was not able to foresee, as David was, the way in which God would answer his prayer.

Life is not easy. Between them the psalmists document every kind of suffering – sickness and death, wilful disobedience and unmerited misfortune. Death offers us a sharp reminder of the precariousness of our lives, and history provides a road map which helps us to avoid the obvious pitfalls into which we may otherwise fall. Through it all, the psalmists beckon us into a new and different future, one which we may experience in part here as we deepen our relationship with God, but into which we will enter fully only on the other side of time.

We are ready to enter the next stage of our journey.

7

A difficult conversation

No one has ever learned or achieved anything worth having without being stretched beyond themselves, till their bones crack.

George Steiner[1]

The next step

The Psalter encourages us to acknowledge that pain is an inevitable part of life, and that it should therefore be an inevitable part of our conversation with God. Following the example of the psalmists, we started our journey through the Psalms by resolving not to suppress our discomfort, but to face it head on. Borrowing their words we began, cautiously, to bring our suffering and our uncertainties to God. We reminded ourselves that God knows and loves us, that our struggles have not gone unseen, and that we are not alone. Emboldened by this thought, we lifted our heads and began to look for signs of God's presence in the world around us. Setting out to walk through the landscape that he created, we invited God to speak to us in it and through it. We became increasingly thankful for the provision he has made for us, and reminded ourselves that the patterns of growth and loss we experience in our own lives echo the patterns of life and death which regulate life in the world around us. Acknowledging the cruelty of death, we began to see our own lives as part of the ebb and flow of human history, and sought to learn from the experience of those who have gone before us.

---

1 From the novella 'Proofs', in *The Deeps of the Sea and Other Fiction* (Faber and Faber, 1996), p. 349.

We have come a long way: our exploration of these themes within the Psalter has helped us to place our personal difficulties in a much broader context, and provided us with a perspective which will stand us in good stead as we come now to the most difficult part of our journey. It is time to do what so often the psalmists have done before us: to go back to the painful emotions with which we began, to re-evaluate them in the light of our growing understanding of who we are in the sight of God, and to ask two questions: what does God require of us, and what help is God able to give us?

We may begin by reminding ourselves that suffering is not only inevitable, but necessary. 'There are many blessings we will never receive until we are willing to pay the price of pain, for the path of suffering is the only way to reach them,' J.R. Miller observes.[2] The price seems high – too high, we may feel. In her study of Paul's spirituality of suffering and joy, Laura Reece Hogan acknowledges that 'pain can be a nightmare, and it can seem to last forever, and it can have us gripped in a relentless and merciless grasp. It can issue from wounds which are so wide and deep and cruel that it seems they could never be healed in a lifetime. Pain can hold us in a headlock against a cold brick wall, and push us to anguished limits. Pain is very real, and very miserable, and sometimes that excruciating grip is beyond words.' And yet she notes too that psychologists have found that many people experience what they term post-traumatic growth: when honestly faced, suffering can make us stronger, opening up new possibilities and transforming our sense of priorities. It seems that the changes are deepest in those who acknowledge a spiritual dimension to their lives; it may be, Hogan suggests, that only God can be with us in the full measure of our suffering and pain – that only God can help us move through to a new and better place.[3]

Of all the biblical texts, it is the Psalms which are the most firmly

---

[2] *Streams in the Desert*, ed. L.B. Cowman (Zondervan, 1997), pp. 356–67.

[3] *I Live, No Longer I: Paul's spirituality of suffering, transformation, and joy* (Wipf and Stock, 2017), ch. 6. Hogan cites research by R.G. Tedeschi and L.G. Calhoun, 'Posttraumatic growth: conceptual foundations', *Psychological Inquiry*, 15:1 (2004).

committed to this process. The psalmists invite us to recognise that whereas we may be tempted to focus on the positive and preserve the illusion that we are in control, the elephant-sized reality is that life is full of pitfalls and threats. The Psalms are there to help us grow through our suffering rather than be crushed by it.

Teach me your way: Psalm 119

How then should we live? We have seen that the Psalter offers us a choice: will we be like the green tree or the dead chaff; will we follow the path of the Lord or will we pursue our own? We have reflected on the choices of those who have gone before us, and pondered the starkly different outcomes which followed from the decisions they made. It is clear that if we choose the path of the Lord, we will, to use the terminology of the Psalter, be counted among the righteous, who receive God's blessing and support; if not, then among the wicked, who must struggle on alone. The distinction may trouble us at first, for we are likely to feel that we cannot comfortably describe ourselves as righteous, and that we should not rush to label others as wicked. And yet, properly understood, these two terms are profoundly helpful, for they refer not to our moral status but to our fundamental allegiance: for the psalmist, the 'righteous' are those who prioritise their relationship with God, depending on him for love, forgiveness and protection, and seeking to live in a way which honours him; the 'wicked' are those who prioritise their own interest, relying on their own resources and pursuing their own agendas.[4] To align ourselves with God's righteousness is no small undertaking, and the psalmist knows that if we are to live as God intends we will need both help and guidance – guidance which God provides in the form of *torah*. In English we translate *torah*

---

4 See Jerome Creach, 'The righteous and the wicked' in William P. Brown (ed.), *The Oxford Handbook of the Psalms* (Oxford University Press, 2014). The nature of the wicked is clearly portrayed in Psalms 10 (those who say in their hearts, 'You will not call us to account') and 36 ('There is no fear of God before their eyes'); that of the righteous in Psalms 112 (those who fear the Lord and delight in his commandments) and 128 (those who walk in his ways). The two groups are contrasted in Psalms 34 and 37. David states his own desire to follow God's way in Psalms 18, 25, 27, 32, 37, 39, 51, 86, 101 and 143 – and yet, as we shall see, he is fully aware of his own sinful shortcomings.

as 'law' – but it is best understood not as a legal code but as a body of teaching and instruction to be followed in the context of a relationship with a faithful and loving God. What it means to live by *torah* is a theme which runs throughout the Psalter: first flagged up in Psalm 1 and repeated in Psalm 19, it finds its fullest expression in Psalm 119.

Psalm 119 is the longest of all the psalms, running to a 176 verses arranged in 22 sections. It follows an acrostic or alphabetical pattern: each section begins with a different letter of the Hebrew alphabet, and every verse within a section starts with that same letter. The law of the Lord, the psalmist declares, provides a complete alphabet of life: here is the alpha and omega of living, spelt out in a pattern which encompasses everything we need to know if we are to enjoy a fruitful and protective relationship with God. For the non-Hebrew reader, deprived of the alphabetic structure, this long psalm can seem a bit of a jumble, but if we listen for the core words which reverberate through the 22 sections – law, decree, commandment, statute, precept, ordinance, word, promise – we can perhaps recapture something of the way in which these hidden alphabetic waves repeatedly cast the same concepts onto the shore of our consciousness.

If in Psalm 19 God's words were first made visible in creation, here in Psalm 119 they are explored as direct verbal revelation; what we have seen, so now we hear, articulated to us not in the heavens and the firmament, the day and the night, but in the patterns of our own human speech. The righteous person, Psalm 119 affirms, is the one who accepts this divinely appointed order and seeks to live within the framework it provides. This is the way of life urged by the psalmist; a way reinforced both in this psalm and in the Psalter as a whole by the repeated use of metaphors of walking, and later to be incarnated in the person and teaching of Jesus – who is himself the Word of God, the Alpha and Omega, the way, the truth and the life.[5] So important

---

5 Two different words for 'path' (*derek* and *orah*) occur six times in the first 16 verses of Psalm 119, and 68 times in the Psalter as a whole. For Jesus see John 1:1–18; Revelation 22:12ff. For his claim to be the way, the truth and the life see John 14:6; note also the adoption of the term 'The Way' to denote the Christian faith in Acts 18:25–26; 19:9; 22:4; 24:14.

is this message that it is not only here expounded in the longest of all the Psalms, but reflected in the structure of the entire collection, its division into five books recalling the five books of the Pentateuch, also known as Torah.

And yet the psalmist is aware that things are not always as straightforward as they seem. We may lose our way, and we may find our path obstructed by adverse circumstances or stymied by the actions of others. All these eventualities are foreseen in Psalm 119.

The psalmist is the first to acknowledge that although he is committed to following the path laid out by God, he is prone to taking wrong turnings. Accepting that he is easily led astray by the desire for selfish gain and the pursuit of worldly vanities, he pleads that God will protect him from shame and disgrace, asks repeatedly for forgiveness, and recommits himself to living according to God's word. He ends with a final acknowledgement that, try as he might, he does not always get things right: 'I have gone astray like a lost sheep,' he confesses; 'seek out your servant, for I do not forget your commandments.'[6] The problem is that he doesn't always manage to keep them.

Dealing with failure: the Penitential Psalms

Despite his obvious willingness to continue the conversation, God, it must be said, takes a dim view of sin. No fewer than eleven psalms deal with the uncomfortable reality that God will discipline us for our transgressions.[7] The most poignant cries are those of David: 'Lord, do not rebuke me in your anger, or discipline me in your wrath,' he pleads; 'I am worn down by the blows of your hand.' Confronted by the gravity of his own mistakes, David is in frequent despair: 'my iniquities have overtaken me,' he laments, for 'they are more than the hairs on my head'; 'I am utterly spent and crushed; I groan because of the tumult

---

6   The psalmist acknowledges his weakness in vv. 5–8, 25–31, 36–39, 67–71, 78, 120, 176.
7   Psalms 6, 38, 39, 60, 81, 90, 94, 118, 119, 141, 143.

of my heart.' He begs for mercy: do not judge me, he implores, 'for no one living is righteous before you.'[8]

Despite their discomfort, the psalmists recognise that the discipline they are receiving is intended to be corrective. 'Before I was humbled, I went astray,' the author of Psalm 119 laments; 'it is good for me that I was humbled, so that I might learn your statutes.' 'Happy are those whom you discipline, and whom you teach out of your law,' agrees Psalm 94. Solomon takes up the theme: 'Do not despise the Lord's discipline or be weary of his reproof,' he counsels, 'for the Lord reproves the one he loves, as a father the son in whom he delights.' It's an enduring message: discipline seems painful rather than pleasant at the time, the letter to the Hebrews confirms; but it yields the peaceful fruit of righteousness to those who have been trained by it – so strengthen your weak hands and knees, follow the Lord's path, and be healed.[9]

In our unforgiving culture, any personal failure is frequently the beginning of the end: an infringement of the law, a moral lapse, an error of judgment can lead to the abrupt termination of a career, followed by the public shame the psalmist so clearly dreads. With God, however, it opens the way for a new conversation, for God is interested not in condemnation but in restoration. Indeed, the greatest biblical heroes turn out to be flawed characters whose lives have been marked by personal failure and deliberate transgression; as Charles Swindoll has pointed out, 'God does some of his best work with those who think they are finished.'[10] The same is true today. 'I went through defeat, disgrace, divorce, bankruptcy and jail,' former MP Jonathan Aitken said after his conviction for perjury; 'I know what it feels like to be submerged in a slough of despond as a result of one's own misjudgments, mistakes and failings.' How did he cope? Well, 'one book I would advise anyone going through this sort of ordeal to look at,' Jonathan said, 'is the Book

---

8 Psalms 6:1 and 38:1; 39:10; 40:12; 38:8; 143:2; see also 41:4.

9 Psalms 119:67, 71; 94:12; Proverbs 3:11–13, quoted in Hebrews 12:5–13.

10 *The Grace Awakening* (Word, 1990), p. 289. See for example the lives of Abraham (idolatry), Joseph (arrogance), Jacob (deceit), Moses (murder), Jonah (rebellion), Peter (assault and denial), and Paul (persecution).

of Psalms. One of the things about having a great fall is that it makes change much easier. I find it rather exciting.'[11]

The process of restoration always begins in the same way: with repentance. Seven psalms in particular have become known as the Penitential Psalms; of these, the most familiar is Psalm 51 – written by David, according to the heading in the Hebrew text, after a chain of events which today would undoubtedly have led to lasting disgrace.[12] The facts are outlined in 2 Samuel 11—12. Spotting a beautiful woman bathing, David had summoned her to his bed, only to learn to his horror that she had conceived a child. Arranging for her absent and loyal husband to be killed in battle, he hastily married her, hoping that would be the end of the matter. God, who as we may recall is acquainted with all David's ways, sends the prophet Nathan to rebuke him. Having hidden the awful truth not only from others but also, one suspects, from himself, David is forced to abandon the cover-up. He falls apart. 'I have sinned against the Lord,' he gasps. David then produces the most heartfelt prayer of repentance in the entire Bible. Horrified by this new perspective on his own behaviour, he becomes suddenly and painfully aware how far short he falls of God's standards. He acknowledges that God is quite right to judge him: recognising that this is not an isolated incident but the culmination of a lifetime of selfishness, David implores God to wash, cleanse, purge and renew him. He asks to be delivered from the guilt of bloodshed, and for his sins to be blotted out – if indeed every day of his life is written in God's book, David's plea is that these particular days be struck from the record. Finally, confessing that his spirit is broken and his heart crushed, he begs God not to discard him, but to restore him: 'Open my lips,' he cries in the familiar words, 'and my mouth will declare your praise!' It's a remarkable prayer – an invitation to not gloss over our failings, bury our guilt in the recesses of our minds or pretend our performance is pretty much up to scratch,

---

11 From an interview with Valentine Low, *The Times* 22 November 2019. Jonathan eventually embarked on a new life as a prison chaplain – and wrote an excellent book on the Psalms.

12 The Penitential Psalms were first so named by Cassiodorus in his sixth-century commentary on the Psalms. They are 6, 32, 38, 51, 102, 130, 143. Confessions of sin are also found in Psalms 25, 39, 40, 41, 65, 79, 90.

but instead to face the unpleasant reality that whether we are guilty of murder and adultery or simply, as Jesus will explain, of angry words and lustful glances, we too suffer from a pervasive and terminal illness called sin. 'The one spiritual disease,' wrote G.K. Chesterton, 'is thinking that one is quite well.'[13]

Building on the insights of Sigmund Freud, modern psychotherapy recognises that our tendency to deny and repress our guilt lies at the root of much mental illness; it is said that a London psychologist once told evangelist Billy Graham that 70 per cent of people in mental hospitals could be released if only they could find forgiveness.[14] Perhaps Freud, with his Jewish background, was simply bringing the insights of the Psalms back into view. It certainly seems that the effect of God's forgiveness on David was transformative.

Psalm 32 takes up the tale. With his usual emotional articulacy, David bounces from despair to exultation: 'Happy are those whose transgression is forgiven, whose sin is covered,' he exclaims. He had, he confesses, tried to keep silent about his sins, iniquities and transgressions, to the detriment of his physical health; but, waking one morning resolved to confess his misdeeds to the Lord, he had been forgiven. Instantly, just as Nathan had said – although, as Nathan pointed out, he would still have to live with the consequences. So pray, David advises, just keep praying, and the rising waters will not reach you; God will instruct and guide you, and you will, despite your sins, be reckoned among the righteous.

He returns to the subject in Psalm 103, where in an echo of Exodus 34 he urges us to thank God who heals and forgives us, who is full of compassion and mercy, who will not remain angry or deal with us as we deserve – for God has removed our sins from us as far as east is from west. As I reflect on my own failings, I find it peculiarly liberating to

---

13 Quoted by Gordon MacDonald, *Rebuilding Your Broken World* (Highland Books, 1998), p. 95. For the teaching of Jesus see Matthew 5:21–30.

14 Billy Graham Evangelistic Association of Canada website, **billygraham.ca/stories/the-cleansing-confession-psalm-51**.

know that whereas I may be sitting here in England, my sins have been detached from me with the same clinical efficiency with which I was once parted from my grumbling appendix, and discarded somewhere in the middle of the Pacific Ocean.

All too often, things don't work out as we expected; hidden faults undermine the happy simplicity of our world view, failure stains the edges of the success we had so earnestly and confidently sought, and we become painfully aware of our own weaknesses and vulnerabilities. God's requirement is that we recognise and confess our failings, not so that we may be punished, but so that we may learn from them and move on. The gift of forgiveness with which he responds is an extraordinary thing – and yet it leaves us with one final challenge, for we must persuade ourselves to accept it. Only then can we truly start afresh. Perhaps this is why David insists that the best response to our undeserved acquittal is praise; we need to shift our attention from our own shortcomings to the God who has overcome them, and look not to yesterday but to tomorrow, for it is with those who recognise their own fallibility that God seems most willing to work. If we want to walk closely with God, Gordon MacDonald suggests, we must learn to live as perpetually broken people: 'The freest person in the world is the one with an open heart, a broken spirit, and a new direction in which to travel.'[15]

What to do, then, with your own sins, iniquities and transgressions? 'The healthy attitude towards a fault made or a sin committed is surely a vigorous shake of one's moral shoulders,' writes Elizabeth von Arnim; 'the sin itself was a sad waste of time and happiness, and absolutely no more should be wasted in lugubriously reflecting on it. Shall we, poor human beings at such a disadvantage from the first in the fight with fate through the many weaknesses and ailments of our bodies, load our souls as well with an ever-growing burden of regret and penitence? Every morning comes the light, and a fresh chance of doing better.' Wisely, she takes a walk. 'All the way I had squirrels for

---

15 *Rebuilding Your Broken World*, p. 185.

company, chattering and enjoying themselves as sensible squirrels living only in the present do; and larks over my head singing in careless ecstasy just because they had no idea they were probably bad larks with pasts.' The thought makes me chuckle every time I watch a lark rise into the sky. We cannot live in our pasts.[16]

'For me,' writes Archbishop John Sentamu, 'it is God's constant forgiveness of my sin that daily causes me to stand in awe of him as nothing else does.'[17]

The cords of the wicked ensnare me

'I find it almost impossible to reconcile the beauty that I saw this morning, as my train pulled through a blue sky and past gleaming poplar trees and wide green playing fields, with the interminable pain and difficulty of living,' my daughter Katy wrote recently. 'Everywhere I look there are people doubled over with anxiety or grief or illness or some other private pain. Living and thriving is what we were all told we would do, but happiness and straightforwardness seem a dream too far away to touch. We are flung out into the world, such a wide and complicated world, with no experience and no knowledge of how to find our way through its treacly mess, and we are crippled by it. And yet at the same time when the actors dance in the theatre and the sun shines on the poplar trees and I wake up in a house which knows the Spirit of God, my joy feels deep and overflowing. The fact that these two things coexist baffles me utterly.'

One of the major causes of devastating grief and confusion, Donald Carson warns, is that our expectations are unrealistic; we do not give the subject of evil and suffering the thought it deserves until we ourselves

---

16 From her novel *Adventures of Elizabeth in Rügen* (Virago Press, 1990; first published 1904), pp. 155–57.

17 *Reflections on the Psalms* (Church House Publishing, Aimer Media, 2015), commentary to Psalm 130.

are confronted with tragedy.[18] Surrounded by the hidden pitfalls and illusory promises of a secular culture, we are liable to assume that as individuals loved by God we will be protected from much of the pain which comes to those who do not know him. Nothing in scripture supports this view; if anything the reverse is true. And yet, as Katy reminds us, there is more to be said, for if God does not promise to protect us from pain, he is almost tangibly present in the midst of it.

The author of Psalm 119, devoted as he was to the joys of following the path laid out by God, was aware not only of his own propensity to make mistakes, but also of the suffering he would experience at the hands of others. Having dealt with the former, he turns to the latter, pouring out the pain he feels as he considers the way, as he puts it in verse 61, that the cords of the wicked have ensnared him. 'The arrogant smear me with lies and subvert me with guile, he cries to God; they taunt and deride me, persecute me without cause and seek to destroy me. They flout your law and ignore your commands – will you not act?'[19] The 'songs of praise' which are the Psalms include an astonishing 62 poems which speak of the psalmist's enemies, assailants, adversaries and foes, and a further 30 which rail against those who do evil. The word 'wicked' is, in the English NRSV translation, the tenth most common word in the Psalter, occurring 104 times, followed by 'deliver' at 75 times and 'shame' at 42 times.[20] It is clear that there is no attempt, in the Psalms, to cover up the painful reality within which we must live.

If Psalm 119 offers an alphabet of godly living, the Psalter as a whole traces its way through a shadow alphabet of pain; in psalm after psalm we read of assaults and afflictions which are as real now as they were then. First comes betrayal, an experience which echoed through David's life – a son who plotted to kill him and seize the throne for himself, and a succession of followers whose loyalty vanished in the pursuit of personal gain. Betrayal hurts most when it comes from those closest

---

18 *How Long, O Lord? Reflections on suffering and evil*, second edition (IVP, 2006), p. 11.

19 Paraphrased from Psalm 119:61, 69, 78, 42, 51, 86, 95, 158, 126.

20 Excluding articles, pronouns, prepositions and common verbs (be, have, etc), and taking together wicked, wickedly and wickedness.

to us, those we have loved and trusted. David's experiences find their echoes in ordinary family and office life all over the world. Melanie, who discovered her husband had had four affairs, and changed all her passwords to 'brutal'.[21] Mike, made homeless by the legal action of a friend in whose failed company he had agreed to invest. Ann, abused by her boss, betrayed by colleagues who chose not to see what was happening, nursing her wounds alone at home. The psalmist understands: even my bosom friend in whom I trusted, who ate of my bread, has lifted his heel against me; my companion violated a covenant with me, with speech smoother than butter but with a heart set on war, he cries. Hurt to the core as he thinks of former friends, he struggles to come to terms with the fact that they have repaid his love by attacking him without cause, even as he prayed for them.[22]

Moving on through the alphabet, we find that the psalmists are not afraid to tackle the perennial problem of bullying. For the young David, this came from a king threatened by his ability and popularity, who sought first to intimidate and then to kill him. Today, bullying includes everything from cruel words in a school playground to creating a hostile work environment in order to force out an employee. It is so pervasive that we are provided with state-funded conciliation services and given access to tribunals which support victims of constructive dismissal. We may be bullied because of our age, appearance, gender, ethnicity, lifestyle choices, or simply because we are more able or successful than our colleagues. As long as people are afraid of their own inadequacies, filled with unresolved anger, driven by the desire for power and status, there will be bullying. The psalmists provide us with the words we need to express our pain. 'For how long will you threaten a person, for how long will you batter your victim, as you would a leaning wall, a tottering fence?' David demands of his enemies in Psalm 62; 'their only plan,' he complains, 'is to bring down a person of prominence.' He turns to God. 'Insults have broken my heart, so that I am in despair,'

---

21 Melanie's experience is one of many related by Christina Patterson, *The Art of Not Falling Apart* (Atlantic Books, 2018), p. 147.

22 Paraphrased from Psalms 41:9; 55:20–21; 109:2–4.

he laments in Psalm 69; 'I looked for pity, but there was none; and for comforters, but I found none.'[23]

Bullying goes hand in hand with false accusation, and here too the passing of the centuries has brought little relief. In 2016 researchers at Oxford University produced a harrowing report into the cases of people falsely accused of abuse; interviewees reported ruined careers, devastating damage to family members, and long-lasting mental trauma. Many had suffered from crippling self-blame despite knowing themselves to be innocent; a quarter reported feeling suicidal.[24] The stress of being falsely accused is so great that we may find our faith on a knife edge: whereas five of the Oxford participants reported that the experience had strengthened their faith, three said they had lost it altogether. David understands their pain: 'My enemies accuse me falsely'; 'for the words of their lips, let them be trapped in their pride,' he cries. 'They open wide their mouths against me,' he wails, saying 'Aha, aha, our eyes have seen it!' 'They have venom like the venom of a serpent,' he mutters.[25] Such behaviour receives particularly harsh treatment in the Psalms. No fewer than 43 psalms deal with the destructive power of the tongue, and the ninth commandment (false witness) is echoed more frequently than any of the others. David urges us to remember that God is with us. 'For no transgression or sin of mine, O Lord, for no fault of mine, they run and make ready,' he declares. 'I put my trust in you,' he says determinedly as he calls out his accusers; 'I am not afraid; what can flesh do to me?' The psalmists' determination to lay before God what is happening stands them in good stead: 'I kept my faith,' confirms the author of Psalm 116, 'even when I said, "I am greatly afflicted".'[26]

The alphabet of pain continues to wend its way through the Psalms.

---

23 Psalm 62:3–4 (paraphrased); 69:20–21.

24 Carolyn Hoyle et al, *The Impact of Being Wrongly Accused of Abuse in Occupations of Trust: Victims' voices* (University of Oxford Centre for Criminology, 2016).

25 From Psalms 69:4; 59:12; 35:21; 58:4.

26 Psalms 59:3–4; 56:3–4; 116:10–11. The word 'trust' occurs 42 times in the psalms – the same number as the word 'shame'.

Between them the psalmists have endured hypocrisy, injustice, malice, persecution and theft. Hypocritical enemies speak peace with their neighbours while mischief is in their hearts, smiling their way through words that seem smoother than butter but in fact bite like sharpened swords. Injustice lurks round every corner, as the wicked shoot from ambush at the blameless and lay secret snares to trap them. Malice fills their hearts as they utter curses and tell blatant lies, persecution is relentless as they fire in the dark at the upright in heart, and dishonesty leads to theft as they take bribes and demand that the psalmist 'give back' what he has not stolen.[27] The capacity of outwardly irreproachable people to cloak reprehensible behaviour in garments of respectability is horrifying – and yet both David and Jesus warn us to expect it, not just as we go about our worldly business, but even amongst those who most stridently proclaim their allegiance to God.[28] Often, we are left with nowhere to go – except, borrowing the psalmists' cries of protest, to God himself.

Finally, people seek to vilify the psalmist and bring shame upon him. This is a growing problem in our own society, where the rise of new media platforms has increased our ability to hurt one another without leaving the comfort of our homes. Journalist Jon Ronson has examined numerous cases of people subjected to public vilification through social media, not for any conspicuous wickedness, but for offences as trivial as a quotation discovered to be inaccurate, a joke deemed to be in poor taste, a tweet judged to be inappropriately phrased. Banished publicly to the far side of a fictional line of depravity, the victims find their jobs are lost, their self-esteem shattered and their lives wrecked.[29] David knows what it feels like, and as ever he has the words to express the fear and anger which rise within him when he finds himself condemned in this underhand way: 'Do not let me be put to shame,' he begs repeatedly; 'do not let my enemies exult over me.' Worried that the assault on his own reputation will undermine others, he asks God to protect them too. And then he asks for justice,

---

27 Psalms 28:3; 55:21; 64:4–5; 59:12; 15:5; 11:2; 69:4.

28 E.g. Matthew 13:24–30, the parable of the wheat and the tares.

29 *So You've Been Publicly Shamed* (Picador, 2015).

requesting that those who have sought to shame him will themselves be exposed and shamed.[30]

We have seen that David is the first to acknowledge his own failures, but he is strident too in his rejection of those who would bring shame upon him in order to gratify their own disordered desires or boost their own personal standing. Often, he says, they behave in this way not because he is himself flawed, but because he has remained faithful to God and sought to honour him. It's an enduring problem today: victims of the growing vogue for public shaming and ostracism, be they public figures who have used politically incorrect terminology, academics with unfashionable views or ordinary people who have offended complete strangers, all find their pain articulated in a remarkable 23 separate psalms.[31] Perhaps it is in his portrayal of shame that David's words bite most sharply into our times.

Owning our fear: Psalm 35

There are many ways of dealing with pain – the standard psychiatric handbook lists over 30 defence mechanisms we use to shield ourselves from what it terms 'unwanted or untenable facets of reality'.[32] Some things hurt so much that we cannot bring ourselves even to think about them, never mind put them into words. It may take years for a person who has been abused to recognise the reality and enormity of what has been done to them; the swelling tide of emotion may be so violent, the sense of shame so overwhelming, that the only safe option seems to be to repress it. Denial and distraction may offer some relief; my own techniques for dealing with corrosive feelings have included the compensatory purchase of pot plants, the voracious reading of historical novels, and night-time dedication to synchronised swimming

---

30 For the psalmist's pleas not to be put to shame see Psalms 25:2–3, 20; 31:1, 17; 69:6–7, 19; 71:1; 119:6, 31, 46, 80, 116. For the request that God shame his oppressors see Psalms 40:14; 57:3; 70:2; 71:13, 24; 119:78.

31 Psalms 4, 6, 22, 25, 31, 35, 37, 40, 44, 53, 57, 69, 70, 71, 74, 83, 86, 89, 97, 109, 119, 127, 129.

32 Appendix to the *Diagnostic and Statistical Manual of Mental Disorders*, fourth (revised) edition (American Psychiatric Association, 1994).

contests. Hot milk and honey is more effective than alcohol; chocolate is actually good for you. Family and friends come into their own. But nothing is more helpful than the Psalms. 'The Psalter is not for those whose life is one of uninterrupted continuity and equilibrium,' Walter Brueggemann warns; 'such people should stay safely in the book of Proverbs.' In reality, few of us live that kind of life, he points out; 'if we think we do, we have been numbed, desensitized, and suppressed so that we are cut off from what is really going on in our lives. The Psalms are not used in a vacuum, but in a history where we are dying and rising, where God is at work.'[33]

How then should we approach God when we find ourselves suffering and oppressed? The secret of the Psalms is that they do not seek to minimise our complaint, but rather to exaggerate it. Whereas we may dare to whisper that we are upset, the psalmist bellows it from the rooftops. Whereas we may confess that we would like to see negative consequences for those who have hurt us, the psalmist calls boldly for dreadful things to be done to them. Whereas we may feel that what has happened to us is not fair, the psalmist demands swift and public vindication. All this is not in order to help us indulge our most unattractive feelings, but to enable us to own them and move on from them. 'Some things are better put into plain speech than lying diffused and darkening, like poisonous mists in the heart,' Alexander MacLaren observed long ago; 'a thought, good or bad, can be dealt with when it is made articulate.'[34] In their insistence that we put our true feelings into words, the Psalms are the chemotherapy to our cancer.

The three most troublesome human emotions are generally recognised to be guilt, fear and anger, and these are the ones most likely to sweep through us when things go wrong. Having expressed his guilt in Psalms 51 and 32, David now turns to face his fears. Running like a refrain through many of the psalms, fear comes to the fore in Psalm 35. We may experience fear as we confront any of the threats we have just looked

---

[33] *Praying the Psalms*, second edition (Cascade Books, 2007), p. 14.
[34] Commentary to Psalm 77 in *The Expositor's Bible: The Psalms*, vol. 2 (Hodder and Stoughton, 1906), p. 376.

at; in this poem, David fears for both his reputation and his life. As we approach the psalm, the curtains rise to reveal the wide expanse of a treeless savannah. Hunters armed with shield and spear stride across the landscape, heading for a pit they have dug in which to catch their prey, cleverly concealed by a net covered with grass and leaves. The object of the hunt is David; his fear is that of the target animal – the antelope, the deer. Driven towards the pit, David calls out to God to take up his own weapons and rush to the rescue. We feel the terror of the hunt; adrenaline flows through our bodies, our hearts beat faster, we seek desperately for a way out.

It seems there is none, for the scene changes abruptly to a courtroom; David, now captured, is in the dock. Ruthless witnesses step forward. They have prepared their words carefully; they ask questions they know he cannot answer. He knows these people well; they are men for whom he has prayed when they were ill, men whose misfortunes he has mourned as he would mourn for his own brother. It dawns on him that the case has been meticulously planned: a record has been kept of his mistakes; criticisms and slanderous statements have been circulated; ridicule has been used to demean him in the eyes of those to whom he might turn for support. Sneering, the witnesses claim to have first-hand knowledge of David's crimes; smiling regretfully as they take turns to speak, they are confident of success.

David, however, is not. As the scene shifts again in his living nightmare, his accusers are transformed into lions, gathering in anticipation, baring their teeth in readiness for the kill. He cries out to God for rescue: wake up, wake up, he implores – how long, Lord, will you stand by and watch this? You know what they are doing; you know that their accusations are false; you know that they want to dispossess me and take my place themselves – will you not speak for me? Lord, you have a track record of rescuing the poor from those too strong for them, from those who rob them – will you not vindicate me? Desperate, he comes up with suggestions. You could send an angel to sweep them away like chaff before the wind, or chase them down a dark and slippery path; or might they not, perhaps, fall themselves into the pit they dug for me, to their own ruin? You could seek out those who delight in my downfall; you could shame those who wish to disgrace me – for I cannot bear the thought of seeing them come out of this the winners. Lord, he begs, say to me 'I am your salvation' – and then I will rejoice and give thanks to you; I will proclaim your righteousness and sing your praises. There David stops. But we know that the nightmare did come to an end, that God did wake up, that David did live to see another day. Often, when I have been overwhelmed by fear, this psalm has helped me to identify and articulate my feelings; often, it has felt that David himself is walking alongside me – that, desperate though I may feel, I am not alone. One day, Jesus himself would echo this psalm – for Jesus too would experience these things.[35]

Expressing our anger: Psalm 109

Fear is a natural first response to threat – but it is rarely the last. As our circumstances improve and our fear turns to relief, all too often we find anger welling up in its place. We have cried out for rescue; now we want justice. It's another natural response, for we are made in the image of a God who insists, from the first page of the Bible to the last, that justice will follow misdemeanour as predictably as night follows day. But not, of course, necessarily immediately.

The Psalms contain some of the most vehement and graphic expressions of anger found anywhere in literature. 'Some of the prayers given here are ones that we, as Christians, should not pray,' one highly respected commentary warns; 'it is difficult to infuse this Psalm with any sense compatible to the Christian spirit,' worries another. The Revised Common Lectionary deals with these passages more circumspectly – it simply leaves them out.[36] And yet this particular Christian is willing to

---

[35] John 15:25. See also Psalm 64, where David makes similar complaints against those who seek to bring him down, and Psalm 55:4–6, where his experiences trigger what today we would describe as a panic attack.

[36] Tokunboh Adeyemo (ed.), *Africa Bible Commentary* (Zondervan, 2006), p. 714; C.H. Spurgeon, *The Treasury of David*, updated edition, ed. R.H. Clarke (Thomas Nelson, 1998), p. 1008. The Revised Common Lectionary excludes the angry passages from

confess that she has at times found David's outbursts of anger extraordinarily helpful. Trying to work out why, I find myself thinking back to a particularly difficult miscarriage. I didn't know what I felt, or why – I just knew I felt bad. Very bad. Sitting down one evening with my husband, I listened to him trying to put my feelings into words for me. I still look back on the conversation with some wonder – how did he know? The most remarkable thing was that by the time I got up from the sofa, the painful emotions had disappeared; as if a boil had been lanced, and the poison released. This is what David does for us in the Psalms: by giving us the words we need to express our angst, he enables us to let go of it. Words, as scripture is at pains to point out, are powerful things.

The Psalm we are advised not to pray, and whose outbursts of anger are among those that fail to appear in the lectionary, is Psalm 109; even Walter Brueggemann warns that it is the most difficult and embarrassing psalm for conventional piety.[37] The sentiments expressed are so challenging, he points out, that the NRSV translation of the Bible adds the words 'They say', thus neatly transferring the vengeful words from David to his accusers. But the Hebrew text does not include this mitigating phrase: the outburst is David's own. Rather than engage with the text, the translators have actually rewritten it.

In Psalm 109 David again presents himself as a defendant in a court of law, on trial for his life. The complainants are pressing their case, which is destructive and slanderous; they speak with words of evil and hate, attacking him without cause, piling lie upon lie, cursing him and demanding that he be condemned to death. After a brief outline of the context, David seizes the witness stand and launches into a 16-verse tirade presenting his own case to God – this, he exclaims with furious eloquence, is the sentence that should be passed, not on him, but on each one of his accusers. In effect we are now watching a trial

---

Psalms 49 (13–20), 68 (21–23), 69 (18–29), 109 (1–20) and 139 (19–23). The Sunday lectionary of the Church of England omits Psalm 109 altogether, along with Psalms 58 and 83, both notable for their eloquent pleas for vengeance.

[37] W. Brueggemann and W.H. Bellinger, *Psalms*, New Cambridge Bible Commentary (Cambridge University Press, 2014), p. 473.

for perjury, with David as the prosecutor and his accusers standing silent in the dock. As David presses his case, it becomes clear that he is demanding that they be subject to comprehensive, public and long-lasting punishment. To be precise, he wants each one of them deprived of his position, his prayers ignored and his days cut short. He wants to see his wife widowed and his children forced to beg; he wants his assets seized, his reputation destroyed, and the sins of his father and mother exposed. He wants him cursed with the same curses he spoke so ruthlessly over others; cursed so that the words soak into his body like water and seep into his bones like oil – for he has worn cursing like a coat. In sum, David ends, this is the sentence I demand: may the evil that my accusers tried to do to me be done to them instead. And, he adds – let them know, God, that it is not me but you that have done this. Thank you; I rest my case.

David rarely seems to have acted on these feelings. The biblical account of his life shows him to have been remarkably generous in the treatment of his enemies, repeatedly turning down opportunities for revenge and willing to forgive even those who had betrayed him. Perhaps it was precisely because David could share his feelings so eloquently with God that he was able to let go of them and leave the matter in God's hands, where it properly belongs.[38] Once, we watched a young woman who had been horrifically abused stare in silence at these words from Psalm 109 and, for the first time, begin to get in touch with her feelings. It was the beginning of a process which would lead to her healing.

We do not always know what to do with the anger that wells up inside us when we are wounded by others. Tried and tested methods range from uttering short expletives to kicking the cat; we may honk furiously at complete strangers on the road or wonder whether it does in fact work to stick pins into wax models; we may accept prescriptions for antidepressant medication, comfort ourselves with cake or attempt

---

38 See for example 1 Samuel 24:11–12: 'I have not sinned against you, though you are hunting me to take my life... May the Lord avenge me on you; but my hand shall not be against you.' The statement that vengeance belongs not to us but to God appears in Deuteronomy 32:35, reaffirmed in both Romans 12:19 and Hebrews 10:30.

to drown our sorrows with alcohol. We may find, though, that it is considerably more liberating to turn to the psalmist for off-the-shelf expressions of fury. Psalm 58 is particularly helpful: 'Let them vanish like water that runs away; like grass let them be trodden down and wither. Let them be like the snail that dissolves into slime,' thunders David. Warming to his theme, he asks in Psalm 68 that his enemies be driven away like smoke in the wind and melted like wax in the fire, and in Psalm 141 that their bones be scattered like soil turned over by a plough. Asaph joins in: 'Make them like whirling dust, like chaff before the wind,' he cries in Psalm 83. 'Let them be like grass on the housetops that withers before it grows,' adds the anonymous author of Psalm 129 – after reminding God that these are the guys who actually tried to plough furrows down his back.

How does this work? Viewing our enemies as a trail of mucus left by a garden snail helps us get our troubles into perspective; using the words of the psalmist makes us feel that someone out there understands us, and that someone even bigger is listening; our delight in his inventiveness (this is so much better than those four-letter words) brings a smile to our face. The whole thing is, to use the technical term, cathartic. Baulk as we may, these passages are there for a reason: they sustain us in situations which otherwise might break us.

Seeking protection: Psalm 23

Once he has given voice to the terror which fills his soul and the anger which sweeps through him as he thinks about those responsible, David's thoughts turn to the question of what happens next. Powerless to act himself, he realises that his immediate need is for protection. He turns again to prayer.

Protection is a theme which runs throughout the Psalms. The psalmists beg to be protected from the consequences of their own failings; they ask for help when ill and afraid for their lives, and call upon God when they are threatened by others. They seek protection not only for themselves as individuals, but on behalf of the entire community; and they express their hope that this protection will be both immediate and eternal. Reminding themselves that the Lord is the strength of his people and a safe refuge for his anointed, they resolve to trust only in him – for while some put their trust in chariots and some in horses, we will call only on the name of the Lord, they declare. Confident in a positive outcome, the psalmists encourage us too to call upon God for protection: 'Though we stumble, we shall not fall headlong, for the Lord holds us by the hand,' David promises.[39]

Sometimes these promises reach us in unexpected ways. Three months into Roger's new job, there was a knock at the door. Jane, a member of our church, explained that she had come with a message for me. It was Psalm 23. 'Thank you,' I said politely. 'No,' said Jane, 'it's not what you think. I want to read it to you, otherwise you won't hear it.' We sat down; I listened. 'The Lord is my shepherd,' Jane began. Then, following David's sudden switch from talking about God to talking to God, she looked me straight in the eye: 'Even though I walk through the darkest valley, I fear no evil, for you are with me. You prepare a table before me in the presence of my enemies; you anoint my head with oil.' 'That,' said Jane, 'is what God wants you to remember.'

Within days, dark clouds began to gather on the horizon – clouds which would cast a shadow over our lives for many months to come. Bemused, I pondered the words. Psalm 23 has been called 'the nightingale of the Psalms'; a song sung in darkness, a song which 'has charmed more griefs to rest than all the philosophy of the world' – and, as the days and weeks passed and the storm intensified, that became true for me too.[40] Someone else drew Roger's attention to Psalm 37, also by David: 'Be still before the Lord, and wait patiently for him; do not fret. Yet a little while, and the wicked will be no more; though you look diligently for their place, they will not be there.' Unsure what to do as

---

39 Psalm 37:24. See also Psalms 28:8 (refuge) and 20:7 (chariots). 'Refuge' is another of the Psalter's key words, present in 31 psalms (NRSV).

40 Rabbi Daniel Silver, quoted by Jonathan Magonet, *A Rabbi Reads the Psalms* (SCM Press, 1994), p. 66.

conflict erupted all around us, we sought the advice of Bill Westwood, Bishop of Peterborough. 'Religion,' said the bishop disconcertingly, 'brings out the worst in people. Stand firm.' Strengthened by the words from the Psalms, we did. One by one, we were saddened to see those involved, for a whole host of different reasons, leaving the church. Five years later I found myself standing in a cathedral, my head quite literally being anointed with oil in a eucharistic service of ordination, in preparation for ministry in that same church. Despite Jane's visit, it was not an outcome I had anticipated.

Awaiting salvation: Psalm 63

It is tempting, when things go wrong, to believe that God is not with us; and yet these are the times, as David knew, when we most need him. The psalmists' pleas for protection were clearly written in the midst of trouble far more profound than most of us are likely ever to face. David is thought to have composed many of his psalms during the years when he lived as a refugee fleeing from the threats of King Saul; others are assumed to have been written during the years in which, as Saul's anointed successor, he battled against those who wished to overthrow him. Psalm 63 bears the inscription 'A Psalm of David, when he was in the wilderness of Judah.' It is peculiarly instructive.

David starts, as ever, with his feelings. Trapped in a dry and weary land where there is no water, David finds the physical needs of his body mirrored in his urgent desire for spiritual succour: he thirsts and faints for God. Lying awake at night, his mind floats back to happier times, when he would praise God in the temple. Far from the temple now, a different image comes to mind. Remembering that God is everywhere, he visualises the Lord's protection not in the strong stones of the temple building, but in the floating wings of a soaring bird: 'In the shadow of your wings I sing for joy,' he sighs.

In difficult times it helps, we are often told, to call to mind a happy place or time; to imagine ourselves not in our current situation but far away in a place where we felt safe and contented, protected from the dangers of the outside world. It's a technique familiar to the psalmists, and one they use repeatedly as they invite us to seek solace from our troubles until such time as rescue comes. We have seen David, at the peak of a crisis, portraying the terror of his circumstances in terms of hunting lions, savage warriors and unjust court cases; in his calmer moments he turns to happier images, and the nightmare of his current reality yields to a dream of a future shaped by the memories of a tranquil past. A new set of images comes into play as the psalmist reminds himself of sanctuary and throne, strong rocks and impregnable fortresses, protective hills and fertile valleys, flowing streams and abundant feasts. David's psalms bear witness to his extraordinary ability to enter a world profoundly at odds with his current reality. 'For God alone my soul waits in silence; he alone is my rock and my salvation,' he sings in Psalm 62. 'Whoever lives in the shadow of the Almighty,' he reassures himself in Psalm 91, 'will say to the Lord, "My refuge and my fortress; my God, in whom I trust."'[41]

Comforted by these assurances, David lifts his eyes to the horizon, and notices another eagle: 'He will cover you with his feathers, and under his wings you will find refuge,' he reminds himself. Distant hills speak to him too: 'Those who trust in the Lord are like Mount Zion,' he reflects in Psalm 125; 'as the mountains surround Jerusalem, so the Lord surrounds his people.' The same thoughts are found in Psalm 71, where an unnamed psalmist expresses equal determination, if less certainty: 'Be to me a rock of refuge, a strong fortress,' he pleads, 'for my strength is spent, and my enemies consult together.'[42] Casting his mind back to better times, he too looks forward to being able to sing God's praises once again. It's a powerful lesson: when things are bad, it helps to call to mind the protection we have enjoyed in the past, and to remind ourselves that as pain sweeps in from the horizon, so we may trust that it will once again be dispelled by the returning sun – for in terms of our relationship with God, nothing has changed.

---

41 Paraphrased from Psalms 62:1–2; 91:1–2.
42 Psalms 91:4 (NIV); 125:1–2; from Psalm 71:3, 9–10.

I have had to learn this lesson repeatedly. Each time life has thrown up an unpleasant challenge, I have hoped that it would be the last; only to find, a few years later, that another was on its way. After the third, I thought that surely the trials were now over, and that I had, with God's help, learned to stand fast. And then came another. Shaking my head in disbelief and seeking once again to make David's prayers my own, I took a few days out to walk with my daughter in the Brecon Beacons. The air was full of unseasonal mists and the hills were cloaked in grey, their summits emerging into view only as we climbed. On one there was a Bronze Age barrow. A wooden fingerpost lay on its side, pointing to the centre of the horseshoe arrangement of stones. 'Jesus loves you,' it said, improbably. Perhaps he does, I thought, gazing at it in astonishment. I just need to trust him. Again.

For eight long years James Stockdale was tortured in a Vietnamese POW camp. Asked afterwards how it was that he had managed to keep going, he explained that he never doubted either that he would get out or that this experience would become the defining event of his life, which in retrospect he would not be without. 'You must never confuse faith that you will prevail in the end – which you can never afford to lose – with the discipline to confront the brutal facts of your current reality, whatever they might be,' he said.[43] It's a good lesson for us as we battle our way through the various (probably rather lesser) disasters which befall us. Like Stockdale, I would not trade my most painful experiences for a life of uninterrupted peace; for it is through them that I have learned that I can depend on God and that, sooner or later, his promises will be fulfilled. 'Happy are those,' sings the author of Psalm 84, 'whose strength is in God, for as they travel through a valley of tears they make it a place of springs; they go from strength to strength. Happy are they who trust in him.'[44] The happiness does not come, I note, from an absence of suffering, but from the protection God provides as we endure it. And that has been true for me too.

---

[43] Story told by Andrew Watson, *Confidence in the Living God: David and Goliath revisited* (BRF, 2009), pp. 34–35.

[44] Paraphrased from Psalm 84:5–7, 12.

Life, I reflect as I dive beneath the cool surface of the Psalms, is both as easy as breathing, and as hard as sailing through a storm in a leaking boat.

8

Putting things right

When others desert us, God remains faithful. When people turn against us, God stays for us. When the world condemns us, God will vindicate us. Faith in the God of justice frees us not only to pray God's blessing upon ourselves but even to seek it for those who turn against us.
Christopher Cocksworth[1]

A resource for corporate prayer

As a guide for private prayer the Psalter is without parallel. The psalmists help us chart our way through choppy waters, encouraging us to face up to our own failings and enabling us to draw closer to God when we suffer at the hands of others. But however helpful the Psalms may be to us personally, we must bear in mind that this was not the primary intention of those who compiled them. Although some of the psalms may be more than 3,000 years old, the Psalter we have in our Bibles today is the result of a painstaking editorial process which may not have been completed until the third century BC. First brought together during the Babylonian exile, the psalms were carefully selected, gathered into five books, provided with titles and musical directions, sung each day in the restored temple and prescribed for use at the festivals held in Jerusalem at fixed times of the year.[2] Effective though it may now be as a resource for private devotion, the Psalter is primarily intended as a collection of songs selected for regular recital in the context of

---

1 Commentary to Psalm 109, in *Reflections on the Psalms* (Church House Publishing, 2015).

2 For the date of the Psalter see chapter 2, note 2. For regular use of the Psalms in the temple see William P. Brown (ed.), *The Oxford Handbook of the Psalms* (Oxford University Press, 2014), p. 9.

public worship. The breadth of material contained within it reveals this wider purpose: the Psalter aims to provide worshippers with a historical, ethical, theological and prophetic guide to their shared identity as the people of God.

This has clear implications, often overlooked, for the use of the Psalms in Christian worship today. The psalmists wish not simply to help us draw closer to God as individuals, but to guide and sustain us as a community of faith, enabling us to live peacefully together as a sign of the coming kingdom. For Christians the Psalter, the gospel text of the Old Testament, serves to model and mould the ministry of the church; through the deliberate act of singing these songs, we implicitly commit ourselves to living by them. The Psalms, as Gordon Wenham observes, are designed to function as powerful shapers of both individual virtues and social attitudes, effective now as when they were first composed.[3]

In the last chapter we traced the path of David and his colleagues as they looked to God for guidance in right living, confessed their personal failures, expressed their anguish when oppressed by others, and prayed for protection. All these themes reappear in the Psalter at a corporate level. The psalmists plunge straight in with guidance: if Psalm 1 urges us to delight in the law of the Lord, Psalm 2 points out that this is not just advice for individuals but a principle of government for kings.[4] As we continue through the Psalter we find that nearly a third of the psalms express the prayers not of the individual but of the community, and that their themes mirror the more personal prayers which we have looked at so far. Collective anguish, complaint, lament and cries for help are all here; so too are acceptance of God's discipline and the need for corporate repentance; so too are thanks and praise as the people renew their determination to walk in the way of the Lord and express their gratitude for his faithfulness.[5] Together these psalms call us into

---

3 *The Psalter Reclaimed: Praying and praising with the Psalms* (Crossway, 2013), pp. 13–14.

4 See also Psalms 21, 72 and 101 (which cover the rule and conduct of kings), 132 (of priests), and 115, 133 (of the people).

5 Psalms 44, 74, 89 express communal complaint; Psalms 79, 80, 81, 85, 90, 106 acknowledge collective sinfulness; Psalms 52, 85 acknowledge God's discipline; Psalms 14, 60, 68, 79, 80, 114 plead for restoration; Psalms 9, 75, 76, 82, 83 ask for justice; Psalms

a distinctive identity in which the pervasive values of a disordered world are rejected by a faithful community called to live in submission to God. These are the parameters within which together we will most fully enjoy God's blessing.

Hear, O my people, while I admonish you: Psalm 81

The psalmists are united in their view that God is steadfast in love towards us, both as individuals and as a community. The word used to describe this attribute of God is *hesed*. Hard to trace in English because it is translated in different ways in different contexts, in the Hebrew Bible *hesed* appears 245 times, of which more than half occur in the Psalms. *Hesed* is how God himself wishes us to understand him, and it is how he had described himself to Moses: 'a God merciful and gracious, slow to anger, and abounding in steadfast love and faithfulness, forgiving iniquity and transgression and sin' – words echoed in Psalms 86, 103 and 145, and emphasised in the repeated assurance of Psalm 136: 'for his steadfast love endures forever'. Affirmed repeatedly throughout history, God's steadfast love is embedded in the covenant of faithful commitment made in turn with Abraham, Moses and David, pointing towards a future which will culminate in the coming of Jesus.[6]

It therefore pains God when David fails to live within the parameters which guarantee our well-being; and it pains him still more when the entire nation does the same. Taking God's love for granted, they abandon their promises, leave the path of the Lord and walk in the ways of the wicked. The result is a gradual corruption of their society, which by David's time was characterised by the oppression and injustice which he portrays so vividly in his psalms – for it is not the threats of Israel's

---

27, 42, 46, 48, 63, 81, 84, 87 celebrate community worship; Psalms 112, 115, 121, 124, 125, 126 express corporate trust; Psalms 65–67, 124, 129 proclaim communal thanksgiving.

6 *Hesed* is also a key theme of Psalm 107 (see chapter 2). For a fuller discussion see Wenham, *The Psalter Reclaimed*, pp. 123–26. For God's words to Moses see Exodus 34:6–7 and Psalm 103:1–14; for the covenant with Abraham see Genesis 17:1–9 and Psalm 105:8–9; for that with David see Psalm 89.

enemies that David most fears, but those which arise from within the community of faith itself. Distressed by their betrayal, God speaks out: 'I hear a voice I had not known,' reports Asaph in Psalm 81: 'Hear, O my people, while I admonish you.' Speaking through Asaph, God laments that his people have refused to listen to him, offering him little alternative but to leave them to follow their own inclinations. 'O, that my people would listen to me and walk in my ways,' God laments.[7] Longing to feed them with wheat and honey, he is left to watch them suffer the consequences of their own choices. It's a very clear warning.

As we have seen with David, God responds to those who stray from the ethical parameters he sets for us by providing corrective discipline, hoping that this will provoke repentance and thus open the door to healing and restoration. The discipline takes the form of rebuke and withdrawal; the loss of God's protection and presence is intended to prompt us to review our actions. For David the separation is spiritual ('Do not take your holy spirit from me'). For the community as a whole it is geographical, and comes in the form of exile. Even as the people plead with God to deliver them from their enemies, those enemies become the agents of his displeasure and the means by which he delivers his rebuke: the temple is destroyed, the king overthrown and the people carried off to a foreign land.[8] David had responded readily to the rebuke administered by Nathan; for the less attentive community, the lesson will be learned the hard way.

The people respond with songs of corporate lament, the most vivid of which are collected in Book Three of the Psalter. To start with they had protested their innocence, as we all tend to do when things go wrong: 'All this has come upon us, yet we have not forgotten you, or been false to your covenant,' the Korahites had complained in Psalm 44 after a defeat in war – even as we read of the betrayal, bullying, false accusation, hypocrisy, injustice, malice, persecution, theft and vilification which flourished within the community. Gradually they

---

[7] From Psalm 81:5, 8, 13.

[8] The story is told in 2 Kings 24—25 and by the prophets (notably Jeremiah 39); the people's grief is expressed in the book of Lamentations.

accept that God is angry with them – although, like David over the matter of Bathsheba and Uriah, it takes a little time before they come to terms with the magnitude of their own failings. 'Why does your anger smoke against the sheep of your pasture?' Asaph asks piteously as he describes the smashing of the temple in Psalm 74. 'How long will your wrath burn like fire?' Ethan demands in Psalm 89, as he reminds God of his longstanding commitment to the covenant. It is true, he admits, that you had made it clear that if we forsook your law you would punish us; but you did say, he reminds God, that you would not remove your steadfast love from David and his descendants – so where is that love now? he asks plaintively. You are feeding us, reproaches Asaph in Psalm 80, with the bread of tears. Eventually they get the point, and in Psalm 85 the Korahites lead in a prayer of collective repentance: you forgave us before; will you not revive us again? they plead; for we trust that our renewed faithfulness will be met once more by your steadfast love. This is an act of hope, an echo of David's own prayer and an anticipation of the one that Jesus himself will invite us to pray.

Book Four will bring resolution. Shaping the book as a response to the crisis of exile so painfully articulated in Book Three, the Psalter's editors will help us to move from despair to a renewed experience of God's steadfast love. For the moment, God's people feel themselves to be alone, forgotten and far from home.

Praying the Psalms today

It's often said that, since the demise of the overtly Christian culture in which we once lived, the Christian church today is living in exile: formerly positioned at the heart of civic life, the church has become an ever-shrinking community of faith surrounded by a secular society which accords it little respect. Like the exiled Israelites, we too are inclined to feel sorry for ourselves, and we too respond by hoping things will get better. But is there an alternative reading to this common narrative – a reading suggested by the Psalms? If the Psalms are intended as a guide to the spiritual life not just of the individual but of the community of faith as a whole, we must expect them to retain their relevance as we pray them within our own community of faith, the church.

The psalmists are clear that the seeds of the exile to come are sown not in Babylon but among the people themselves: in walking away from God, the community of faith had distanced itself from the source of its own life. It is only when they recognise the enormity of their failure that God is able to restore them, return becomes possible, and the temple can be rebuilt for a new generation – who begin afresh with collective readings of the scriptures and daily recitals of the Psalms.[9] Could it be that we, like those whose mistakes are lamented in the Psalms, have failed to walk in the path of the Lord; that our current decline arises not simply from the hostility of the culture which surrounds us, but from our own failure to depend on God and to live in accordance with his will? Should we consider the possibility that we are in fact being disciplined by God, and that our exile, like theirs, might be the result of our own shortcomings? If indeed this is the case, there will be, for us as for the psalmic community, only one possible route back: repentance, not just individual but also corporate.

There are many ways in which we might seek the answer to this question, many avenues we might explore to help us determine whether the life and ministry of the Christian church is indeed falling short in its witness to *hesed*, the steadfast love of God. But perhaps one stands out, not least because it was as dear to Jesus as it had been to David, and it's related to the question we looked at in chapter 7 – who are the righteous, and who are the wicked? And whose job is it to place people in one category or the other? We have listened to David's cries for forgiveness for his own sins and for deliverance from those who would judge and condemn him. We are well aware that Jesus calls us both to seek and to offer forgiveness, and mindful of his warning not to treat others as David's enemies treated him: 'Do not judge, and you will

---

[9] The story of the return to Jerusalem is told in the book of Nehemiah, where Nehemiah's personal repentance (ch. 1) is followed by the fulsome confession and recommitment of the people (ch. 9). The confession echoes that of Psalm 106.

not be judged; do not condemn, and you will not be condemned,' he said.[10] God alone is judge, both David and Jesus remind us repeatedly; and a keen sense of our own failings should prevent us from leaping to condemn others. So how are we doing?

Out of the mouths of babes and infants

George (5) and Freddie (3) emerged from Sunday School. 'Write down your sins,' said George, thrusting a pad of post-it notes and a pencil into my hand. 'What, all of them?' I asked. 'Yes. Write them down!' 'Have you written your sins down?' I asked. 'No! Write them down. Do it now!' Cautiously, but accurately, I wrote, 'I am not always patient.' George took back the pad, tore off the top sheet and pressed it firmly onto my jumper. 'There!' he said triumphantly. Freddie too had a pad of post-it notes. 'Write down your sins,' he commanded, frowning imperiously. 'Okay. What about you? Have you got any sins?' I asked. 'No! Write them down!' Not yet able to read or write, Freddie was not inclined to wait for the details; so the post-it note was torn off blank, and stuck beside its fellow on my jumper. In the meantime George had warmed to his task, and several other members of the congregation now also sported post-it notes. 'What happens now?' I asked Freddie. 'God,' said Freddie firmly. 'Does God forgive my sins?' I asked, hopefully. 'No! God is the policeman! The policeman comes!' Janet watched ruefully. 'Some of my Sunday School lessons work well,' she said. 'Some of them, clearly, don't.'

It turned out that Janet had been encouraging the children to think about Matthew chapter 7, where Jesus issues a graphic warning against the folly of focusing on the specks in other people's eyes whilst ignoring the planks in our own. 'Do not judge, so that you may not be judged,' he thunders; 'for with the judgment you make you will be judged, and the measure you give will be the measure you get.' George and Freddie

---

10 Luke 6:37. God's unique role as judge is affirmed repeatedly by the psalmists – e.g. Psalms 7, 9, 36, 51, 143 (David), 50, 75 (Asaph); see also Psalms 96, 97, 98, 119.
The gospel of John tells us that God will judge through his Son Jesus (John 5:26–27).

had put their fingers on one of the ways in which we most often fail one another. Rather than directing fellow believers to the life-saving prayers of the psalmist and the forgiveness promised by God in response, we have an alarming tendency to focus on one another's faults. The results can be devastating; instead of leading people gently towards God, judgment slams the door in their faces. David, prepared to admit his own failings, describes in painful detail what it feels like to be accused of misdemeanours by people who are less willing to be honest about themselves than he is. If there is one thing David hates, it is being put in the dock by people who wish to accuse, judge and destroy him. And yet the impulse arises within us all. 'Is that your inner Nazi speaking?' my daughter asked with a twinkle in her eye as I remarked one day upon the lamentable behaviour of a complete stranger.

When former believers are asked why they have given up on their faith, many say that it is because of the way they have been treated by the church – either because the church had nothing to offer when they were in pain or, more devastatingly, because it was itself the cause of that pain; in the midst of their struggles they had been rejected instead of loved, judged instead of forgiven, blamed instead of healed. 'Over and over again,' John Marriott reports, 'those who have lost their faith tell stories of being hit by Friendly Fire in the form of judgment and condemnation from fellow-believers.' 'Those who have been the most hurtful, those who have been the most unkind, those who have betrayed, slandered, and undermined me have been those who have also called themselves by God's name,' writes Anne Graham Lotz sadly; and 'the wounds have hurt even more when the wounders wrapped their behavior in a semblance of religion or piety.' Sometimes the wounds are inflicted by individuals, but all too often, Marriott finds, by entire church elderships, who are inclined to treat those who have taken wrong turnings not as people in need of help but as moral delinquents who have forfeited their right to belong. 'The greatest tragedy,' confirms William Hendricks as he interviewed church leavers, 'was that a system promising forgiveness and freedom from guilt ended up by making so many of them feel guilty.'[11] 'There is no help for you in God,' David's accusers had said in Psalm 3 as they sought to break his spirit and destroy his faith; but David knew not only that this wasn't true, but that it could never be true.[12]

I think of Rose, a young woman whom I once invited to come with me to church. Could she, Rose asked in a nervous whisper, go forward for communion? A man in the row in front turned round. 'If you want to gossip during the service, could you please do it outside,' he snapped. It was Rose's first, and last, visit to church. I think of Clive, recovering in hospital after a life-threatening accident. 'God must be punishing you for your sins,' said a visiting church member, a shadow on his brow. I think of Mark, clinging to his faith after a messy divorce, and the pain in his eyes as he told how his pastor had explained he was no longer welcome in church.

And yet I think too of those who have been dealt with more gently. Over the years Roger and I have prayed with hundreds of people who wished they had lived differently, people trapped by their experiences, ashamed of their responses – people with secret addictions, hidden failures, ungodly habits. 'I have slept with 50 men,' said Tracy; 'they say you can help – but I don't want anything religious.' And, two hours later, 'I am going home to start my new life.' 'I was dismissed,' confessed Joe, 'for taking some money from the till.' Helped to understand why he had done this, Joe found another job and went on to play a key part in the life of the church. 'I have been looking at porn sites,' explained Nigel uncomfortably, wincing as he shared his own childhood experiences. Every one of these people needed the forgiveness and healing which only God can provide. Any one of them could have been me. The church, notes Francis Spufford, is not meant to be the high ground of

---

11 John Marriot, *A Recipe for Disaster: Four ways churches and parents prepare individuals to lose their faith* (Wipf and Stock, 2018), ch. 8; Anne Graham Lotz did not leave the church, but reflected on her experiences in her book *Wounded by God's People* (Hodder, 2013), pp. 18, 32; William Hendricks, *Exit Interviews: Revealing stories of why people are leaving the church* (Moody Press, 1995), pp. 266–67.

12 Psalm 3:2. See also Psalm 71:11, where the psalmist's accusers assert confidently that God has forsaken him, and that he is now on his own.

virtue, but a harbour for the guilty: 'We are supposed to be on the side of goodness in the sense that we *need* it, not that we *are* it.'[13]

The psalmists know from bitter experience that none of us stands justified before God, and that God does not deal with us according to our sins or punish us for our iniquities; for God, as Walter Brueggemann notes in his commentary to Psalm 103, operates not out of a precise moral calculus but out of immeasurable and transforming compassion and grace.[14] And grace, as David knew, is ministered not through condemnation and exclusion, but through repentance and restoration. This is what the good news actually is: whoever we are, whatever we have done, God stands alongside us, ready not to judge and condemn but to forgive and restore. It's a message sorely needed in our increasingly judgmental culture, and it is uniquely ours to bring.

And yet it seems that this desire to judge others may not only be a problem within our local fellowships, where inevitably people who have failed to grasp what it means to be loved by God will be inclined to throw hand grenades into one another's spiritual lives, but more extensively within the leadership of our denominations. What is the best way for Christian leaders to contribute to society as a whole? When we speak, write, post, or tweet about our national life, when we comment on the conduct of public figures or offer our views on government policy, do we do so out of a prayerful and servant-hearted desire to model a godly way of living to those who may not yet know God, or do we sound disconcertingly like George and Freddie, calling into question the moral integrity of those with whom we do not agree and ringing the bells of condemnation whenever we detect a whiff of imperfection? The church, suggested Professor Chris Baker, commenting on a barrage of disapproving tweets from church leaders, 'must

---

13 *Unapologetic: Why, despite everything, Christianity can still make surprising emotional sense* (Faber and Faber, 2012), p. 188. Italics mine.

14 Walter Brueggemann and William H. Bellinger, *Psalms*, New Cambridge Bible Commentary (Cambridge University Press, 2014), pp. 442–43. See also Psalms 130:3 ('If you should mark iniquities, Lord, who could stand?)'; and 143:2 ('No one living is righteous before you').

reflect urgently on how, and with what narrative, it intervenes in the public sphere'.[15]

And when we are afraid that our own institutional shortcomings – widespread sexual abuse, dubious investments, increasing centralisation of power, to name but a few – have become only too obvious, do we pour our energies into binding up the wounds of the poor, the needy and the broken-hearted, or do we look for scapegoats and hope that public sacrifice will deflect attention from our failures?[16] It is all too easy to sound more like moral policemen than bearers of good news; all too easy to focus on the specks in other people's eyes instead of taking the planks out of our own. Our primary calling is not to comment on the conduct of others, but to model something entirely different; our first responsibility before God, the psalmists insist, is to put our own house in order, to live in a way which reflects our commitment to a God who is merciful and gracious, abounding in steadfast love – and to reflect that love ourselves in the way we treat others. Otherwise we will come across, as Jesus said in a characteristically blunt one-word summary, as hypocrites.

So the Psalms offer us another opportunity, an invitation to lament our failures and confess our sins, not just individually but also collectively. The decline of western Christianity, David Smith suggests, should be viewed in a similar manner to the exile in Babylon: 'as a tragedy which conceals an unasked-for blessing, opening up entirely new spaces for repentance, recovery and renewal and so gifting us an opportunity to read the gospel with new lenses capable of overcoming our tragic blind spots.'[17] If we wish to express our faith coherently and credibly, we would be wise to consider the possibility that we may be complicit

---

15 Writing in *The Church Times*, 27 May 2020.

16 The Church of England and the Roman Catholic Church have faced extensive public enquiry and received numerous complaints on these aspects of their corporate life in recent years. Both have seen sharp declines in attendance. Psalm 109:16 offers a salutary warning.

17 *Stumbling Toward Zion: Recovering the biblical tradition of lament in the era of world Christianity* (Langham, 2020), p. 28.

in our own demise, and to remind ourselves that exile, for us as for the people of God in the sixth century BC, is God's last resort.

You thought I was just like you: Psalm 50

If the psalmists take a little time to get to grips with the need for corporate repentance, they do not shirk their responsibility once they have grasped the issues. Asaph issues the call in Psalm 50 (which we note is carefully placed alongside David's personal repentance in Psalm 51). God does not keep silence, Asaph warns, but calls us to account as a community. Your beautiful services and your prayerful offerings are all very well, God says – but there are some among you who recite my statutes whilst ignoring my word, who slander and speak against your own people. You thought I was just like you, God continues, and up to now I have said nothing – but if you do not mend your ways, *I will tear you apart*.[18] Sharply dividing appearance from reality, stripping away the cloak of religious pretence, this is an uncompromising call to the community to take a hard look at its corporate life.

Faced with this clarity, the community responds, again through Asaph – but not before God has been forced to carry out his warning. The temple has been destroyed, Jerusalem razed to the ground, and the scattered survivors brought to their knees. 'Do not remember against us the iniquities of our ancestors,' they plead in Psalm 79; 'deliver us, and forgive our sins.' The Korahites continue the prayer in Psalm 85, but it is only in Book Four that the people offer a full and frank confession of failure. 'Both we *and* our ancestors have sinned,' the author of Psalm 106 declares as he catalogues the iniquities of the people – ingratitude, rebellion, jealousy, worshipping idols, grumbling, eating sacrifices, not trusting or obeying God, shedding innocent blood and adopting the values of the surrounding cultures. But God, he reminds them, has

---

18 Psalm 50:22.

forgiven and delivered them many times before, and can be trusted to do so again – for God is, after all, steadfast in love.[19]

I was once part of a church which, although well attended and active in ministry to the community, had a history of pride and conflict which had in recent years nearly destroyed it. A visiting preacher suggested we might like to gather together, repent of our failings and those of our predecessors, and ask God to cleanse and forgive us. 'Both we and our ancestors have sinned,' we admitted. As we celebrated the Eucharist together, people reported a sense of light and warmth flooding into the building. A few days later our surveyor came to the surprised conclusion that there was, in fact, no further trace of the extensive dry rot he had been called in to investigate. The following Sunday, we experienced a remarkable outpouring of the Holy Spirit during the service. 'The angels are back,' said one of the older members happily.

Back in Jerusalem, the facts have been faced, and confession has been made. Psalm 106 brings Book Four of the Psalter to a close, and as we move on into Book Five we find ourselves invited to join the people of God as they sing hymns of thanksgiving. Psalm 126 is a song of joy; God has listened and responded. Now restored to Jerusalem, it all seems like a bad dream, they say; once again we laugh and shout, and other nations say that God has done great things for us. And then, in Psalm 132, comes the line we repeat so often, perhaps without paying due attention to the fact that it represents the end, and not the beginning, of a long and painful process: 'Let your priests be clothed with righteousness, and let your faithful shout for joy.' We may remind ourselves that righteousness comes not through human perfectibility, but through a willingness to face our own failures and ask God for help. That should be our prayer today: as Gordon Wenham points out, the Psalms leave us in no doubt that a faith community that fails to uphold a biblical ethic cannot expect to enjoy God's covenant blessings.[20]

---

19 Verses 24 to 39 of Psalm 106, which detail the sins of the people, are omitted from the Revised Common Lectionary.

20 *The Psalter Reclaimed*, p. 159.

The cry for justice

Having encouraged us to confess our own sins and advised us to turn to God for protection, the psalmists now urge us to consider the possibility that we may need to repeat this same process as a community, recognising our failures and seeking forgiveness for our collective, and sometimes catastrophic, failure to live as the people of God. In telling their own story, they remind us that when the community of faith responds to God's rebuke, he not only forgives but also restores. As we pray the Psalms, we learn that this can be true for us too, and that blessing may once again become part of our corporate experience.

But what happens in the meantime? Is that it, we find ourselves asking; don't we need more than that? Even as we accept the call to put our own house in order and seek forgiveness for the way we have damaged others, we may feel compelled to ask what redress we have against those who are not similarly willing to acknowledge the wounds they have inflicted on us. It's clear what we are to do with our own feelings of guilt – but how are we to deal with the fear and anger which flood through us as a result of the damaging actions of others? If God is indeed steadfast in love, if he is indeed a God of justice, should we not expect him to take action on our behalf? In other words, what *does* happen to the wicked, the people who live by their own agenda, the people who have trampled us or our friends underfoot in the relentless pursuit of their own interests? How *do* we respond if we ourselves have been judged and condemned, abused and rejected by members of our family, by our colleagues, neighbours or even by the Christian community in which we have so longed to find acceptance?

I think of Rob, forced to hand over a growing ministry which he had built up from scratch to an ambitious outsider sent in to take over from him. Angry and depressed, Rob was forced to watch from the sidelines as it all fell apart. I think of Moira, who alerted her church elders to the presence of financial irregularities in the minister's accounts. Bullied out of the fellowship and betrayed by a leadership which preferred to prioritise reputational management, Moira accepted their verdict that she had let God down, and attempted suicide. I think of those sexually abused by priests they had trusted, abused again by an institutional church which ignored their complaints and muffled their voices – presumably in the hope that what the world did not see, God would not see either. Most have suffered long-lasting trauma; some have taken their own lives.[21] And I think of those subjected to the over-compensatory disciplinary processes of the Anglican and Catholic churches, established to investigate complaints of any kind against the clergy but so notoriously open to abuse that they leave 40 per cent of those subjected to them also contemplating suicide. The abuse, it has been suggested, has not been resolved but simply displaced.[22] And as the psalmist knew only too well, it is excruciatingly difficult to believe that God is on your side when those who accuse, reject and condemn you claim to be doing so in his name.

So what can we expect from God, we may find ourselves asking, while we wait for things to be put right? Don't we need more than an assurance that God is displeased? Yet again, the psalmists spring to our aid: some of the most remarkable psalms are those which put into words the agonising cries for vindication which echo from the lips of those who have been persecuted and exploited by others. These are the psalms we can pray when, traumatised by our experiences, we realise that final resolution will come only when things are finally put right. As we read on, we find that we are being offered a threefold invitation: to ask, to trust, and to wait – for God will indeed act.

---

21 The extent of sexual abuse within the Church of England and the Roman Catholic Church, and the extent to which it was covered up, was laid bare by the Independent Inquiry into Child Sexual Abuse which reported in 2020. Many have told their stories in Janet Fife and Gilo (eds), *Letters to a Broken Church* (Ekklesia Publishing, 2019).

22 The alarming findings of a report by Carl Senior and Alena Nash of Aston University into the disciplinary processes of the Church of England were published in 2020 by Sarah Horsman of the Sheldon Community. A thorough review is now under way.

Ask: Psalm 7

David's first great plea for justice comes in Psalm 7. He is being accused of wrongdoing, the inscription suggests, by a man named Cush, a Benjaminite. We do not know who Cush was, but we do know that members of the tribe of Benjamin were implacably opposed to David and actively seeking his downfall; David confirms that Cush was not acting alone.[23]

Once again, David pictures himself in court, surrounded by aggressive litigants who accuse him of acting unjustly, of harming his friends and robbing his opponents. Have I really done this – for if I have, then let me be found guilty, he cries. It's a question which haunts every victim of personal or institutional abuse, every person falsely accused, everyone who has been deliberately damaged by others – could my accusers be right, am I in fact what they say I am? We have already seen David ask himself this question in Psalm 139, for it's one which comes naturally when disaster strikes. But once again David rallies; no, the problem lies not in me, he reflects, but in them – a simple test of the heart will prove that. So 'rise up, Lord, in your anger,' he pleads; you have heard their case – make a judgment! Examine me, and then them! Reminding himself that God is a righteous judge, David reflects that unless Cush and his friends repent and seek forgiveness, they will themselves suffer the fate that they are so determined to inflict on him – for God will sharpen his sword and string his bow; the tables will be turned, and it will be they who are in the dock. Even though this is an outcome yet to come, relief floods into his heart: God will deliver just judgment; God will act.

Long before I had got to grips with the Psalms, I found myself struggling with the same internal conflict which David describes here. For six years I had found the criticisms of those whose expectations I was unable to meet increasingly difficult to bear. One morning, in the midst of the routine task of making breakfast, I was swept suddenly and

---

23 See 2 Samuel 16, 20.

unexpectedly into another realm. I too saw myself standing before the Lord in a court of law, surrounded by the voices of accusation which so troubled me in real life. The allegation was not primarily that I had done this or that – I didn't even know if I had – but that I was a certain kind (the wrong kind) of person. As I stood in the dock my accusers, in a muddle of their voices and my own, informed the Lord that they knew what I was really like, and that those who thought otherwise were simply not in possession of the facts. The voices died down; a moment of pin-dropping silence followed. Then an arm, a hammer, a crash: 'Not guilty!' rang out the verdict. In that instant I shed a burden so heavy that I felt gravity had lost its grip; tension drained with such speed from my body that my arms and legs went floppy, as if I were no longer flexing them against a raging wind but floating on a rising thermal. In that split-second encounter with God, all my anger and resentment vanished. I managed not to drop the breakfast – but walked about very cautiously for the rest of the day, smiling generously at everyone I met, giving to the Lord the thanks due to his righteousness and singing praises to his name, as David puts it in this psalm. Even 30 years later, it remains one of the defining moments of my life.

Trust: Psalm 37

As the years go by, David becomes increasingly confident that although God may not respond instantly to our pleas, he can nonetheless be trusted to provide us with justice. And so the ageing David composes a very different psalm: drawing on a lifetime of experience, he sets out to provide reassurance and guidance for those who struggle with injustice and abuse. Without minimising our pain, Psalm 37 offers a full and comprehensive assurance that our oppressors will be dealt with, that God will make our vindication shine like the light, that the shadows which surround us will be dismissed and the justice of our cause will gleam in the midday sun. Everything, David promises, will be dealt with.

In the meantime, what is required of us is trust. 'Do not fret because of the wicked,' he counsels; 'commit your way to the Lord; trust in him, and he will act.' It's another long psalm, and like Psalm 119 it comes in the ordered, reassuring form of an acrostic. Taking as its subject the troubling prosperity of those who seek to destroy us, couplet after couplet offers advice on how to cope, assuring us that though we stumble, we will not fall, for the Lord holds us by the hand. Injustice may unfold through the alphabet of our experience, the psalmist suggests; but each successive letter serves to move us gradually towards the inevitable outcome: a full reckoning will be held. You may fear your oppressors, but the Lord laughs at them, for their days are numbered. Your own future, by contrast, is assured, for the Lord is your refuge, and your inheritance is secure. Listen, David says, to the advice of an old man; just keep walking, keep trusting, and all will be well.

Over the years Roger and I have prayed for a number of people who have been sexually abused, some as children, others as adults. All of them have had to own and express their anger, and to place their unresolved pain in God's hands – for although we long for justice, we are often required to accept that we will not, in the short run at least, see that justice administered. And yet release is possible, even while we wait. For me this was vividly demonstrated when I found myself praying, alongside a ministry partner, for Carol. Carol had been abused as a child; still under the care of a psychiatrist, she had remained dependent on regular therapy and antidepressant medication. As we prayed together, Carol was overwhelmed by the reality of God's love. We encouraged her to accept David's advice and to place her abuser's future in the hands of God, secure in the knowledge that he, and not she, would take responsibility for the outcome. Could she let go, we asked? 'I'd never thought of letting go,' Carol admitted. Bravely, she said she would like to try. Together we read the words of the prophet Zephaniah, who had struggled with the same issues on behalf of a whole people. Rejoice, my daughter, the Lord had said through Zephaniah, for I am with you, and you will fear disaster no more. I will deal with your oppressors, and change your shame into praise; I will rejoice over you with singing, and renew you with my love.[24] Then we waited together. Within minutes Carol was laughing and crying, as the reality of who she was before God dawned on her. 'Daughter!' she gasped, a radiant smile creeping slowly across her face. The next morning Carol looked like a completely different person; as if the load of a lifetime had been lifted from her shoulders.

Wait: Psalm 94

So we ask, and we trust. Our third task is to wait. What is it, exactly, that we are waiting for? The answer comes in Psalm 94, shaped as a credal statement of justice. God, begins the psalmist, is the God of vengeance, the judge of the earth. Vengeance, Walter Brueggemann explains, is to be understood in this context not as an emotion, a hate reaction, but as a specific act to restore justice where the regular legal processes have failed.[25] Injustices do occur, Psalm 94 acknowledges – through the arrogance of those who crush God's people and undermine their inheritance, or through the social abuse of women, foreigners and children. Those who do these things appear to believe that God is not watching. But God *is* watching, the psalmist insists. Reminding us that we should welcome God's discipline, which keeps us heading in the right direction even as we suffer at the hands of others, he promises that for those who ignore God there will be firm and decisive retribution. Not to put too fine a point on it, he says, *God will wipe them out*. In the meantime we must thank God for the life-changing consolation and interim protection that he provides for us, and wait.

Pondering these things one sunny autumn day as I walked over the Quantocks, I followed a rutted old drove road beneath thickly gnarled beeches and found myself emerging beside a little church. I went inside. It was cool and dark, with carved Tudor pew ends and golden roof bosses – a place, I thought, where whole generations must have

---

24 See Zephaniah 3:14–20.

25 Brueggemann and Bellinger, *Psalms*, p. 406.

come before God to express both their joy and their suffering. A Bible lay open on the lectern at the book of Ezekiel, chapter 18. The people had been complaining, it seems, that God was unfair; specifically, that he was not delivering justice in the way they had expected him to, and that those who repented of their sins were escaping punishment. And indeed they will, God had said to Ezekiel – just as, if you too repent, you will escape punishment for yours. I take no pleasure in the death of anyone, and I would prefer that they turn from their ways and live, he says; for those who do not will die. Is it my ways that are unjust, God concludes – or yours?

This is a tough lesson to learn. It helps to remember that we ourselves are far from perfect; that every single one of us falls short, both within our own souls and in our relationships with others, that we too are in need of forgiveness, and that the distinction God makes is not between good people and bad people, but between those who repent and those who do not. Perhaps, given our own imperfect performances, it's better to allow God to take his time, to trust the outcome to him.

Can we live with this caveat and this delay? Maybe we can. Vengeance, as Walter Brueggemann reminds us, is not a psychological but a theological matter: it belongs properly to God, and not to us: 'Vengeance is mine,' God declares.[26] We do need to express our pain and our anger, and we do need to know that God has heard us and that he cares. But for our own sakes we must leave it there; for if it is truly justice which we seek, and not simply revenge, then we cannot afford to allow bitterness and resentment to find a permanent place within our hearts. Asaph puts it very clearly in Psalm 73: struggling with the conundrum of God's continued failure to take action against his oppressors, he too goes into the sanctuary to pray. Confessing that he had been both envious and angry as he watched his enemies grow in wealth and status, Asaph realises how close he had come to losing his faith altogether – 'I was stupid and ignorant,' he says; no better than a dumb animal. As he

---

26 *Praying the Psalms*, second edition (Cascade Books, 2007), p. 67. See Deuteronomy 32:35, quoted in Romans 12:19 and Hebrews 10:30.

prays, his anger dissolves. One day, he reflects, all this will seem like a bad dream, and these people will have no more solidity than ghosts; when the time comes those who are found to be false will perish, and that is all I need to know. My heart may fail, but God will uphold me; it is good to stick close to him, for he is my refuge, Asaph concludes.[27]

And so the Psalms give the last word not to us, but to God. We confess our pain, we make our case, and we wait, trusting the outcome entirely to him. It's a temporary answer, but it does point clearly to a definitive and permanent one: an answer which will come in the person of the long-awaited king, the successor to David, through whose rule God's covenant promises will be finally and fully fulfilled.[28] For those of us who recognise this hope to have been realised in the person of Jesus, the Psalms point the way to a new future, because the story the psalmists tell is the one that Jesus came to complete – a story of creation and covenant, of disobedience and disaster, but a story too of love and forgiveness, of restoration and redemption. Narrated in both the Psalms and the gospels, this is a story which stretches from the beginning of time to its end: this is our story.

The final step: forgiveness

How should we pray, Jesus' disciples asked him. 'Forgive us our sins, as we forgive those who sin against us,' he replied. If the ultimate answer to injustice and abuse is found in the judgment of God, an interim answer lies within our own hearts. The psalmists encourage us to face the facts: that life, as my father warned me, is not fair. They allow us to mind this, and they help us to complain about it. They urge

---

27 Geoffrey Grogan remarks that 'it is increasingly recognised that 73 is of great importance in the structure of the Psalter... that it virtually sums up the message, not only of the whole Book of Psalms but of the whole Old Testament' – *Prayer, Praise and Prophecy: A theology of the Psalms* (Mentor, 2001), p. 217.

28 For the expected king see Psalms 2, 45, 110; numerous passages from the Psalms are quoted in the New Testament as confirmation of Jesus' identity. For Jesus' own statement see Luke 24:44: 'Everything written about me in the law of Moses, the prophets, and the psalms must be fulfilled.'

us to trust, not to fret, and to wait. In encouraging us to articulate and then let go of our pain, the psalmists enable us to take the first step on a journey which will be completed only through our relationship with Jesus: we must learn to forgive.

The day before his arrest Jesus warns his disciples of what is to come, quoting Psalm 69, in which he finds the harsh predictions of his own humiliation, suffering and death. Perhaps it helps us to imagine ourselves standing on the hill outside Jerusalem, knowing that we too have become part of the scream of pain which echoes throughout human history, culminates in the cry of anguish which first poured from the lips of David in Psalm 22, and now reverberates from the cross: 'My God, my God, why have you forsaken me?' Perhaps it helps us to remember that in the agony of our own suffering we too must trust that the ultimate solution is to be found in that very same God, who has not after all forsaken us; and to whisper the words, this time from Psalm 31, with which Jesus, some hours later, would end his life: 'Into your hands I commit my spirit' – words which would subside into the silence of night, only then to rise again as he creates a path beyond pain into a new and different world. 'Be strong, and let your heart take courage,' David concludes, 'all you who wait for the Lord.'[29]

And yet we must remember too that, without minimising the horror of all this, Jesus will, even as he hangs on the cross, ask God to forgive those who have nailed him there.[30] Forgiveness, we conclude, does not mean pretending that the abuse we have suffered was not wrong, or that we didn't really mind; nor does it mean trying to live as if it didn't happen, or can simply be forgotten. You can't do any of those things from a cross. What it does mean is what the psalmists glimpsed and Jesus will demand: letting go of the desire for retribution and releasing those who have hurt us to God, recognising that he alone is qualified to judge them. It means accepting that in echoing the psalmists' repeated

---

29 Psalm 31:24. For Psalm 69:4 see John 15:25; for 69:21 see John 19:28–29; for the timing see Nick Page, *The Longest Week* (Hodder and Stoughton, 2009), Day Five. For Psalm 22:1 see Matthew 27:46; for Psalm 31:5 see Luke 23:46.

30 Luke 23:34; for the command to forgive see Luke 6:37–38; 11:4.

prayers for forgiveness of our own sins, we must declare ourselves willing to forgive others for theirs. And it means embracing the fact that what really matters (in the words of the psalmist) is that God will receive us, and (in the words of Jesus) that our names are written in heaven.[31] And finally, it means taking all possible steps to open up this pathway to others too.

Meanwhile we wait, recognising that we live in a flawed and complicated world, a world in which Jesus was willing to suffer with us. We remind ourselves that Jesus has promised to return in judgment, at which point every single one of us will be held accountable for our actions, and the righteous, who clung to God, will be finally separated from the wicked, who did not. This judgment will usher in a new world, one in which God will make his home among us, and in which there will be no more mourning or crying or pain.[32] Just once in the Psalms we catch a glimpse of this world, when the broken author of Psalm 102 is filled with a sudden premonition of the future. Reminding himself that God created heaven and earth at the beginning of time, and realising that they will not last forever, it occurs to him that just as we discard our worn clothing and replace it with new, so God will replace this broken world with something altogether different. From that time on, the psalmist foretells, our children will live in perfect security, enjoying the presence of God fully and completely.

In the meantime, looking back, we may even be grateful for the way in which God has allowed us to experience these things, for, like broken Kintsugi pots whose cracks have been mended with gold, or like the blackened trunks of Madagascan tapia trees which depend on fire to bring new growth, we find that, contrary to our expectations, we have become stronger, more realistic about ourselves and about others; that we have come to a deeper awareness of the suffering of Jesus, and emerged better able to stand with others in their own suffering – which we recognise may greatly exceed our own. If we follow the path

---

31 Psalm 49:15; Luke 10:20. For a helpful exploration of forgiveness see R.T. Kendall, *Total Forgiveness: Achieving God's greatest challenge* (Hodder and Stoughton, 2001).

32 Matthew 25:31–46; Revelation 21:1–5.

traced for us by David and completed by Jesus, we may well find that, far from being destroyed by our sufferings, our faith has matured and deepened; that now, perhaps, we truly do, both as individuals and as a community, have something to share.

9

A long walk in another world

Life is not a race but a pace we need to maintain with reality.
Sign on advertising hoarding in Accra

Songs of praise

The month is August, the year 2009, and I find myself in a small, dusty town in the far south of Tanzania. Lying in a broad valley dotted with mango, cashew and coconut trees, Masasi consists of a patchwork of houses scattered on each side of a single tarmac road. It's a place of peace and silence: the wind rustles the dry leaves of the trees, a grasshopper zithers quietly in the grass, white butterflies flutter across the open ground. In the distance a man chops wood; voices hum faintly in the heat of the afternoon. Otherwise all is still; no sound, just the dusty sun on the distant hills which pock the flat landscape, one here, one there. Each night we sleep beneath an astonishing density of stars dusted with distant galaxies; each morning we wake to the sound of a single spoon being struck gently against an empty tin. At 6.00 am, English time, 50 priests enter the cathedral. Robed in spotless white, they sing, faultlessly. Their unaccompanied voices seem to emerge from the stones themselves, rising in waves to the rafters, filling the cool morning air with golden sound. I sit at the back, listening to their ethereal song as they chant the daily office, now singing the psalms, now fading into the silence of prayer. It is, I think to myself, the most beautiful worship I have ever heard.

A week later, the catechists arrive. Among them is John. John is himself a song; as we praise God together it is John's voice which takes the lead. Among the Swahili words, some ring out like bells: I pick out love and praise, God and Lord, blessing and thanks. As John pours joy into the air, 60 voices respond to him as one, now in unison, now dividing in spontaneous harmony: where he leads, they follow; where he calls for praise, they provide it. Where do these songs come from? I ask. We have no idea, they say; we just know them. Not content with a praise-punctuated day, John recruits a choir and teaches them two new songs of his own composition; every evening twelve catechists gather outside my bedroom window and rehearse into the early hours of the morning. On the final day they rise to their feet at the close of the Eucharist and sing their thanks not only to God, but to the visitors who have come to spend time with them. The melodies are rooted in my soul to this day.

What has Africa to offer the world? Richard Dowden asks. Patience, hope, civility – and music, he suggests. 'If you judged the peoples of the world by their music, Africans would rank the most hopeful and contented. If music were wealth Africa would be rich.' Is there some secret source of joy in Africa that the rest of us have forgotten or never knew? he wonders.[1] There is, I thought, as I listened to the psalms pouring from the cathedral. It's not in circumstance – John had arrived with an untreated leg injury caused by a motorbike accident the day before. Here in Masasi, the source is God himself.

So far we have focused on the Psalms as works of poetry, for that is how they present themselves in the pages of our Bibles. But the Psalms are conceived not simply as poems, but as songs. Our English word 'psalm' comes from the Greek *psalmos*, a song with string accompaniment; it's the word used by the authors of the Greek Septuagint Bible to translate the Hebrew title *mizmor*, or 'song set to music', found at the head of many psalms. The usual Hebrew title for the Psalter, *Tehillim*, is derived from the verb *hallel*, to praise – so these are not just songs, but songs of praise. This core intention of praise is reflected by the fact that the word 'praise' is the fourth most common in the Psalter, exceeded only by the words which reverberated through John's songs, 'Lord', 'God'

---

[1] *Africa: Altered states, ordinary miracles* (Portobello Books, 2008), pp. 285–86.

and 'love' – and this despite the fact that many of the Psalms, as we have seen, express profound suffering.[2] There is something peculiarly incongruous about praise.

Songs of the temple: Psalms 100 and 150

The psalmists are adamant that praise is to be a key component of our relationship with God. 'Happy are those who live in your house, ever singing your praise', 'for a day in your courts is better than a thousand elsewhere,' we read in Psalm 84. 'Sing to God, sing praises to his name,' chants David in Psalm 68. 'It is good to give thanks to the Lord, to sing praises to your name,' echoes Psalm 92. 'Let us come into his presence with thanksgiving; let us make a joyful noise to him with songs of praise,' urges Psalm 95. And yet in their exhortation to praise God, the psalmists do not pretend that life is a bed of roses, for every single one of these songs acknowledges the pain and peril of everyday living. Perhaps there is something about praise which generates its own joy; perhaps it's simply that God's steadfast love leads him into responsive action which in turn generates an outpouring of thankfulness. It's certainly the case that as we move through the five books of the Psalter we find the psalmists' praises rising in a gradual crescendo until finally they find full expression in an outpouring of unmitigated joy.

One of the best-known songs of praise comes in Book Four of the Psalter. Titled simply 'A psalm of thanksgiving', Psalm 100 invites us to worship the Lord with gladness, to enter his gates with thanksgiving and his courts with praise, to rejoice in his steadfast love. It is, as Walter Brueggemann observes, a liturgical articulation of the first commandment. Often accompanied today by a melody composed in the mid-16th century for the vernacular Geneva Psalter, and framed in the words of William Kethe's 1561 English translation 'All people that on earth do dwell,' Psalm 100 was sung in procession at the coronation

---

2 The words translated as 'Lord' (791 times) and 'God' (433 times) in the English NRSV translation appear in the original text as *Elohim*, *Adonai* and *YHWH*. The word 'love' appears 160 times; the word 'praise' ('praises', 'praised') 158 times.

of Queen Elizabeth II in 1953 and again on the 50th anniversary of that occasion – fittingly, for it brings to a close a series of psalms celebrating the kingship of YHWH.[3] It retains its place as one of the best-known hymns in the Christian tradition.

If praise comes to the fore in Book Four, providing a natural conclusion to the painful pleas for deliverance from the hands of the enemy in the previous book, it reaches a climax in Book Five, which concludes with a series of short psalms each of which begins and ends with the phrase 'Praise the Lord!' – in Hebrew, 'Hallelujah!' In much of Africa, 'Praise the Lord' remains the greeting which frames every conversation between Christians; and such is the reach of the Psalms that 'Alleluia!' survives as an exclamation of grateful relief even in modern secular English. But the psalmist reminds us that praise is not limited to the human voice alone, for Psalm 150 also specifies the instruments used to accompany our song: trumpets and cymbals, harps and lyres, stringed instruments, tambourines and pipes. We may imagine the scene as David's 288 musicians process into the house of the Lord, singers in front, instrumentalists last, girls playing tambourines in between.[4] We know that this was not occasional but normal, for all these instruments are mentioned elsewhere in the Psalms, many of which are prefaced with instructions for the director of music, along with notations for the melody to be used ('According to… the Lilies, The Deer of the Dawn, Do Not Destroy, The Dove'), and descriptions of musical genre (a *shir*, *mizmor*, *tehilla*, *tepilla*, *maskil*, *miktam*, *shiggaion*, song of ascents).[5] Today we have no certain knowledge of how

---

[3] For the liturgical setting and the psalm's placement at the end of the enthronement series which begins with Psalm 93 see Walter Brueggemann and William H. Bellinger, *Psalms*, New Cambridge Bible Commentary (Cambridge University Press, 2014), p. 428. Other psalms with a royal theme are 45, 72, 110 and 145.

[4] 1 Chronicles 25:1–7; Psalm 68:24–27.

[5] For trumpets see Psalms 47, 81, 98, 150; for tambourines see 68, 81, 149, 150; for pipes or wind instruments see 5, 87 (a bored instrument in the Hebrew), 150; for harps (*kinnor* in the Hebrew) see 33, 43, 49, 57, 71, 81, 92, 98, 108, 137, 147, 149, 150; for lyres (*nebel* in the Hebrew) see 33, 57, 71, 81, 92, 108, 144, 150; for other stringed instruments see 4, 6, 45, 54, 55, 61, 67, 68, 76, 92, 150. Prescribed melody: Psalms 45, 69, 80 ('lilies', see also 60, 'The Lily of the Covenant'); 22 ('Deer of the Dawn'); 57, 58, 59, 75 ('Do Not Destroy'); 56 ('The Dove'); see also Psalms 8, 81, 84 ('The Gittith'); 6, 12 ('The Sheminith'); 53, 88 (*Mahalath*); 9 (*Muth-labben* or 'Death of the Son'); 46 (*Alamoth* or 'maidens'). Song type: many psalms

all this sounded, although the inscriptions suggest that some were intended for choral singing and others to be orchestrated. The poetic structure implies that the psalms may have been sung responsively, in the format demonstrated so beautifully by John and characteristic of African worship today.

Finally, whoever we are, wherever we come from, whatever our circumstances and experiences, Psalm 150 invites and exhorts us to raise our voices in a great symphonic chorus which is not limited to human beings but, as Psalm 148 had so amply illustrated with its inclusion of everything from stars to insects, bursts forth from the whole of creation: 'Let everything that has breath praise the Lord!' It's a foreshadowing of the world to come.[6]

I have participated many times in the informal sung worship practised both in western countries and in Africa, and I have attended many carefully choreographed and beautifully sung formal services of thanksgiving, consecration, ordination and celebration in English cathedrals. But only once have I felt that I was experiencing the full magnificence of the temple worship celebrated in the Psalms. The car park was full. The people were dressed in white, the choirs in blue and purple, the celebrants in red, cream and gold. Beginning with a procession, ending with a party of overwhelming generosity, in between the congregation was caught up into more than four hours of prayer, worship, liturgy, choral singing, hymns, offerings, dancing, reading and preaching. The mood and music shifted from sadness to joy, from slow to fast, from loud (very loud) to breathtakingly quiet as we moved through the various elements of the liturgy, confessing our sins, receiving forgiveness, giving thanks, pledging our allegiance to

---

are titled *shir* (song), *mizmor* (song set to music), *tehilla* (praise), *tepilla* (lament); see also Psalms 32, 42, 44, 45, 52–55, 74, 78, 88, 89, 142 (*maskil*); 16, 56–60 (*miktam*); 7 (*shiggaion*); 121–34 (song of ascents).

6 Psalm 150:6 (NIV). That all of creation unites in praising the Lord is also emphasised in Psalms 65:13 (the meadows and valleys sing for joy), 66:4 (all the earth worships God), 96:12 ('the trees of the forest sing for joy'), 98:8 (the floods clap their hands, the hills sing for joy), and 104:12 (birds sing). For the worship of the world to come see Revelation 7:9–17.

one another and to God. Robes glistened in the artificial lighting, rain thundered down outside, and the service culminated in a deafeningly triumphant broadcast of Handel's Hallelujah chorus. Perhaps I should have expected it, for only the week before we had attended a five-hour service in another parish – where, at the climax of the Eucharist, fairy lights had come on all round the altar. For the first time in my life, I emerged slightly dazed, feeling that I had retraced my entire spiritual journey in a single morning. Where was this? Africa, again – this time in Koforidua, Ghana.

Songs of lament: Psalm 137

Presented by their redactors in five distinct collections, the Psalms reveal a gradual thematic and chronological progression as we move through the five books – but they are not grouped by genre, either within the individual books or within the collection as a whole. Commentators have often sought to classify the Psalms into clearly identifiable categories: thanksgiving psalms, enthronement psalms, praise psalms, lament psalms, wisdom psalms, historical psalms, liturgical psalms and, inevitably, miscellaneous psalms. But perhaps the distinctions don't matter all that much, for as Robert Alter points out, there is no fixed association between genre and theme: a single genre may be put to a range of uses, and different types may be mixed within a particular psalm. In the Psalms, improvisation is the key.[7]

Within this diversity of genre, critics agree that the predominant themes are praise and lament. And yet even this broad distinction does not always enable us to place psalms under one or the other heading – not just because almost all the 'lament' psalms include elements of praise, but because lament itself is not easily defined. Carleen Mandolfo points out that across cultures, lament takes two primary forms: the 'dirge' (a song of mourning) and the 'supplication to the deity' (an appeal

---

[7] 'Psalms', *The Literary Guide to the Bible*, eds Robert Alter and Frank Kermode (Fontana, 1989), pp. 244–63.

for help); and that whereas the Greek tradition understands lament primarily as a cry of mourning, the laments of the Psalter are better understood as crisis language: these Psalms do not so much grieve loss as appeal for the reparation of status.[8] This, though, is a theme which occurs in many of the Psalms, even where the emphasis is elsewhere, with the result that commentators rarely agree on exactly how many of the Psalms should properly be regarded as laments. They do, however, agree that they fall into two basic types: individual laments and communal laments.[9]

We have already considered many of the individual laments contained within the Psalter – particularly those of David as he appeals to God for forgiveness and deliverance; these are found predominantly within the first two books. We have looked too at the appeals for divine intervention as the psalmists witness the assaults of enemy peoples and the destruction of the temple; these communal laments are found predominantly in the third book. An outpouring of corporate thankfulness echoes through Book Four; and so we come to Book Five, the most varied of all the psalm collections. And there, before we reach the concluding psalms of praise, we find a particular kind of lament: lament which arises from a dissonance between past and present, or present and past – the bittersweet memory of past happiness in times of pain, or the poignant memory of past pain in a time of new beginnings.

If Psalm 88 is the darkest of the individual laments contained within the Psalms, Psalm 137 can claim to be its corporate counterpart. After the desecration described so vividly in Psalm 74, the people of God now find themselves transported far from home. 'By the rivers of Babylon,' begins the exiled psalmist, 'there we sat down and there we wept, when we remembered Zion.' So painful were the memories of a joyful past that the people found themselves incapable of song;

---

[8] 'Language of lament in the Psalms' in William P. Brown (ed.), *The Oxford Handbook of the Psalms* (Oxford University Press, 2014), pp. 114–30.

[9] Reckonings vary from 42 (Mandolfo) to 66 (Brueggemann and Bellinger). Artur Weiser points out that themes of lament are frequently found intermingled with other psalm types: *The Psalms: A commentary* (SCM Press, 1962), p. 66.

their harps dripping like tears from the waterside willows on which they had hung them, they had subsided into silence. Like Heman in Psalm 88, they have reached the limit of their emotional and spiritual resources. But do sing to us, their captors demand with consummate cruelty – sing one of those songs from your temple, one of those songs which commemorates your God; for we would like so much to hear you celebrate once more the temple which we smashed, the God whom we overcame when we carried you away from your own land! Stung by the mockery, the psalmists declare that they will *not* allow the muscles with which they play their harps to wither; that they *will* remember Jerusalem: may their tongues cleave to the roof of their mouths if they do not!

And so they sing. What they sing is one of the bits we tend to leave out. Let's remember the Edomites, who rejoiced as they watched the invaders tear down our city, they chant obediently; let's sing of daughter Babylon, let's cheer ourselves up with the thought that sooner or later payback will come – we will be happy then, oh so happy as we watch your babies' heads being smashed against a rock! Ouch, we think. However angry I may be when I find myself mistreated by others, I would not even in my darkest moments wish harm on their children; the thought of smashing in the skulls of defenceless infants fills me with horror. We need not regret that this is here, one commentator suggests, as long as we don't say it's the word of God. This, says another with delicate understatement, is morally problematic. And yet, even as I wonder if we should indeed leave these verses out, I find two avenues of thought helpful.

The first is that this song is framed in these terms not simply as a means of expressing a distastefully bloodthirsty desire for revenge, but as a way of deceiving those to whom it is sung. The song, Rodney Sadler suggests, is intentionally crafted to resemble the requested song of Zion – the words are chosen because they sound like those which are expected, but in fact carry a rather different meaning. 'Sons of Edom' sounds, in Hebrew, like 'sons of Adam' – a phrase which comes four times (translated into English as 'humankind') in Psalm 107 alone.

The word 'daughter' appears disarmingly often in the Psalms in reference to Zion; the phrase 'happy are those' opens the Psalter and recurs at intervals throughout it; the word used for infants, '*owlel*' in Hebrew, sounds remarkably like the expected '*hallel*' (praise); and the final word, rock or '*cela*', echoes the word '*selah*', a term of uncertain meaning which closes many song sections in the Psalms themselves. So to a foreign ear, there might be enough linguistic echoes to make this sound indeed like a song of Zion. You want a song, the psalmists ask? Okay, we'll give you a song![10]

The second thought is that this outburst, harrowing though it is, nonetheless represents progress: stung out of the silent misery into which they so rarely fall, the psalmists are once again expressing their feelings, communicating honestly with God. If we cannot do this, there is no hope for us, for in the face of cruelty and abuse the most dangerous response is to feel nothing – we are only too well aware that some of the greatest atrocities of modern times have been perpetrated by people who have been systematically desensitised to violence and can therefore be compelled to repeat it. Just as the intemperate cursing of Psalm 109 once enabled an abused young woman to begin to deal with her own lacerated feelings, so too this outburst represents the first step in the expression of the post-traumatic numbness of an entire community. But even so, I hear you say – it's a bit much, isn't it?

At intervals over the past 15 years I have been invited to visit northern Mozambique, as part of a small multinational team, in order to support the Anglican Church in its ministry to a people scarred by decades of national and international brutality. So great has the suffering been that it is difficult to put it into words – firstly under an exploitative occupying power which systematically impoverished the entire country; then during the violent struggle for liberation; then at the hands of a communist government which proscribed the church, terrorised

---

10 Rodney Sadler, 'Singing a Subversive Song: Psalm 137 and "Colored Pompey"', in Brown (ed.), *The Oxford Handbook of Psalms*, pp. 447–58. For a true song of Zion see Psalms 46, 48, 76, 84, 87, 125, 132. Asaph had powerfully conveyed the fear of destruction in Psalm 83, which demonstrates the consequent impossibility of singing a song of celebration for the entertainment of those from whom God had failed to rescue them.

Christians, and murdered those thought to oppose it; and finally as a result of nearly 20 years of guerrilla warfare waged by an externally funded rebel movement which led not only to the destruction of entire communities and widespread damage to what little infrastructure the country possessed, but also to the deaths of hundreds of thousands of people and the exile of many more; the last landmines were still being cleared at the time of our first visit. During the few short weeks I have spent there, I have listened to the stories of people who had witnessed the murder of their fathers or learned of the rape of their mothers, I have seen the burnt out churches and the pockmarked buildings, and I have watched the struggles of a once gentle but now brutalised people to regain their dignity and learn again to love one another. But one conversation horrified me more than anything else. 'We have a past,' explained the bishop one morning. 'What our people remember is the rebel gunmen who marched into their villages and made them kill each other. They made them kill their own brothers and sisters. *They made them put their babies in the household mortar and pound them until they were dead* – if they refused, they would be killed themselves. Then they burned the villages. That is where we are coming from.'

At the end of our visit they gave us each a beautiful carved wooden mortar and pestle; this is the heart of every home, they said proudly; now you truly belong here. I treasure it; but I cannot look at it without a shudder. If we, who cannot even imagine these things, feel that the violent verses of Psalm 137 have no place in the conversation between God and his people, perhaps we have not understood what that conversation is actually about.

When the Lord restored our fortunes: Psalm 126

If Psalm 137 is sung in exile, Psalm 126 rises from the lips of those who have experienced the longed-for restoration. Here the exilic memory of happier times gives way to poignant recollection of past pain in a subsequent time of peace. Subtitled 'A harvest of joy', the psalm serves as a reminder of the intimate connection between joy and lament – a connection which arises, perhaps, not only from the realities of our lived experience, but from a fundamental dichotomy in our relationship with the God from whom we remain, as yet, painfully separated.

This short psalm falls into two parts. The first three lines celebrate the Lord's merciful and loving response to the anguish expressed so forcefully in Psalms 74 and 137, with their vivid descriptions of the smashed temple and the bitterness of life in captivity. The Lord has restored our fortunes! We are back home! We can't quite believe it – it feels like a dream, they confess. Their relief pours out in laughter; the language of violence gives way to cries of joy. 'The Lord has done great things for us!' they sing, even as they make their way to the holy city – for this is a song of ascents, a pilgrim psalm; a song, indeed, of Zion.

But the harsh memories are still there, and even this new joy is tinged with sadness. The second half of the song repeats the opening line, but this time in a distinctly minor key: 'Restore our fortunes, O Lord, like the watercourses in the Negeb.' Perhaps pain never quite goes away for, as creatures bound up in time, the past is ever present within us, and even the most confident hope is inevitably experienced in counterpoint to a reality of lived disappointment. Here, it seems, the disappointment is expressed in the imagery of drought. We have sown: surely, with the gift of water, we shall reap. We have mourned: surely, with the blessing of the Lord, we shall rejoice.

And yet the song is not simple, for the distinction between imagery and reality is deliberately blurred. Listening, we can imagine the dry desert watercourses filling with water after seasonal rain; we can imagine the hard graft of sowing, and we can anticipate the joy brought by a plentiful harvest. But the tears of exile persist, for even now the people weep as they sow. Perhaps the imagery picks up on old religious myths which associated the sowing of seeds with death and the harvest of grain with revival. But perhaps too it is tinged with the memory of the suffering endured by the rivers of Babylon; it is, we note, with the imagery of burial and new life that Ezekiel had, five years into the exile and from the banks of those very same rivers, described the longed-for homecoming. One day all these threads will be woven together: the imagery of sowing and death, growth and new life, the agony of exile and the hope of restoration will all reach their fulfilment in the death and resurrection of Jesus; for what you sow, St Paul will explain – even your most fervent hope – does not come to life unless it dies.[11] In the meantime, for these returning exiles, even the simple act of scattering grain triggers the rise of painful memories.

I fear that, in our western cultural commitment to a philosophy of growth and well-being, we have lost the capacity to lament. In Africa, it is not so. Come with me again to Tanzania, much further north this time, to a poorly resourced diocese on the edge of a high plateau which, at the time of my first visit 20 years ago, had no surfaced roads, few schools or clinics, and electricity and running water in only one town. Since then the diocese had experienced a period of remarkable growth, with a revival in church life, a burgeoning membership, and a holistic leadership strategy which had brought huge benefits to remote communities. Perhaps such rapid growth is bound to bring challenges; at any rate, by the time of my fifth visit the diocese had descended into conflict. Everybody, it seemed, had fallen out with everybody else. As the women gathered together to pray, the clergy met with a small team of facilitators. Honest in expressing their grievances and willing to repent for mistakes made, they were open to the possibility of reconciliation. Writing down the things that had angered them, they committed their feelings to God, burned the papers on which they had inscribed their pain, and resolved to forgive one another. By the time we all came together again, the atmosphere was very different; the palpable tension had gone, and 70 faces were wreathed in smiles. 'Today the diocese has been healed,' they said.

---

11 For the parallels in the religious myths of Ugarit and Egypt see Brueggemann and Bellinger, *Psalms* p. 540. Ezekiel was writing from the banks of the river Chebar in the land of the Chaldeans, in the fifth year of the exile of King Jehoiachin (592BC) – see Ezekiel 1:1–2. For the prophecy of return see Ezekiel 37:1–14. For St Paul see 1 Corinthians 15:42ff.

Later that evening, the bishop met with the rural deans in the small tent which served as a supplementary meeting room. As we visitors walked beneath a vast night sky, we were arrested by the sound of gentle, harmonious singing – not the usual vigorous praise, but something different. It came from the tent. As we drew closer, we found ourselves listening to a slow, melodious song of lament, pulsing with quiet emotional power; the sound of trauma being consigned to the past, the modulation of longstanding grief into something altogether more beautiful: the quiet hope that, once again, God would restore their fortunes. The bishop told us the next day that they had remained together until three in the morning. It was only one moment; but it seemed so very biblical. 'Salvation is the message that our God enfolds our broken reality,' Japanese theologian Kazoh Kitamori once wrote.[12] I felt that perhaps I had just listened to him doing it.

We have, in the western church, continued to sing songs of praise – sometimes exuberantly, but often, it has to be said, in forms which are so respectably modulated that our thanksgiving sounds distinctly muted. But whether our own tradition is one of exuberance or restraint, rarely do we find ourselves singing songs of lament. The psalms of lament may retain a place in the repertoire of our cathedral choirs, but I cannot think of a single occasion on which I have sung a song of lament in an ordinary local church. And yet can we really suppose that it is possible to have a relationship with God in which there is only praise, and never lamentation? If joy and sorrow are the twin polarities of our human emotional experience, so too they must find expression in any authentic relationship with God – to think otherwise is to enter into denial. Might the steady stream of weary and hurting people leaving our churches be connected with our inability to lament?

David Smith does not exempt even our most outwardly successful churches from responsibility: perhaps, he suggests, in focusing exclusively on celebration and victory we have unwittingly created an ever-growing fringe of people with aching hearts and profound

---

12 *Theology of the Pain of God* (SCM Press, 1966), p. 20.

questions – questions which they are forced either to suppress or to take elsewhere.[13] Barbara Brown Taylor goes further, pointing out that churches which embrace what she calls a 'full solar spirituality' are forced to deal with darkness by pretending it isn't there – which doesn't help when you find yourself surrounded by it.[14] And might our lack of credibility in the secular world be in part due to our unwillingness to articulate our collective anguish in public conversation with God? It is our duty and our joy to sing praises to God, but if at the same time we turn away from lament and supplication we are liable to find that in times of crisis we are left with a choice between pretence and silence.

Indeed, it seems that this may be happening already: as new uncertainties (global warming, desperate refugees, deadly diseases) loom ever larger on the horizon of our western complacency, it appears that whereas, corporately speaking, we are ever willing to offer our opinions in the political arena, when it comes to our conversation with God, we have nothing to say – as if, unaccountably, we had lost our voice. It is easy to forget that in times of crisis, whether personal or collective, horizontal conversations may not be as effective or helpful as vertical ones: lament and supplication are as necessary now as ever – and yet when disaster strikes we actually close our churches.[15] Maybe this is another dimension of our community life which calls for re-evaluation; something, perhaps, which the Beatles and Bob Dylan got right, and we have got wrong. One day, perhaps, we will once again find the confidence to express our fears and turn to God for help. At the very least, we might find ourselves able to lament with and on behalf of those whose suffering far exceeds our own. The world is a painful place.[16]

---

13 *Stumbling Toward Zion: Recovering the biblical tradition of lament in the era of world Christianity* (Langham Global Library, 2020), p. 6.

14 *Learning to Walk in the Dark* (HarperCollins, 2014), p. 7.

15 A ComRes poll found that during the 2020 Covid lockdown 25% of UK adults prayed about the pandemic, and the proportion attending online services more than doubled compared with normal attendance. The response of the individual was very different from that of the institution, which seems increasingly to prioritise socio-political commentary over the provision of pastoral and spiritual leadership.

16 The tide may be turning: Mark Vroegop, *Dark Clouds, Deep Mercy: Discovering the grace of lament* (Crossway, 2019) and David Smith, *Stumbling Toward Zion*, have written helpfully on the relevance of lament today. Both draw on Claus Westermann's *Praise and Lament in the Psalms* (Westminster John Knox Press, 1987).

What is it about music?

Why is it so important that we do not just read or pray the Psalms, but sing them? What does music add to the words themselves? It's clear that it does add something – we have only to imagine ourselves reciting the lyrics of 'Yesterday' or 'Blowing in the Wind' to realise that without the music they lose their impact. We may reflect, then, that meaning resides not only in words, but also in sounds: the territorial song of a robin, the jingling tune of a passing ice-cream van, the wailing siren of an ambulance all convey a distinct and comprehensible message – this is my patch; come for a treat; get out of the way! We may consider too that meaning may not be simply factual but profoundly emotional, and that music is itself a language in which things that cannot be conveyed adequately in words alone can nonetheless find powerful expression. Films use music to transform us from objective spectator to engaged participant; television programmes beckon us in with distinctive signature tunes; even in nature documentaries music is employed to help us experience the tension of the hunt or relax in the peace of a summer meadow. The music must of course be carefully chosen: we are likely to conclude that Beethoven's Pastoral Symphony will not strike terror into our hearts, that no general has ever asked his army to march to the sound of the Sugar Plum Fairy, and that Verdi's Requiem Mass will not do for a wedding – the emotional content would be all wrong. Nor would the lilting melodies of John's praise songs have helped the rural deans to express their sorrowful trust in a new future. Good music needs no signpost, Robert Schumann said; it carries its own meaning.

To this emotional dimension of music we each add a personal contribution, for music exists not only in the present moment but within our memories – the Berceuse from Fauré's Dolly Suite sweeps me back to *Listen with Mother* and the delight of childhood radio stories; the reason I want to listen to Wagner when I am feeling angry and alone turns out to be that my mother used to find it helpful in drowning out my infant colic; and the second of Schubert's piano impromptus re-evokes the uncertain ripples of emerging love with which I once listened to it in the silent companionship of my future husband. It is odd that music should carry this emotional power, for it is, after all, no more than a series of pitched sounds occurring in a linear sequence. Music, like the thoughts in our heads, has no tangible reality; it exists only as a movement, living in the gaps which lie between the physical components that convey it. The music is not in the notes, but in the silence between, Mozart once said. And yet, as the notes chime boldly in major keys or creep quietly in minor ones, something opens up inside us.

It seems natural, then, to assume that the original musical accompaniments to the Psalms were variously composed in order to convey the emotions articulated by the words. It also seems natural to expect that the music served to embed the Psalms and the prayers they express into the memories of those who so regularly sang them. Would the jaunty tunes of the Pilgrim Psalms have brought back memories of shared festivals? Would the repeated melodies of the historical psalms have helped to build a sense of national identity? Would anyone wishing to confess their sins have heard the tune to Psalm 51 echo within them, and would the celebratory tones of Psalm 100 have reminded its hearers of the many things for which they were truly thankful? And as for the gaps, perhaps music is an integral part of our spirituality, a gateway to another world where reality cannot be held or measured. Perhaps it's in the gaps that we find the things for which we have no words. 'To listen seriously to music, and to perform it,' Archbishop Rowan Williams once said, 'are among our most potent ways of learning what it is to live with and before God. In this obedience of listening and following, we are stretched and deepened. The time we have renounced, given up, is given back to us as a time in which we have become more human, more real, even when we can't say what we have learned, only that we have changed.'[17]

---

17 'Keeping Time', in *A Ray of Darkness* (Cowley Publications, 1995), p. 16.

Singing the Psalms

We no longer have the original musical notation to the Psalms. But we do know that various instruments were employed – sometimes a single harp or a group of flutes, sometimes an entire orchestra – and we infer that some were sung by voices alone. We know that praise was associated with clapping and dancing, and accompanied by cymbals, trumpets, stringed instruments, pipes and drums, but also that David composed his psalms with a lyre. We know that particular melodies were fitted to particular psalms, that certain psalms were prescribed for use on particular occasions, and that different terms were used to denote different types of song. All these things support our conclusion that the great emotional range of the individual psalms must have been reflected in the music first composed to accompany them.[18]

After the Roman siege of Jerusalem in AD70, the Psalms lost their temple setting for the second time. But we know that they remained a constant part of the devotional lives of both Jews and Christians. Jesus and his disciples sang Psalm 118, prescribed for Passover, at the Last Supper; Paul expected the churches in Corinth, Colossae and Ephesus to sing psalms when they met together; and every single New Testament author except Jude quotes from or alludes to the Psalms. The early Christians continued to live, as Tom Wright has remarked, in a psalm-shaped world.[19]

By the third century the Psalms were so regularly sung within the church that many Christians would have known them by heart. In the fourth century Athanasius recommended them for private devotion, explaining that they portray all the movements of the human soul. In the sixth Benedict ruled that the whole Psalter was to be sung weekly,

---

18 Eight psalm inscriptions specify particular instruments, seventeen the melody, and ninety-six the genre. Psalms 38 and 70 accompany a memorial offering, Psalm 30 a dedication, and Psalm 45 is a love song. For use of the psalms in particular cultic settings see Weiser, *The Psalms: A commentary*, p. 22.

19 *Finding God in the Psalms: Sing, pray, live* (SPCK, 2014), p. 11. For Passover see Matthew 26:30; Mark 14:26 (the Greek word *psalmos* is given as 'hymn' in some English translations). For church worship see 1 Corinthians 14:26; Ephesians 5:19; Colossians 3:16.

and in the following centuries the plainsong formula of Gregorian chant was developed to enable this to be done simply. In the ninth century King Alfred, not content with regularly singing and praying the Psalms himself, translated the first 50 from Latin into Old English, and from the 13th the devotional Books of Hours encouraged lay people to pray the Pilgrim and Penitential Psalms daily.[20] But it was during the 16th-century Reformation that the Psalms exploded into the vernacular and became freshly accessible to everyone. 'Whatever may serve to encourage us when we are about to pray to God, is taught us in this book,' said John Calvin, while Martin Luther followed Benedict in insisting that all the Psalms should be sung (with no bits missing) in congregational worship: 'Music is to be praised as second only to the Word of God,' he said, 'because by her are all the emotions swayed.' Encouraged by Luther, commentaries were written, verse translations made in both French and English, and new melodies and settings composed to replace the uniformity of the unaccompanied chant which had dominated the monastic tradition.[21]

By the 18th century, responding to the need to bring a specifically Christian perspective to congregational worship, Isaac Watts was producing a rich variety of new hymns which read the Psalms through the lens of the gospel; to him, among many others, we owe 'O God our help in ages past', drawn from Psalm 90. Re-emerging unexpectedly from my mother's childhood memory, this hymn has proved one of the few things able to comfort her as she faces the fears and challenges of dementia. Together with John and Charles Wesley, Watts created a whole new repertoire of hymns, and by the following century these, with their memorable lines and stirring tunes, had begun to replace

---

20 The Books of Hours grew out of the Little Office of the Blessed Virgin Mary, a pattern of daily prayer developed by the Benedictines, and formed the basis of the daily devotional practice of the laity throughout the late Middle Ages. See Melody Knowles, 'Feminist interpretation of the Psalms' in Brown (ed.), *The Oxford Handbook of the Psalms*, and Eamon Duffy, *Marking the Hours: English people and their prayers 1240–1570* (Yale University Press, 2006).

21 The first complete English Bible, translated by Myles Coverdale, was published in 1535. The first metrical translation of the Psalter was published in 1562; it included musical settings, some based on popular ballads, and remained the standard English version for nearly 200 years. A summary of the history and usage of the English Psalter is given on **churchmusic.ca/BOP4.html**.

the Psalter as the primary mode of sung worship. The trend away from the Psalms has accelerated in our own times with the growth of gospel songs and choruses, to the extent that, for most of us, the Psalms no longer feature directly in our regular Sunday services.[22]

The exception to this general rule is found in our cathedrals, where the legacy of Gregorian chant lives on in the Anglican chant which developed from it in the 16th century as an alternative to the new metrical approach. It's a format which enables the full text to be sung without any need to fit it into a particular rhythm or tune, and in their faithful commitment to daily singing of the psalms our cathedral choirs provide a unique and important link to a biblical resource which we can ill afford to lose. But it's also a format which undoubtedly has the effect of smoothing out not only the highs and lows of the music, but also the heights and depths of the emotions it is able to convey. A verse sung largely on the flat with a simple resolution at the end seems designed to keep our emotions in check rather than to release them: a tiny melodic rise may permit a momentary gladdening of the heart, and an equally modest dip may briefly lower our spirits; but the emotional vibrancy, articulacy and release of the Psalms is inevitably muted. Comparison with the works of the great classical composers shows how much is lost, in emotional if not verbal terms: the haunting lament of Mendelssohn's 'O for the wings of a dove', based on Psalm 56, for example, is so very different in both sound and effect from the jaunty tones of Handel's 'Laudate Pueri', a rendering of Psalm 112, or the triumphant joy of Hayden's Creation Oratorio, based on Psalm 19. Scottish musician Ian White is one of few modern songwriters to have worked through the Psalter, aiming to reflect the full emotional range of the individual psalms; even today, a quarter of a century after he first listened to them, my husband remembers the emotional journey Ian's psalms took him on as he played them over and over again through many sleepless hospital nights. The one that still causes him to choke

---

22 For an overview of the early musical tradition see Brown (ed.), *The Oxford Handbook of the Psalms*, pp. 1–23; individual essays by Kimberly Bracken Long and Michael Morgan explore the musical tradition in more depth.

up begins 'From everlasting to everlasting'; like 'O God our help in ages past', it comes from Psalm 90.[23]

In Africa I have learned that it is possible to express deep joy in uninhibited worship, and that grief can be expressed with equal fervour. And I have learned that this is not an either-or, but a both-and. It's not that the happy people devote themselves to praise, and the suffering people air their misery in lament – it's more complicated than that. We are increasingly aware that emotional health depends on the ability to experience, and then to express, our feelings, right across the register which runs from despair to joy. The Psalms help us both to come to terms with our failings and tribulations, and to rejoice at the steadfast love with which God meets us when we do. They call us back into a world we have forgotten, or to which we have perhaps never been; a world which knows both how to rejoice and how to lament, and which understands that the two are connected.

'To what then will I compare the people of this generation, and what are they like?' Jesus demanded of those who had responded neither to John the Baptist's calls for repentance nor to his own proclamation of good news. 'They are like children sitting in the market-place,' he concluded, 'calling to one another, "We played the flute for you, and you did not dance; we wailed, and you did not weep."'[24] Today we may, with varying degrees of success, try to rejoice; only rarely do we lament. In Africa, they do both. The result is that there is, in African worship, an authenticity which is both striking and inspiring.

In the beginning was the word

Music, then, is an essential component of the Psalms. The words of the psalmists pour themselves into the instrumental or choral clothing

---

23 Ian's psalms are available from his website **littlemistymusic.com**. See also The Psalms Project, a group of musicians currently setting the psalms to music; starting in 2006, they have so far released four albums.

24 Luke 7:31–32.

designed to enhance and complete them. And yet it's not as simple as that, for the words have not been chosen at random, or without concern for their own auditory impact; they bring with them their own music.

We, living in a print age, tend to read poetry with our eyes. But for most of history, poetry has been understood as an auditory phenomenon; until the invention of the printing press in the 15th century, and for most people for centuries after that, poetry was read with the ears. Until very recently, most poets have paid little attention to how their work would look on the page. What matters in a poem is what it sounds like: poetry is, in its essence, verbal music. So instead of following a linear structure determined by grammatical convention, a poem fits its words within a rhythmical or metrical structure. Instead of choosing words solely for their precision of meaning, a poem pays attention to the sound they make or the associations they bring with them. Instead of avoiding repetition, a poem embraces it and sets it to work. In this sense, a poem creates its own music, for words too are sounds, and a text is simply a transcription of those sounds. So part of the task involved in setting a poem to music is to work with the sounds that are already there, to enhance the emotions that have been so carefully expressed in oral form by the author.

For those of us who read the Psalms in translation, our inability to hear the sounds of the original text creates a problem. I was once told by a Hebrew-speaking friend that the Psalms are breathtakingly beautiful in their expression; that whereas translations may remain faithful to the meaning, they invariably fail to do justice to the form. Jewish poet Naphtali Herz Imber explained that in the Psalms 'one finds the deep heartbreaking tones of a Beethoven, as well as the smooth, light, laughing, comic song of an Offenbach; the silent, sweet whisper of love's longing, as well as the wild galloping Hallelujahs suggestive of Wagner's Walküre. In the Psalms is contained the music of the past, present and the future.'[25] He was talking not about their

---

25 Quoted by Jonathan Friedmann, 'Music of the Psalms', *Jewish Magazine*, July 2008, jewishmag.com/125mag/music-psalms/music-psalms.htm.

musical settings, but about the words themselves. Poetry, as Robert Frost famously observed, gets lost in translation. Which perhaps is why many poets have sought not so much as to translate as to reimagine the Psalms in their own idiom – Philip and Mary Sidney in the 16th century, George Herbert in the 17th, Christopher Smart in the 18th and Gerard Manley Hopkins in the 19th all wrote distinctive, moving psalms linked more or less strictly to the original works.[26]

There are, however, some features of the style and structure of the Psalms which survive even in translation. The most striking of these is the use of what is usually called parallelism, or 'the confirmation of sentences', as it was first termed. In a parallel structure, lines come in pairs, the second of which echoes the shape of the first. A simple example is provided by Jesus: 'Ask, and you will receive; seek and you will find.' In the Psalms, the effect of the second line is to reinforce the meaning of the first: sometimes by simply repeating what has just been said but in different words, sometimes by adding some new element or emphasis, and sometimes by setting it against a contrasting statement – but always within the same rhythmic structure. We do this even today when we want to drive a point home: I've said it, I'll say it again! It's not just bad, it's truly awful! Not like this, like that! These three forms are known as symmetrical, synthetic and antithetical parallelism, and they serve to reinforce, develop or intensify what has just been said. It's a form peculiarly suited to choral singing: one voice may sing the first line, with the congregation responding in the second (as John did in Masasi), or one group may sing the first, echoed by an antiphonal group in the second (as in English cathedral worship today). One of the best examples of parallelism in the Psalter is provided by Psalm 19, with its opening words 'The heavens are telling the glory of God; and the firmament proclaims his handiwork.'

Another structural form, this time invisible in translation, is used in psalms which begin each line with a new letter of the alphabet. We have

---

26 For Hopkins, the Psalter served as 'parent text' rather than direct source, particularly in his later poetry of lament. See Peter S. Hawkins, 'The Psalms in poetry', in Brown (ed.), *The Oxford Handbook of the Psalms*, pp. 104–06.

already seen the effect of this acrostic approach in Psalms 119 and 37, where the imperatives of human conduct and the consistency of God's response are reinforced by the reassuring orderliness of the framework in which they are expressed. An acrostic structure is also found in Psalm 145, devoted to the praise offered to God by generation after generation, by faithful people everywhere, by every living creature which experiences his bounty; the same sense of inevitability and completeness develops as we move line by line into ever deeper thankfulness. But an unfolding alphabet can also be used to express suffering; David couches his cries of pain and pleas for deliverance within an acrostic structure in Psalms 9, 10, 25 and 34. We might more readily perceive the impact of this cumulative approach by transposing it from letters of the alphabet to days of the week: on Monday it happened, on Tuesday I suffered, on Wednesday I wept, on Thursday I fell ill – Lord, are you listening? It's a structure employed to good effect in the children's story about the very hungry caterpillar – on Monday he ate an apple, on Tuesday he ate two pears, on Wednesday he ate three plums… and so it goes on, until the caterpillar acquires first a serious stomach ache and then, in the inevitable conclusion, the wings of a butterfly. A measured structure of this kind is easy both to remember and to listen to; I can still remember my son, aged two, settling himself down with the book, 'reading' it from memory: 'On Monday 'e ate, on Tuesday 'e ate…' and so on. Doesn't do much for you on the page – but when read aloud, it comes alive.[27]

Hebrew-speaking commentators have drawn attention to many other features of the Psalms: auditory effects like alliteration and assonance (the repetition of consonants or vowels in a single phrase), structural effects like inclusio (enveloping a psalm or group of psalms within a repeated opening and closing phrase) and chiasmus (reversal of word order in successive phrases), deliberate plays on words, the careful placing of stress – all these and a host of other patterns of sound and meaning are woven into the poems.[28]

---

27 Eric Carle, *The Very Hungry Caterpillar* (World Publishing Company, 1969).

28 For a helpful introduction to the Psalms as Hebrew poetry see Jonathan Magonet, *A Rabbi Reads the Psalms* (SCM Press, 1994).

Seeing what you mean

And yet as we read the Psalms in translation today, it is probably not their rhetorical and structural complexity which strikes us but rather their vivid use of imagery. Here we find a profound and pervasive simplicity, for the psalmists employ all this oral sophistication in order to invite us to look at, and to feel, things which are visually and emotionally not complicated at all. It's as if we are being handed an ornate and beautiful magnifying glass and encouraged, through the preciousness of the gift, to look more closely not at things that are themselves rare and unusual, but at the most basic components of our lives and experiences.

The function of an image is to enable one thing to be described in terms of another, in such a way as to help the hearer to visualise or understand it more accurately. This may be done very simply: her cheeks were red as a rose. In receiving the image, we are invited to identify the characteristic which is being transferred from the thing evoked to the thing described – in this case, the colour red. And yet it's more complicated than that, because the rose brings other characteristics too – beauty, delicacy, fragrance, for example. And so the image doesn't just clarify, it also enhances. Had we read that her nose was red as a beetroot, our thoughts would have been sent in a quite different direction.

Imagery is used most effectively when something concrete and specific is used to describe something abstract and intangible. We have already looked at how the psalmists use concrete images to convey abstract realities – storms represent the assaults of an enemy or the power of the Creator, trees represent people as they flourish or wither according to the choices they have made, paths represent the journey of the individual through life, and so on. But it is striking that whereas many poets draw upon the rare and the unusual in their choice of imagery, the psalmists demonstrate keen observational powers but give no hint of harbouring any interest in literary originality. Familiar plants, birds and animals embody the psalmists' emotions: lions and dogs represent threat, doves convey vulnerability, owls evoke sleepless nights. God too is understood through everyday images: he is sun, shield, rock, fortress, refuge, and stronghold, and he relates to us as mother, shepherd, physician, warrior, archer, midwife, ruler, weaver, employer and judge – all familiar to us from everyday life. The metaphors and images adopted are not complex, and the comparisons they make are not subtle.

And yet this deliberate simplicity works for us on a number of different levels. The immediate consequence is not to dilute the impact but rather to intensify it: the images burst without explanation or adornment into the poem, thrusting us deeper into the reality of our own experience – for we too have seen the gracefulness of deer and dove, and we too have been kept awake by the solitary owl. Even images which are not familiar in everyday western life lurk in our subconscious minds as archetypes: one of my toddlers, on climbing the stairs alone for the very first time, announced with some relief, 'I went upstairs, and no lions did come with me!', neatly demonstrating the way ancient reality lives on within us. It is 13,000 years since lions last stalked England, but they had served to tell us how she felt.

Secondly, perhaps in these simple images we learn something about reality itself. We have remarked that the psalmists do not simply illustrate through creation, but rather understand through it: that lions and trees serve both as a tangible channel for the voice of the God who first spoke them, and as a metaphorical one for our response. The world is itself a language, one which one day Jesus too would bring to life through his parables. The speech of these ancient poets is as uncluttered and open as the created world, the images they use as familiar as the emotions they seek to portray. You are angry? Roar like a lion. Your enemy's words are poisonous? Cast him as a viper. Here we find neither distraction nor obfuscation: the spaces between these simple words and images invite us, whoever we are, to fill them with our own thoughts and experiences, and even a toddler can do it. Language does not, after all, have to be complicated in order to be profound: 'In the beginning was the Word,' wrote John, putting a whole philosophy into a time reference, a verb and a noun. And the simpler the words, as any songwriter knows, the easier it is to sing them.

In this sense too the Psalms take me back to rural Africa – or perhaps it's the other way round, and my visits to rural Africa have taken me more deeply into the Psalms. In Africa I enter a world where threat still does come from marauding lions and hidden snakes, where the sun burns drought into the ground and rivers rush in seasonal torrent, where birds sing and people sow, reap, suffer exile and express their feelings in dance. It's a world of vivid colour and practical living, a world where people walk for miles on dusty paths, a world where languages are spoken but not written, and scripture is not studied in books but memorised through song. And it's a world which knows both suffering and joy – the suffering of disease, violence and famine, and the joy of song and dance, of connectedness and relationship. It's a world, indeed, where the complexities of indoor theology are of little use, a world where pretence crumbles into the reality of lived experience. If at home I have learned to clothe my thoughts in garments of subtlety and abstraction, in Africa I have learned again to make them concrete. If the Psalms transport the western reader to another world, in Africa they reflect and describe the one that is all around you. It's a good place to see and sing the Psalms.

10

Coming home

Praise the Lord!
How good it is to sing praises to our God;
    for he is gracious, and a song of praise is fitting.
The Lord builds up Jerusalem;
    he gathers the outcasts of Israel.
He heals the broken-hearted,
    and binds up their wounds...
Great is our Lord, and abundant in power...
Sing to the Lord with thanksgiving.
PSALM 147:1–3, 5, 7

Interlocking journeys

As I look back over my journey now, I am reminded that I have been reading poetry all my life. Starting with the inevitable delight of nursery rhymes, progressing to set texts at school, wandering happily at university from twelfth-century Anglo-Norman story-poems to the abstractions of 20th-century verse, and then choosing one of the world's greatest poets as the subject of my PhD, over the years I have delighted in poetry, studied it, taught it and shared it; at times I have even found myself writing it. And it's not just me, for poetry is an ancient art form which emerges out of the mists of human prehistory: created orally, first shaped in writing some 4,500 years ago, poetry has echoed within our souls for longer than we can remember.[1] Still today, poetry

---

1 The earliest named poet known to us is Enheduanna, a Sumerian priestess living in the city of Ur in the 23rd century BC. The oldest poetic texts to come down to us are Sumerian temple hymns (27th century BC), Egyptian pyramid inscriptions (24th century BC) and parts of the Sumerian Epic of Gilgamesh (22nd century BC).

reaches across cultures and backgrounds: children write it at school, young people rap it in cities, radio ads and greetings cards declaim it, gravestones say goodbye with it. A London church once ran a poetry workshop for those attending its soup kitchen, displaying their work on the railings outside; and just last week I passed a house in a well-to-do village where the poems of local residents had been inscribed onto slates arranged on an external wall. Poetry, says Stephen Fry, is a primal impulse within us all; it is 'songwriting, confessional, diary-keeping, speculation, problem-solving, storytelling, therapy, anger management, craftmanship, relaxation, concentration and spiritual adventure all in one inexpensive package.'[2] And all these elements are found within the Psalms, one of the oldest and most widely read collections of poetry ever produced.

We do not know for certain when the Psalter reached its final form, and until quite recently it was regarded as an anthology of disparate elements assembled without any obvious governing order or principle. The psalms it contains may be classified by genre (hymns, laments, thanksgiving, royal psalms, wisdom psalms), by theme (creation, law, history, messiah, suffering, guilt), by cultic setting (use within the temple on set occasions), by literary form (lament, praise), and by relational development (orientation, disorientation, reorientation); but psalms in all these categories are distributed throughout the Psalter. Many psalms seem to have been part of smaller, pre-existing collections which can be identified by their opening inscriptions or their use of key terms and phrases (Davidic, Korahite, Asaphite psalms; Songs of Ascents; Elohistic, Enthronement and Hallelujah psalms). These survive to some extent as collections within a collection, or at least as footprints left by the compilers.[3] The emerging Psalter played a key part in helping an estranged people maintain their faith in a foreign land, and

---

2 *The Ode Less Travelled* (Arrow, 2007), p. xii.

3 Susan Gillingham suggests that the final compilers may have been the Levites, temple servants whose role was to provide music, singing and teaching in the temple – 'The Levites and the editorial composition of the Psalms' in William P. Brown (ed.), *The Oxford Handbook of the Psalms* (Oxford University Press, 2014), pp. 201–13. There is some repetition – Psalm 14 reappears as 53, part of Psalm 40 recurs in 70, and parts of Psalms 57 and 60 are repeated in 108.

following the return to Jerusalem some 50 years later it took its place, with the addition of new works, as the hymnbook for temple worship.

Over the last decade I have edited two poetry anthologies, each including over 100 poems dating from between the tenth century BC and the 21st century AD, and contributed by poets writing from within very different contexts and traditions. Pondering how to order them, I decided to structure each collection not by author or date, but in such a way as to support the emotional and spiritual journey of the reader. For the first, I spread all the poems out on the floor and moved them around until I felt they could be read sequentially, irrespective of when they were written or by whom, rather as one might read a novel. For the second I adopted a more visible structure, grouping poems into five stages which reflect our experiences as we move from cradle to grave, inviting the reader to remind herself of highs as well as lows, and encouraging him to blend those experiences together into a settled, coherent whole. I wanted the poems to echo and express the journey each of us takes with our lives.[4]

It seems that a more sophisticated version of this process may lie behind the formation of the Psalter. In recent years critics have become increasingly aware that the Psalms were subjected to careful editing, and that the compilers trod a delicate path between simply pulling together existing collections and shaping them in such a way as to form a coherent whole. While each psalm undoubtedly stands as a work in its own right, we now accept that individual psalms were placed within the Psalter neither randomly nor according to simple historical provenance, but purposefully, in such a way as to give the finished collection a function and meaning which is greater than the sum of its parts. The Psalter, it seems, was carefully and intentionally crafted in such a way as to carry its own theological message.[5]

---

4 The first anthology is out of print; the second is *Something Understood* (The Mathetes Trust, 2017).

5 See Nancy deClaissé-Walford, 'The meta-narrative of the Psalter' in Brown (ed.), *The Oxford Handbook of the Psalms*, pp. 355–56. A helpful summary of this narrative approach is given by Jerome Creach, *Discovering the Psalms* (Eerdmans, 2020), ch. 6; see also Geoffrey Grogan, *Prayer, Praise and Prophecy: A theology of the psalms* (Mentor, 2001), ch. 15.

Viewing the Psalter as a whole, then, we may discern a clear movement within it, one which is at the same time chronological, theological, and profoundly personal. The five books demonstrate a historical progression, moving from the reign of David (Book 1, Psalms 1—41) through that of Solomon (Book 2, Psalms 42—72), to the story of foreign invasion (Book 3, Psalms 73—89), deportation and exile (Book 4, Psalms 90—106), and finally to restoration (Book 5, Psalms 107—150). Nestling within this historical framework we find a parallel evolution in theological perspective, as the focus shifts gradually from earthly kingship (David and his successors) to divine kingship (the rule of the Lord himself). And this theological development is accompanied in turn by an emotional shift, as a focus on lament gradually gives way to an inclination to praise; this emotional shift takes place, furthermore, on both a personal and a corporate level.[6]

The Psalms, in other words, take us on a journey: a journey which is at the same time historical, theological and experiential, which is both individual and corporate, and which points forward to a final resolution in a new and different future. It's a journey whose pattern we are invited to recognise in our own lives, for which the Psalms will provide us with the resources we need, and in the course of which a single overarching message emerges – the message that, however difficult it may be at times to believe it, God is sovereign and God is with us. Three markers define the itinerary: trust the Lord, Psalm 1 advises at the outset of the journey; expect to suffer, Psalm 88 warns from the low point in the centre of the collection; you will again praise him, promises Psalm 150 as we reach the end.[7]

---

[6] For the chronological and theological development see the essays by William Brown, J. Clinton-McCann and Nancy deClaissé-Walford in Brown (ed.), *The Oxford Handbook of The Psalms*; for the emotional shift see Claus Westermann, *Praise and Lament in the Psalms* (Westminster John Knox Press, 1987).

[7] Measured by volume of words rather than by number of Psalms, Psalm 88 stands at the centre of the Psalter – with the result that the Psalter as a whole takes the same chiastic (in and out) form as many of the individual psalms within it (e.g. Psalms 25, 92, 145). A chiastic structure creates a pivotal point which marks a change in direction.

The coming king: Psalms of enthronement

In the foregoing chapters I have wanted to treat the Psalter as a text in its own right, as a free-standing guide to the perils and pitfalls of life on earth, traced in time through the experiences of an individual and a people in the context of a relationship with God. But the Psalms are deliberately open-ended, drawing past into present but pointing too to an as yet unfulfilled future, a future in which David's earthly kingship will be followed by a divine kingship of an entirely different kind. Christians recognise these Psalms as prophetic, and identify the coming king as Jesus. The Psalms tell a story which Jesus came to complete – a story which unfolds slowly, and which continues to unfold even today.

The overthrow of the monarchy following the Babylonian invasion had come as a devastating blow for a people who had held firmly to God's covenantal promise of a permanent kingdom governed by a descendant of David. 'Your house and your kingdom shall be made sure forever before me; your throne shall be established forever,' God had told David. The promise is echoed in Psalm 2, composed perhaps as part of the historic coronation festivities for David: 'I have set my king on Zion,' God says; 'I will make the nations your heritage.' It recurs again in Psalm 72, in which David signs off with a prayer seeking its fulfilment through the reign of Solomon and his successors; here the compilers note that 'the prayers of David son of Jesse are ended.' And yet within a few hundred years the kingdom had been overthrown.[8] The agonised disbelief which greeted its loss is vividly portrayed in Psalm 89, centrally placed beside Psalm 88 and bringing to a close the exilic laments of Book Three of the Psalter. If the people of God were to preserve their faith, it was clear that a major shift in expectation would be required: and a shift is exactly what the compilers provide. Book Four opens with Psalm 90, the only psalm in the entire collection to be attributed to Moses: reaching back to the ancient memory of the Exodus, it stands here as a clear marker of a new search for historical

---

8 2 Samuel 7:16 (see also 1 Chronicles 17:11–15; Psalm 132:11–12); Psalms 2:6, 8; 72:20.

and theological continuity. Human life is fragile, Moses reminds us; thousands of years sweep past like a dream, and our iniquities bring the wrath of God down on our heads – but we know him to be steadfast in love, and we ask now for a new future: Lord, would you make us glad for as many days as you have afflicted us?

Psalm 90 paves the way for a new series of songs known as royal or Enthronement psalms.[9] Pointing back to Psalms 2 and 21, they celebrate the rule of a great king – not David, this time, but the Lord himself. The Lord is king, robed in majesty, Psalm 93 announces; a great King above all gods, adds Psalm 95; ruling all peoples and coming to judge the earth, affirms Psalm 96. Righteousness and justice are the foundation of his throne, proclaims Psalm 97; he is victorious over the nations, says Psalm 98; he has been with us throughout history, just as he was with Moses and Aaron and Samuel, concludes Psalm 99. As we read these psalms we realise that the world is being reimagined, the past reclaimed and the future security of the people affirmed; the longstanding themes of creation, history, victory and justice are all being brought together as the process of reorientation takes place before our eyes. And we, of course, know the end of the story, for the New Testament makes clear that this divine king, who is both the descendant of David and yet the Lord himself, has come in the person of Jesus. Looking back, we find the seed was sown from the very beginning: in Psalm 2 the king set on the throne of Zion is the Lord's 'anointed' – in Hebrew, the *mâshîyach*, or Messiah.

Praise the Lord: Hallel Psalms

The appropriate response to all this, of course, is praise, and this becomes the dominant theme of Book Five, which brings the Psalter to a close. Psalm 110 looks back to the Enthronement Psalms, forming a bridge to a new series traditionally referred to as the Hallel (praise)

---

9 The Enthronement Psalms are usually reckoned as Psalms 93, 95—99; see also Psalms 47, 82.

Psalms.[10] Attributed to David, Psalm 110 repeats and develops the promises of Psalm 2: the anointed ruler will be not only king but also priest and judge; he will sit at the right hand of the Lord and reign forever. The voice of David, like that of Moses, provides a reassuring sense of continuity, suggesting that we are not breaking with the past but simply re-evaluating it. In placing this psalm here, the compilers are affirming that it was right to cling to the promises, but that their implications are only now coming into full view. Psalm 110 is widely cited in the New Testament as confirmation of the messianic identity of Jesus, and Jesus himself will use it to zip the Pharisees neatly into the straitjacket of their own convictions. What do you think about the Messiah, the anointed king we are all waiting for, he asks – whose son is he? The son of David, of course, they dutifully reply. Right, so what about Psalm 110, then, Jesus continues, where David calls that king his lord? If he's his lord, how can he also be his son? Are you sure, Jesus is saying, that we are looking for an earthly monarch here – might not there be a conundrum in the middle of all this, a king who is descended both from David and from God himself? A few weeks later, Peter rams it home with unambiguous clarity: 'Therefore let all Israel be assured of this: God has made this Jesus, *whom you crucified*, both Lord and Messiah.'[11]

So all is not lost. God has the matter in hand. Despite the setbacks we can trust him, and we must praise him. And this is exactly what happens next, in a series of psalms which echo with the phrase 'Hallelujah', 'Praise the Lord!'[12] These Hallel Psalms look back with thanks for the great historical rescue of the people from slavery in Egypt (Psalm 114); mixing together gratitude for defeat of idol-worshipping nations (Psalm 115) with thanks for personal healing and deliverance (Psalm 116), they mark a new beginning in the life of the people of God: a

---

10 The intervening psalms focus on God's saving provision for his people through both creation and history; Psalm 101 offers a reminder of the characteristics of a godly king.

11 Jesus and the Pharisees: Matthew 22:44–46; Peter: Acts 2:36 (NIV, italics mine); see also Hebrews 1:5–14.

12 Psalms 113–118 are the classic Hallel Psalms, recited each year as part of the Passover festival. Together with a wider grouping (Psalms 111—112; 146—150) they are also known, from their opening phrase, as the Hallelujah Psalms.

recovery of confidence, a restored faith in the future. The despair of exile has given way to the new reality of salvation, and the pain of the past is dispelled by the shortest psalm in the entire collection, Psalm 117: 'Praise the Lord, all you nations! Extol him, all you peoples! For great is his steadfast love towards us, and the faithfulness of the Lord endures forever. Praise the Lord!'

As to the future, that too is secure: the last of the series, Psalm 118, invites us to give thanks that the stone that the builders rejected has become the cornerstone of an entirely new building. Haven't you read it? Jesus asked the Pharisees. Again, it's Peter who spells it out: '*Jesus is "the stone you builders rejected, which has become the cornerstone". Salvation is found in no one else.*'[13] As we have already seen, the Hallel Psalms were regularly sung as part of the Passover festival, and this psalm is likely to have been the one sung by Jesus and the disciples on the evening before his death.[14] It was, as it turned out, the last evening of the old order, the beginning of a new era ushered in by a sacrificial death to which these festivities had pointed for centuries – another act of deliverance, providing an eternal fulfilment for the deliverance already experienced through the exodus from Egypt and the return from exile in Babylon. And so bit by bit the authors of the New Testament pick up the threads left hanging out of the Psalms and weave them into the long-awaited story of Jesus.

Making sense of the past

The death of Jesus was received by his followers as a tragedy, the loss of all their hopes. Perhaps they had shared the common expectation that the Messiah would come as a conquering king: Simon was a political activist, the ambitious mother of James and John had put in a request for high office for her sons, and Judas had clearly been horrified by Jesus' casual attitude to money. Jesus' arrival in Jerusalem

---

13 Jesus and the Pharisees: Matthew 21:42; Peter: Acts 4:11–12 (NIV, italics mine); see also 1 Peter 2:6–7.
14 Matthew 26:30.

had been greeted by the ancient equivalent of flags and red carpets, and celebrated with the joyful public proclamation of Psalm 118: 'Blessed is the one who comes in the name of the Lord!' *Are* you the Messiah? the chief priests asked, nervously. And yet it all ended not with a coronation but with an ignominious execution. Apparently not.[15]

It seems, as Jesus pointed out three days later to two disciples walking on the road to Emmaus, that a more attentive reading of the scriptures in general and perhaps the Psalms in particular might have led to a different conclusion. The Psalter offers us two contrasting pictures of David: he is not only God's anointed king, but also a man who suffers at the hands of others. It tells the story of a man who experiences rejection, opposition and persecution, a man who does not come as a powerful conqueror, but who through suffering nonetheless inherits an eternal kingdom. Had you not realised that it was necessary, Jesus asked the two walkers, that the Messiah should suffer these things?[16]

Throughout his ministry, Jesus had both cited and prayed the Psalms, and he returns now to Jerusalem to emphasise the point: '*Everything*,' he repeats, 'written about me in the law of Moses, the prophets, and the psalms must be fulfilled' – specifically, he points out, that the Messiah will suffer and rise from the dead on the third day, and that repentance and forgiveness of sins will be proclaimed in his name to all nations.[17]

And so the Psalms take their place as prophetic texts finding fulfilment through the life and death of Jesus. Eagerly embraced by the New Testament authors, quotations and allusions to the Psalms are found in every New Testament book except the shortest letters, with

---

15 Psalm 118:26. The Hebrew word for salvation, *yeshua*, occurs twice in Psalm 118; it became the name of Jesus himself, whose coming fulfilled the promises of the psalm. See Megan Daffern, *Songs of the Spirit* (SPCK, 2017), pp. 167–71. For the chief priests' question see Luke 22:67.

16 Luke 24:13–27.

17 Luke 24:44 (italics mine). Jesus had prayed from Psalms 22 and 31 on the cross, and cited Psalms 2, 41, 110 and 118 in his teaching; Psalm 69 is quoted by all four gospel accounts as a prophecy of his death.

no fewer than 129 out of the full 150 psalms mentioned.[18] Psalms 2 and 110, which speak directly of the king who is to come, receive special attention in the teaching of Peter and Paul, both of whom draw extensively on the Psalms in the evangelistic addresses recorded in Acts 2 and Acts 13. The letter to the Hebrews draws on no fewer than eleven psalms in order to demonstrate the divinity of Jesus.[19] And it's not a matter of simple quotation, for the gospel writers rely on the Psalms not only as a prophetic authentication of their message but as a source of language and imagery to express the suffering of Jesus, son of David, himself: the Psalms not only inform their thinking but provide the words in which to express it.[20]

As the compilers of the Psalms draw to the end of their work, it is to David that they return. It's been a long and unexpected journey, and now David brings us back to the thoughts of Moses: human life is like a breath, and our days pass like a shadow, he says in Psalm 144. And yet the outcome of this fragility is to bring us into deeper dependence on God; happy are those whose God is the Lord, David concludes, before moving into a call to celebrate the steadfast love of God in the closing collection of songs of praise. All the faithful shall bless you, he cries in Psalm 145, and speak of the glory of your kingdom – an everlasting kingdom which will endure throughout all generations! It's all come right, the compilers suggest: David, himself, the great king with whom the covenant was made, is able to proclaim his satisfaction with the revealed outcome. The remaining psalms invite us to join our voices in unmitigated praise and thanksgiving: Praise the Lord!

---

[18] The exceptions are 2 and 3 John, 1 Thessalonians, Philemon and Jude.

[19] Peter cites Psalms 10, 16 and 110 in Acts 2, and 118 in Acts 4; Paul cites Psalms 2 and 16 in Acts 13. Hebrews cites Psalms 2, 8, 22, 34, 40, 45, 95, 104, 110, 118 and 135. A helpful list of psalms cited in the NT is given by Christopher Ash, *Psalms for You* (The Good Book Company, 2020), pp. 275–77. See also Gordon Wenham, *The Psalter Reclaimed: Praying and praising with the Psalms* (Crossway, 2013), ch. 4.

[20] For the suffering of David and its fulfilment in the life of Jesus see Wenham, *The Psalter Reclaimed*, pp. 98–99, and Stephen Ahearne-Kroll, 'Psalms in the New Testament' in Brown (ed.), *The Oxford Handbook of the Psalms*, p. 272.

A map for the journey: Psalm 121

One of the glories of modern Britain is the Ordnance Survey series of maps. Painstakingly created over more than two centuries, they offer us a detailed representation of the entire country at a scale which enables us to identify every field, stream and footpath. Over the last decade or so I have been following the paths within a 25-mile radius of my home, highlighting each one with a coloured pen on the map as I complete it. The area closest to our house now appears as a tangle of intersecting coloured lines, each one walked many times and in many combinations. I feel a curious sense of satisfaction as I look at it; it traces where I have been, gives tangible form to my journey.

As I have plunged ever more deeply into the Psalms, I have come to feel that they too offer a kind of map. We saw in chapter 4 that the Psalter is conceived as a journey undertaken on foot, a chart of the difficulties and the joys which we encounter as we make our way towards God. We have found ourselves passing through raging torrents and walking by quiet streams, pausing to appreciate the beauty of flowers or catch our breath after a hasty scramble over rocks. We have endured terrifying storms and relaxed in lush valleys, gazed at distant hills and watched eagles soar far above our heads. We have threaded our way past hidden snares and concealed pits, endured the heat of the midday sun, and stood in awe beneath a canopy of stars. And throughout it all, constantly afraid that we will be led astray, we have done our best to follow the signposts which mark out the way of the Lord. Perhaps it is not surprising that journey should be the metaphor which lies at the heart of the Psalter, for recent research by neuroscientists suggests that the deepest and oldest part of our brain is that in which we first learned to find our way around the world; both memory and language are rooted in concepts of physical space.[21]

One of my favourite psalms, perhaps because it most clearly embodies

---

21 Michael Bond, *Wayfinding: The art and science of how we find and lose our way* (Picador, 2020), ch. 4.

this sense of life as a journey through physical space, is Psalm 121. It's another of the Pilgrim Psalms, the little collection which we looked at in chapter 4, and which we now find follows on from the Hallel Psalms; the two collections are separated only by Psalm 119, the compass-setting 'psalm of the way' par excellence.

Psalm 121 is the traveller's psalm. As the pilgrims set out on their long walk to Jerusalem, they fix their eyes on the mountains which lie ahead, and pray for protection from the hidden perils which may await them – for in the mountains lurk rebels and fugitives, robbers and bandits. Perhaps there are spiritual dangers too, for in these hills foreign gods are worshipped and cruel sacrifices made.[22] Few such fears may trouble me as I set out to drive up the M5, but travelling in Africa has taught me to take the psalmists' prayers for protection seriously, for in Africa travel remains as precarious an undertaking as it was in ancient Israel. There, people know better than to take such a casual approach, and every journey begins and ends with prayer – even, I have discovered, when you arrive exhausted at four in the morning. Over the years prayer has provided me with a sense of security when stranded by punctures on remote rural roads, when plunging as the light fades into the great dust bowl which interrupts the old track across the Masai steppe, when plagued by wild bees whilst waiting patiently in open country beside an overturned vehicle. The prayers of my companions sustained me during a lonely cross-examination at the Congo border as I sought common ground with a gun-bearing functionary seated beneath a dim light bulb and a paper-thin hornet nest; in Madagascar as we set off in a convey of buses for a long night drive through bandit country; and in Tanzania as cars were washed off the road ahead of us by a flash flood. 'From where will my help come?' cry the pilgrims. 'From the Lord, who made heaven and earth,' comes the reply. Despite our nonchalance at home, it seems that his help is available even on the M5: my husband, hastening home after a long day, fell asleep at the wheel. At least, he thinks he did, for he woke with a start to find

---

22 Including infanticide – see Deuteronomy 12:31; Jeremiah 19:5.

himself not on the motorway but neatly positioned within a parking bay beside an off-road service station.

The Lord will keep you safe, the psalm continues – and, unlike the god Baal worshipped in the hills by the Canaanites, he will not fall asleep on the job.[23] He will protect you as you travel by day and as you travel by night; he will keep you from all evil. 'Defend us from all perils and dangers of this night,' the Anglican evening liturgy begs, following the ancient daily pattern of the monastic tradition, itself based on the recommendations of Psalm 119.[24] We may find ourselves wondering, from the comfort of our solid suburban homes, what those dangers might be, for here the night offers us relaxation and rest, cosy evenings in front of the telly, silent sleep in comfortable beds. Again it is in Africa that I have come to appreciate the prayerful insistence of the Psalms – indeed, I only agreed to go in the first place because I heard God speaking to me repeatedly through the assurances of Psalm 91: he will command his angels to guard you in all your ways, so that you will tread on the lion and the adder, promises the psalmist. 'Those who love me, I will deliver; when they call to me, I will answer them; I will be with them in trouble' confirms the Lord himself.[25] And in Africa, the dangers of the night are as real as those of the day. I have lain in bed listening to the unearthly screaming of hyenas; I have tied little knots all over ragged mosquito nets to minimise the risk of mosquito-borne diseases; I have resisted the desire to venture out under the night sky to visit the straw-walled toilet in case the watchman should mistake me for an intruder and unleash one of his poison-tipped arrows in my direction. A toddler snatched by a prowling lion, a deadly mamba snake curled beneath the bed, a bishop who secures his windows with iron bars and Bibles to protect his family, for he has received death threats – all these things I have known. I once fell nervously asleep in a lakeshore hut wondering what might be the intentions of the

---

23 See the story of the competition between Elijah and the prophets of Baal in 1 Kings 18, where Elijah suggests that Baal must be asleep.

24 Psalm 119:62 ('At midnight I rise to praise you') and 119:164 ('Seven times a day I praise you') are the texts which led Benedict to set up the daily pattern of prayer specified in his Rule.

25 Psalm 91:14–15.

old man lying across the threshold outside. The next morning they told me it was the village chief, who had insisted on taking personal responsibility for my safety. We thank you, Lord, for bringing us safely through the night.

It is worth noting that Psalm 121, in common with all the Psalms, does not anticipate that a life of faith, a determination to follow the way of the Lord, will prevent us from encountering danger, difficulty and suffering – indeed, both David and Jesus knew only too well that it may be our very desire to honour God which will cause us to experience these things. The author of Psalm 121 seeks not prevention but protection, the kind of protection I have experienced in Africa: as we travel along the road laid out for us, he concludes, the Lord will keep our life, our going out and our coming in – from this time on and forevermore. I sang it to my husband as he faced the real possibility that his life was at an end; we read it to my mother as she struggles through her last years. 'That's nice,' she says each time, as her angst subsides.

Psalm 121 is the second of the 15 Pilgrim Psalms. It is followed by Psalm 122, which helps the pilgrims express their thanks as they reach the end of their journey, pass through the gates of Jerusalem and enter the house of the Lord. Psalm 125 celebrates the protection which the Lord offers to those who place their trust in him, and Psalm 127 reminds them that their good fortune is due not to their own efforts but to the generosity of his provision. Psalm 128 expresses the joy of those whose determination to follow the way of the Lord has been rewarded with blessing, and Psalm 133 rejoices in the unity which, at last, seems to have fallen into their laps. The psalmists know that it is important to acknowledge that this peace has not been easily won: for if the Lord had not been on our side, David cries in Psalm 124, our enemies would have swallowed us alive, and we would have been swept away by the raging waters of defeat – but the Lord *was* with us, he says, and we have escaped like a bird from the snare of the fowlers. Me too, I thought once as I watched a forest guide cut a neat wire loop from the fallen log to which it had been fixed; me too.

The journey, of course, is not quite over, and a little group of psalms within this collection remind us of our need for ongoing protection: restoration is a continuous process, our enemies have not gone away, and our need for forgiveness is lifelong.[26] But we are able to reflect that despite all that has happened the Lord has indeed fulfilled his covenant with David, and we end the day standing in the dark in the house of the Lord, offering him our thanks and praise – praise which, as we have already seen, will increase in confidence and strength until it reaches a climax in the five Hallelujah Psalms which bring the Psalter to a close.

The journey becomes a story: Psalms 30 and 138

As I reflect now on my travels through the Psalms, I realise that a journey, with hindsight, becomes a story – not just the story of a people, but the story of each and every one of us. Individually, the Psalms are helpful, providing us with the resources we need as we travel: each has its own message, each comes to life in its own way. But taken together their impact is far greater, for they enable us to find a place for our varied and inconsistent experiences within a single narrative, one that has both a starting point – our conception – and an end point – our arrival in heaven. Within the narrative there is room for everything we find in an ordinary human life: success and failure, triumph and disaster, joy and disappointment. All these things become chapters in an unfolding story which, given that our desire is to move towards God and not away from him, take us ever closer to our destination. The psalmists have taught us that instead of ignoring the furious elephants and resenting the spiritual hurdle of the wall, we must accept that setbacks and suffering are necessary stimuli to our own spiritual growth; they have helped us come to terms with both our flaws and our wounds. As I look back now, I realise that the Psalms have enabled me to recognise afresh that I am in need of the mercy and grace of God, and to rejoice in all that I have been given. They have given me permission to be who I actually am.

---

26 Psalms 123, 129, 130.

As I think about the story of my life, two psalms in particular serve as bookmarks. Psalm 30 comes halfway through the first book and is sung by David as he confronts the difficulties which will dominate the next chapter of his life. Enjoying the Lord's favour, David had been brought from obscurity to a position of status and strength – a position which he had not sought but which had given him great joy. His position was, he thought, unassailable. 'As for me,' he notes, 'I said in my prosperity, "I shall never be moved."' But then, David says, it all went wrong. Faced with unexpected opposition and sudden failure, David cried out to the Lord – who failed to act. David, distraught, threw himself into anguished prayer – is that it, are you just going to let me die, then? And the Lord responded. We don't know what the precise circumstances were – David speaks both of enemies and of illness. But the psalm marks a moment of real crisis in the life of a man who thought he had reached a position of settled stability. The obvious shock with which he cries out to God is repeated all too often in our own lives today, as the stories shared in this book have shown. Life is like being on a giant wheel turned by Fortune, they used to say in the Middle Ages: one minute you are up, and the next you are down – you haven't seen it coming, and there is absolutely nothing you can do about it. That's how it was for David, and how, in smaller ways, it has been for me.

The second bookmark lies much further on in the collection, among the pages of Book Five. Psalm 138 is also by David, and it seems to come from a point much later in his life. It's a song of thanksgiving. David thinks back to that earlier moment of crisis, and notes that on the day he called, the Lord answered him, giving him the strength he needed to keep going. He has known other times of trouble since then, he reflects; but he recognises now that always the Lord has walked with him, protecting him from those who would destroy him. The troubles did indeed come; but the doubts went. 'The Lord,' David can now say with confidence, '*will* fulfil his purpose for me.'

I once listened to this psalm in a small parish church in Ghana, where the congregation had gathered with Paul, their priest, to join with him in giving thanks for his 25 years of ordained ministry. The preacher was

Paul's former mentor, now retired from his own duties as archbishop. Paul, the archbishop said, has known both success and disappointment, triumph and disaster; but he has persisted through it all, he has remained faithful, and he has much to thank God for – for God too has remained faithful. Perhaps the people knew more of Paul's story than we did, but the very vagueness of the allusions brought the sermon to life – for Paul's story, David's story, is the story of each one of us. Looking back that day over the 25 years of my own ministry, I found the psalm both moving and encouraging. Though I live surrounded by trouble, I thought, once more borrowing the words of the psalmist, you stretch out your hand and save me. And I too am grateful.

Coming home

It's autumn. Yesterday afternoon I went for a walk in our local woods, a plantation of conifers scattered over the mossy bumps and lumps which rise and sink between them, the solid gruffy ghosts of 2,000 years of lead mining in the limestone hills of the Mendips. I had gone to look for crossbills, but found myself gazing instead at fallen beech leaves and tree stumps spangled with all sizes and shapes of fungi, splashes and curves of orange and cream and russet and grey against the dark, mossy wood. It's a funny time, autumn, I thought, and I suppose I am in the autumn of my own life. Gone the nervous, delicate shoots of spring, gone the energy-rich growth of summer; now the strange forms of fungi emerge, mottled, multicoloured, beneath the full-grown trees of my past. Thinking back over the ups and downs of my life and reflecting on the traumatic experiences of those who have shared their stories with me, it seems that much of the time life is filled with grief and loss. Life, sometimes, seems to be closing in on us.

And yet, and yet. Autumn, I have always thought, is the most beautiful time of the year. It is the time when all that has gone before is gathered into fruitfulness, the time when the steady green of summer emerges in a kaleidoscope of rich and unique colours, and each plant is clothed in the glorious hues of its own fulfilment. Here in the orchards of

Somerset the apples glow red and yellow like lamps among the trees. I have downloaded an app to help with the fungi, and am learning their names, just as I began a few years ago to learn the names of flowers: turkeytail, spectacular rustgill, the Miller. The viral pandemic which dominated our lives for so many months has brought us closer as a family, I have recovered aspects of myself which I had thought gone for ever, and new opportunities have opened up before me. I feel freer than I have done for decades; I stand on the brink of another world.

I reread Psalm 83. 'God sometimes hides his face from the world,' observes the commentary; 'but his hiddenness does not mean he is absent' – any more, I reflect, than the life of the all-pervading fungus is absent when it remains below ground, as it does for most of the year. 'The ultimate reason to live confidently in a hostile world,' continues the commentary, 'is that Jesus Christ has prevailed over our greatest enemies: sin, guilt, Satan and death.' I have known all those, I thought, and read on. 'In Christ we are invincible, for Jesus was raised bodily, and we are now united to him by faith. Our future could not be brighter, whatever adversity washes over us in this fallen world.'[27] That, I thought, is true.

Over the years in which I have been praying the Psalms, I have been astonished by the sheer variety of emotional and spiritual resources contained within them. Nodding their head wisely in the presence of the trumpeting elephants, the psalmists have invited me to sit down and remember that I am the imperfect but nonetheless beloved child of God. They have encouraged me to raise my head above the parapet of my own concerns and reconnect with that God, who is both the creator of the world and the power present within it. They have helped me to place my own journey in the geographical context of the land in which I live, and to reflect that my trajectory through life is but a small part of the historical journey of God's people, who are also my people. They have encouraged me to take delight in the beauty and intricacy of little things, and to allow God to speak to me through them. As I began

---

27 *ESV Devotional Psalter* (Crossway, 2016), pp. 82–83.

to recover my spiritual footing, the psalmists insisted that I face up to the violence of my own feelings, and enabled me to express them to God without either pretence or fear. Reassuring me that forgiveness and justice are available to me, they required me to place my trust in God and in the future that he has planned, and escorted me firmly into his presence in order that I might do so. Finally, they suggested that I might find it both helpful and appropriate to acknowledge the assistance that I have received by offering my thanks and praise to God – not just for what he does, but for who he is.

In short, the psalmists have enabled me, in the midst of the trials which come to us all, to re-examine my expectations of what it is to be human, caught in the gap between creation and redemption, and to move confidently forward into the next stage of my life on earth, knowing that this is but part of the pilgrimage which will lead me eventually into the direct presence of the Lord himself. And they have done this not with any sense of do-good superiority, but by daring to cry that they too have felt the things which I have felt, that they too have experienced the setbacks which I have experienced, that they too have had to learn to trust, and that they too, both individually and on behalf of an entire people, have surrendered their lives afresh to God.

I have saved one psalm until now, because it has always spoken vividly to me. It's Psalm 131, the remaining Pilgrim Psalm. It needs no commentary:

> O Lord, my heart is not lifted up,
>   my eyes are not raised too high;
> I do not occupy myself with things
>   too great and too marvellous for me.
> But I have calmed and quieted my soul,
>   like a weaned child with its mother;
>   my soul is like the weaned child that is with me.

I sat down to write this book in January. It's now mid-November, and a day of rain has been broken by an interlude of sunshine. Glancing outside, I find a double rainbow glowing with suspended beauty, high over the Mendip hills.

For further reflection

If you would like to spend some time reflecting on your own spiritual journey, you may find the following pointers helpful. Use them to guide your own prayers as you complete each chapter, perhaps taking one question each day and moving on to the next chapter only when you are ready. Or you may prefer to set them aside to be followed over a longer period once you have read the whole book. They can also be used as a basis for shared discussion if you are reading *World Turned Upside Down* as a group.

Chapter 1: Making sense of life

1 Reflection on Psalm 23

Read Psalm 23 aloud, pausing at the end of each phrase to allow the familiar words to settle into your mind and heart.

Now listen to the psalm as it is sung. You could search for the traditional version sung to the tune Crimond, the contemporary version by Howard Goodall, or the popular worship version by Stuart Townend.

2 Stepping into the psalm

Close your eyes and imagine you are standing in a lush meadow beside a stream of fresh, running water. Pause to take in the scene. Reflect that you have walked a long way to reach this beautiful spot. But your walk hasn't been as pleasant as you expected. Were there obstacles on the path? Did you take a wrong turning, or meet some unhelpful people?

Now think about the spiritual meaning of all this imagery. What has troubled you most in your life? Are you walking through a dark valley at the moment? What does the darkness consist of?

3 Seeking solace

Allow yourself to notice that someone is walking with you. Have you ever experienced this? What is it like, for example, to rely on a guide as you enter a cave? To be blind, and depend on the expert care of a guide dog? What exactly does a shepherd do for his sheep?

Can you begin to think that there might be an invisible, divine presence padding along beside you? Remain quiet for a while until the presence of God becomes a reality for you.

4 Reaching safety

Dark valleys do not go on forever. As you emerge from the shadows, look down and notice that a picnic has been laid out on the grass. The sun is shining, the stream trickling, the birds singing. The people who have troubled you are nowhere to be seen. It's a scene of perfect peace.

Can you accept that this might be what the Lord has in mind for you, as you begin to travel through the Psalms in his presence?

Chapter 2: An anatomy of pain

1 Sleepless nights

When we are upset, angry or afraid we may find we cannot sleep; we toss and turn, struggling with the dark thoughts we suppress in the day only to find them running riot at night. The psalmist knows exactly what this feels like – and perhaps you do too.

Read again the section of this chapter 'Songs of suffering'. What goes through your mind when you are so disturbed that you can't sleep? Are you, like the psalmist, able to cling to the hope that God will help you through this experience, even if you can't yet see how?

2 An anatomy of pain

Psalm 107 identifies four distinct sets of painful life circumstances. Do any of the pictures used to conjure up the anguish of those whose lives have fallen apart seem relevant to your own experience? If so, are you able to cry to the Lord in your trouble, and trust him to deliver you from your distress?

Spend some time thinking about the last two sections of the psalm (vv. 33–38; 39–43). What do these verses tell us about the kind of relationship God expects to have with us?

3 How bad does it get?

The Psalms make it clear to us that trouble is to be expected, and that quick fixes may not be provided. Psalm 88 expresses Heman's anguish as he tries to come to terms with this uncomfortable reality. This psalm gives us permission to scream aloud at God as we get to grips with our most negative and destructive feelings. Do you think you can be as honest with God as Heman was?

4 A note of hope

We began our reflections with Psalm 23, which offers a long-term view of our spiritual journey. Try reading Psalm 24, where David continues the story. The comfort provided to us individually will one day find expression in the praise of a whole community as those who have sought God come into his presence and find peace. We know from Psalm 107 that this will include all those who turn to God even as they suffer the consequences of their own mistakes. It will also include you.

Can you believe that this is so, and begin to thank God that as well as a beginning, there will be an end?

Chapter 3: Who am I?

1 Who are you?

If you were to find yourself in another land, speaking to a stranger who had asked the simple question, 'Who are you?', how would you respond? Does Psalm 139 help you to answer that question?

Would you answer the question 'Who are you?' in the same way you would answer the question 'What do you do?', or differently?

2 Kill the wicked!

When we find ourselves on the receiving end of criticism, selfish opposition, hatred or malice, we may struggle to retain our sense of self-esteem. Have you ever experienced this?

Although (or perhaps because!) David is doing his best to live close to God, he finds that he is subject to violent persecution. Psalm 139 shows us how he responded: he faced and articulated his anger, he reminded himself that God is with him, and he asked God to intervene. Can you accept that it's okay to be angry? Are you able to get in touch with your anger, pour it out to God and ask for his help?

3 Search me, and know my heart

You know that God made you and that God is with you. You have expressed your anger and asked God to deal with those who pay no regard to him. Are you willing now to invite him to search your heart and mind, and to ask if there is anything in your own life and behaviour which needs to change?

Chapter 4: Who is God?

1 Relying on a God of power

Psalm 74 paints a picture of smashed sanctuaries and violent storms, and expresses the terror of a defenceless people. For many today the burning and looting of churches or the destructive power of water remains an ever-present reality. And yet Asaph insists that God has the power to deal with these things.

Thinking about the destruction you have experienced in your own life, are you able to trust that this is so? Reread Psalm 29 and ask God to intervene against the forces which threaten you or your community.

2 Looking at the stars

In Psalm 8 David gazes in awe at the heavenly canopy which rises above his head each night, and reflects on the astonishing fact that the God who spread out this glorious dusting of light is the same God who cares about each one of us.

See if you can find a place far from human habitation where you too can see the stars – if you live in a built-up area, an internet search for 'dark sky map' will help you identify a good location. Sit or lie down quietly for half an hour, then read Psalm 8. How do you feel?

3 Going for a walk

The Pilgrim Psalms (120—134) are designed to be sung whilst walking. Download Psalm 125 onto your phone, and take it outdoors. Allow the rhythm of your feet and the solidity of the landscape to calm and strengthen you as you meditate on the psalm.

Psalm 136 reflects on God's presence in the historical landscape. Whether you live in a city or in the countryside, you live in an environment which has been shaped over millennia. Plan another walk, and think about those who have inhabited that environment before you. What has been the spiritual history of this place? Does learning to read the landscape help you to gain a perspective on the joys and troubles of your own life?

Chapter 5: Connecting with God

1 The book of the universe

How strong is your relationship with the created world? Do you expect to hear God speaking to you through it? How would you start, or advise someone else to start?

2 The landscape comes to life

Read Psalm 65 slowly. Make a list of all the things God does, focusing on the verbs in the second person – 'You answer, forgive, choose', and so on.

Now read the psalm again, reversing the order of the three stanzas. Consider the way God blesses the land; the way he sets boundaries for the forces of nature; the way he acts in the lives of people. Does starting with God's provision for the natural world help you to trust in his provision for you?

3 Medicine for the soul

Psalm 104 is a hymn of praise, focused on God's creation of the earth and on the way he renews it each day. The seven stanzas describe different aspects of God's creative activity. Which seems the most vivid to you?

Can you engage more deeply with God through the world he has created? Could you pay renewed attention to birds or flowers, write your own poem or paint one of the scenes described by the psalmist?

Close by echoing the psalmist's prayer in verses 33–34. How would you like to respond to verse 35?

Chapter 6: Travelling with God

1 The anguish of death

Read Psalm 22. What strikes you most about this psalm? Is it David's anguish at the thought that he might die? Is it his desperate plea for protection from those who want to destroy him? Is it the cry of Jesus on the cross, as he adopted David's words to express his own despair?

The psalm marks a turning point in the history of our relationship with God. Think now of those you have loved and lost, or of your own limited lifespan. Does knowing the end of the story help? Are you able to thank God for his eternal answer to this prayer?

2 Walking backwards into the future

In Psalms 77—78 and 105—106, the psalmist looks back over history, contrasting the faithfulness of God with the failings of his people. What do you know about the history of your own family or community? Can you see a similar pattern? What lessons are there to be learned?

Read Psalm 77 slowly and prayerfully. Do you identify with the pain that Asaph expresses in the first half of the psalm? Can you call to mind the ways in which God has been faithful to you in the past, and place your trust in him for the future?

3 The fragility of life

Close your meditation by reading Psalm 90. Make a note of your feelings as you do so. Are you able to accept the twin realities of your own fragility, and God's steadfast love?

Chapter 7: A difficult conversation

1 Dealing with guilt

Think back to Psalm 139, and David's closing prayer that God would search his thoughts and heart. Did you pray it too? Did God speak to you?

Now read Psalm 51. Do you share David's desire for forgiveness? Would you find it helpful to pour out your own sense of failure to God, asking him to cleanse your heart and renew your spirit? Conclude your prayer by reading aloud from Psalm 103:8–14, and thank God for giving you a new start.

2 Dealing with fear

The psalmists give graphic descriptions of the painful and malicious ways they have been treated by others. Have any of their experiences found an echo in your own life? Have you ever been abused, bullied, betrayed, falsely accused, or shamed?

In Psalm 35 David expresses his fear as people hunt him, put him on trial, and seek to shame him. He begs for protection and expresses his confidence that he will receive it. You may or may not have been chased down dark streets at night, accused of crimes you did not commit, slandered or libelled – but these remain common experiences today. Do you find any comfort in allowing David to express your feelings for you?

3 Dealing with anger

The third negative emotion which is most likely to trouble us is anger. How good do you think you are at acknowledging and expressing your anger? As Christians we are urged to offer forgiveness to those who hurt us. Do you think that angry psalms like Psalm 109 can help us to do that? Do you dare to pray it?

Chapter 8: Putting things right

1 Acting together

Read Psalm 81, in which God appeals to his people to listen and submit to him; and Psalm 50, in which he makes clear that he's looking for inner change and not religious activity. Think about your own group or Christian community. Is there anything in your shared life, past or present, which you need to put right?

2 Asking for justice

Read Psalm 7 slowly and carefully. Think of a situation in which you feel you have been treated unjustly by others. Ask God to hear your complaint, knowing that he is a righteous judge who experiences anger every day as he watches people hurting each other. Can you, like David, accept that if those who have harmed you do not repent, they will answer not to you but to God himself? How do you feel about that?

3 Deciding to trust

David knows that although God can be trusted to act, he may not act immediately. Read Psalm 37 and quieten yourself before God. Ask God to help you to stop thinking about those who have trampled over you, and to trust him. Remind yourself that although you may stumble, you will not fall – for God himself holds you by the hand. You may like to learn verse 4 by heart: 'Take delight in the Lord, and he will give you the desires of your heart.'

4 Learning to wait

Look at Psalm 73:21–22, where Asaph realises the stupidity of nursing resentment in the way that he has. Now read Psalm 94. Thank God for the way he has taught and guided you, even when you have found that painful. Reflect that those who have harmed you will one day face God's judgment. Imagine them standing in the dock. Take one last look, and leave the room – you do not need to be there. Ask God to give you peace as you place your trust in him.

Close your meditation by praying that the Lord will forgive you your sins, remembering that he requires you to forgive those who have sinned against you. Have you done that?

Chapter 9: A long walk in another world

1 Songs of thanks

Now that you have brought your most painful experiences to God and placed your trust in him, perhaps you are ready to thank and praise him.

Start by listening to Psalm 100 or Psalm 150. The online database **Hymnary.org** lists hundreds of musical settings for these psalms, and the Choral Public Domain Library (**cpdl.org**) allows you to search by composer, language or translation. You can also search for a particular psalm on YouTube or Spotify. See if you can find three versions in different styles, and listen to them.

2 Songs of lament

We began this book with Psalm 88, the darkest of all the personal laments. Now we read Psalm 137, its corporate counterpart. Do you find this psalm helpful, or just horrifying? Can you imagine what it must have been like to be in the situation the psalmist is describing, or in its modern counterpart today?

Now read Psalm 126, which tells the next part of the story. Have you ever experienced this kind of relief? If you are struggling now, can you think back to a time when God has rescued and restored you? Can you picture yourself in the second stanza of the psalm, coming home after a long, hard day, carrying the harvest which will sustain you?

3 Seeing what you mean

Think back over the psalms you have encountered so far, focusing on those which employ imagery from the natural world – you may like to look again at chapter 5, and the section 'A new vocabulary of prayer'.

See how many of these images you can list – plants, birds, animals. Does looking at the natural world help you to find your own language of prayer? Go for a walk, allowing the things you see to become words in which God may be speaking to you, or in which you may speak to God.

Chapter 10: Coming home

1 A map for the journey

Many of the psalms present human life as a journey, a path followed on foot through an ever-changing landscape. Read Psalm 121 and think about your own life. Do you find psalmist's words comforting?

2 The journey becomes a story

Now read Psalm 30, where David thanks God for his faithfulness. 'Weeping may linger for the night, but joy comes with the morning,' he sings. Has that been true for you; or are you now able to believe that it will become so?

3 Coming home

We began our journey by reading Psalm 23, placing our trust in God to lead us through dark valleys and to protect us from evil. Has reading this book helped you to find that trust? Would you like to begin your own journey through the Psalms, praying one each day, or following the lectionary readings?

Whatever your life experiences have been, and whatever your current circumstances now are, end your reflection by praying Psalm 131. God is not only your father, but also your mother. Allow yourself to feel God's arms around you, and relax, knowing that you do not have to have all the answers.

4 Saying thank you

A good mother reads stories to her children. End your journey by turning to Psalm 147, and invite God, your mother, to read it to you as a story. The story comes with pictures. Allow the pictures to form in your mind as you listen – if you can, you may like to draw them.

Thank God for bringing you home.

Index of psalms

Italics indicates the citation is only in the footnotes on that page. **Bold** indicates a focus on that psalm.

1	*82*, 90, *96*, 127, 129, 135, 160, 212	23	**13–15**, 19–20, *82*, **153–55**
2	*82*, 160, *179*, 213–15, *217*, 218	24	231
3	167	25	*82, 135, 139, 147*, 205, *212*
4	*147, 186*	26	*82*
5	*82, 186*	27	*82, 135, 161*
6	30, **137–42**, *147, 186*	28	31, *117*, 146, *154*
7	31, *96, 165*, **174–75**, *187*	29	**68–71**, 72, 83
8	30, **75–77**, *82*, 83, *186*, 218	30	*199*, **223–25**
9	*160, 165, 186*, 205	31	30, *147*, 180, *217*
10	*82, 135*, 205, *218*	32	*82, 135*, **137–42**, 148, *187*
11	146	33	72, *186*
12	*186*	34	*135*, 205, *218*
13	31	35	31, *82, 96*, **147–50**
14	*160, 209*	36	*82, 96, 135, 165*
15	*82*, 146	37	*82, 135, 147, 154*, **175–77**, 204–05
16	*82, 187*, 218	38	**137–42**, *199*
17	31, *82, 96*	39	*38, 82, 135*, 137–38, *139*
18	30, 67, *82, 96, 135*	40	31, *82*, 137–38, *139*, *147*, 209, *218*
19	72, 135, 201, 204	41	*138, 139*, 144, *217*
20	*154*	42	31, *82, 161, 187*
21	*160*, 214	43	31, *82, 186*
22	29, 30, 31, 39, *96*, **117–21**, *147*, 180, *186, 217, 218*	44	*82*, 118, *147*, 160, *187*
		45	*96, 179*, 186–87, *199*, 218

46 .... 19, *161*, *186*, *191*	*160*, 163, *187*, 189, 193
47 .... *186*, *214*	75 .... 63, *160*, *165*, *186*
48 .... *82*, *161*, *191*	76 .... 63, *160*, *186*, *191*
49 .... *150–51*, 181, *186*	77 .... 30, 63, 67, *82*, **130–32**
50 .... 63, *82*, *165*, **170–71**	78 .... 63, *82*, **125–30**, *187*
51 .... 34, *82*, *135*, **137–42**, 148, *165*, 170, 198	79 .... 63, *139*, *160*, 170
52 .... 90, *96*, *160*, *187*	80 .... 63, *82*, *96*, *160*, 163, *186*
53 .... *147*, *186–87*, *209*	81 .... 63, *82*, *96*, *137*, *160*, **161–63**, *186*
54 .... *186–87*	82 .... 63, *82*, *160*, *214*
55 .... 31, *82*, *117*, 144, 146, *150*, *186–87*	83 .... 63, *96*, *147*, *151*, 153, *160*, *191*, 226
56 .... 31, *82*, 145, *186–87*, 201	84 .... *82*, 96–97, 157, *161*, 185, *186*, *191*
57 .... *82*, *96*, *147*, *186–87*, *209*	85 .... *82*, *160*, 163, 170
58 .... *96*, 145, *151*, 153, *186–87*	86 .... *82*, *135*, *147*, 161
59 .... *96*, 145, 146, *186–87*	87 .... *161*, *186*, *191*
60 .... *137*, *160*, *186–87*, *209*	88 .... **42–44**, 106, 118, *186–87*, 189, 212, 213
61 .... 31, *96*, *186*	
62 .... 144, 156	89 .... 67, *82*, 113, 118, *147*, *160*, *161*, 163, *187*, 213
63 .... *161*, **155–58**	
64 .... 146, *150*	90 .... 15, **113–32**, *137*, *139*, *160*, 200, 201–02, 213–14
65 .... 72, **90–92**, *96*, *139*, *161*, *187*	
	91 .... *82*, *96*, 156, 221
66 .... *161*, *187*	92 .... 90, *96*, 185, *186*, *212*
67 .... *82*, *161*, *186*	93 214
68 .... *82*, *96*, *150–51*, 153, *160*, 185, *186*	94 .... *137*, 138, **177–79**
	95 .... 72, *82*, 185, 214, *218*
69 .... 31, *117*, 144–46, *147*, *150–51*, 180, *186*, *217*	96 .... *96*, *165*, *187*, 214
	97 .... 70, *147*, *165*, 214
70 .... *147*, 199, *209*	98 .... *165*, *186*, *187*, 214
71 .... 31, *147*, 156, *167*, *186*	99 214
72 .... 89, *96*, *160*, *186*, 213	100 .... **185–88**, 198
73 .... 63, *82*, 178–79	101 .... *82*, *135*, *160*, 215
74 .... 31, **63–68**, *82*, 83, *96*, *147*,	

Index of psalms

102 .... 30, 31, *96* , **137–42**, 181	126 .... 78–79, *161*, 171, **192–96**
103 .... *38*, *82*, *96*, 140, 161, 168	127 .... 78–79, 89, *147*, 222
104 .... 19–20, *96*, **100–106**, *187*, *218*	128 .... 78–79, *82*, *96*, *135*, 222
105 .... **125–30**, *161*	129 .... 78–79, *96*, *147*, 153, *161*, *223*
106 ..... **125–30**, *160*, *164*, 170, 171	130 .... 78–79, **137–42**, *168*, *223*
107 .... **34–38**, *82*, *96*, 129, *161*, 190	131 .... 78–79, **227**
108 .... *186*, *209*	132 .... 78–79, *160*, 171, *191*
109 .... 31, 144, *147*, **150–53**, *169*, 191	133 .... 78–79, *160*, 222
110 .... *82*, *179*, *186*, **214–15**, *217*, 218	134 78–79
111 .... *215*	135 .... **125–30**, *218*
112 .... *135*, *161*, 201, *215*	136 .... **82–88**, **125–30**, 161
113 .... *215*	137 .... *186*, **188–92**, 193
114 .... *160*, 215	138 .... *82*, **223–25**
115 .... *82*, *160–61*, 215	139 .... 19, 30, **48–62**, 68, *82*, *150–51*, 174
116 .... *82*, 145, 215	140 .... *96*
117 216	141 .... *137*, 153
118 ...... *96*, *137*, 199, 216, 217, *218*	142 .... 31, *82*, *187*
119 .... 72, *82*, 129, **135–37**, 138, 143, *147*, *165*, 176, 204–05, 221	143 .... 30, *82*, *135*, **137–42**, *165*, *168*
120 78–79	144 .... *186*, 218
121 ... 32, 78–79, *161*, *187*, **219–23**	145 ...... *82*, 161, *186*, 205, *212*, 218
122 .... 78–79, *82*, *187*, 222	146 .... 30, *82*, *215*
123 .... 78–79, *187*, *223*	147 .... *96*, **109–11**, *186*, 209, *215*
124 .... 30, 78–79, *96*, *161*, *187*, 222	148 .... *96*, **109–11**, 187, *215*
125 .... **78–82**, 156, *161*, *191*, 222	149 .... *186*, *215*
	150 .... **185–88**, 212, *215*

Select bibliography

Works on the Psalms

Adeyemo, Tokunboh (ed.), *Africa Bible Commentary* (Zondervan, 2006)

Aitken, Jonathan, *Psalms for People Under Pressure* (Continuum, 2004)

Alter, Robert and Frank Kermode (eds), *The Literary Guide to the Bible* (Fontana Press, 1989)

Anderson, A.A., *The New Century Bible Commentary – Psalms 73—150* (Marshall Morgan and Scott, 1971)

Ash, Christopher, *Psalms for You* (The Good Book Company, 2020)

Atkinson, David, *A Light for the Pathway: Exploring the Psalms* (Wipf and Stock, 2021)

Augustine, *Enarrationes in Psalmos*, in *Patrologia Latina*, ed. J.P. Migne, vol. 36

Bell, John, *Living the Psalms* (SPCK, 2020)

Bonhoeffer, Dietrich, *Psalms: The prayer book of the Bible* (1966)

Booker, George, 'Musical instruments in the Psalms', *Psalms Studies Book 1*, **christadelphianbooks.org/booker/psalms1**

Brown, William P. (ed.), *The Oxford Handbook of the Psalms* (Oxford University Press, 2014)

Brown, William P., *Seeing the Psalms: A theology of metaphor* (Westminster John Knox Press, 2002)

Brueggemann, Walter, *From Whom No Secrets Are Hid: Introducing the Psalms* (Westminster John Knox Press, 2014)

Brueggemann, Walter, *Praying the Psalms: Engaging scripture and the life of the Spirit*, second edition (Cascade Books, 2007)

Brueggemann, Walter, *Spirituality of the Psalms* (Fortress Press, 2002)

Brueggemann, Walter, *The Message of the Psalms: A theological commentary* (Augsburg, 1984)

Brueggemann, Walter and William Bellinger, *Psalms*, New Cambridge Bible Commentary (Cambridge University Press, 2014)

Brueggemann, Walter and Steve Frost, *Psalmist's Cry: Scripts for embracing lament* (House Studio, 2010)

Church House Publishing, *Reflections on the Psalms* (Church House Publishing, 2015)

Clements, Roy, *Songs of Experience: Relating to God emotionally* (Christian Focus, 1993)

Creach, Jerome F.D., *Discovering the Psalms: Content, interpretation, reception* (Eerdmans, 2020)

Daffern, Megan, *Songs of the Spirit* (SPCK, 2017)

Dickson, David, *Psalms* (Banner of Truth Trust, 1959)

ESV Devotional Psalter (Crossway, 2016)

Friedmann, Jonathan, 'Music of the Psalms' in *The Jewish Magazine*, July 2008

Grogan, Geoffrey, *Prayer, Praise and Prophecy: A theology of the Psalms* (Mentor, 2001)

Horsfall, Tony, *Deep Calls to Deep: Spiritual formation in the hard places of life* (BRF, 2021)

Johnston, Philip and David Firth, *Interpreting the Psalms: Issues and approaches* (Apollos, 2005)

Law-Turner, Frederica, *The Ormesby Psalter* (Bodleian Library, 2017)

Leonard, Richard, 'Singing the Psalms: A brief history of Psalmody', Laudemont Ministries, 1997, **laudemont.org/a-stp.pdf**

Lewis, C.S., *Reflections on the Psalms* (Fontana, 1961)

Kidner, Derek, *Psalms 1—72* (IVP, 1973)

MacLaren, Alexander, *The Expositor's Bible: The Psalms*, volume 2 (Hodder and Stoughton, 1906)

Magonet, Jonathan, *A Rabbi Reads the Psalms* (SCM Press, 1994)

McCann, J.C. Jr, 'Book of Psalms', in L.E. Keck et al. (eds), *The New Interpreter's Bible Commentary*, volume 4 (Abingdon Press, 1996)

Morales, Michael, 'Jesus and the Psalms', **thegospelcoalition.org**

Reissig, Courtney, *Teach Me to Feel: Worshiping through the Psalms in every season of life* (Good Book Company, 2020)

Smith, David W., *Stumbling Toward Zion: Recovering the biblical tradition of lament in the era of world Christianity* (Langham Global Library, 2020)

Spurgeon, Charles H., *The Treasury of David*, updated edition, ed. R.H. Clarke (Thomas Nelson, 1998)

Varughese, Alex, 'Types and original uses of Psalms', **nph.com/vcmedia/2410/2410351.pdf**

Vroegop, Mark, *Dark Clouds, Deep Mercy: Discovering the grace of lament* (Crossway, 2019)

Ware, Bruce A., 'The gospel in the Psalms', **crossway.org/articles/the-gospel-in-psalms** (adapted from *ESV Gospel Transformation Study Bible*)

Weiser, Artur, *The Psalms: A commentary*, trans. Herbert Hartwell (SCM Press, 1962)

Wellington, James, *Praying the Psalms with Jesus: A journey of discovery and recognition* (Grove, 2015)

Wenham, Gordon, *The Psalter Reclaimed: Praying and praising with the Psalms* (Crossway, 2013)

Westermann, Claus, *Praise and Lament in the Psalms* (Westminster John Knox Press, 1987)

Wilson, Gerald H., *The Editing of the Hebrew Psalter* (Society of Biblical Literature, 1985)

Woodhouse, Patrick, *Life in the Psalms: Contemporary meaning in ancient texts* (Continuum, 2015)

Wright, Tom, *Finding God in the Psalms: Sing, pray, live* (SPCK, 2014)

Zenger, Erich, *A God of Vengeance? Understanding the psalms of divine wrath*, trans. Linda M. Maloney (Westminster John Knox Press, 1996)

Other works cited

Asser, Bishop, 'Life of King Alfred', in *Alfred the Great: Asser's life of king alfred and other contemporary sources*, ed. Simon Keynes (Penguin, 1983)

Badè, W.F., *The Life and Letters of John Muir* (Houghton Mifflin, 1924)

Bochen, C.M. (ed.), *Thomas Merton: Essential writings* (Orbis, 2000)

Bonaventure, *The Soul's Journey into God*, trans. E. Cousins (Paulist Press, 1978)

Bond, Michael, *Wayfinding: The art and science of how we find and lose our way* (Picador, 2020)

Brueggemann, Walter, *The Land: Place as gift, promise, and challenge in biblical faith* (Fortress Press, 2002)

Bryson, Bill, *The Body: A guide for occupants* (Doubleday, 2019)

Buechner, Frederick, *Now and Then* (Harper and Row, 1983)

Buechner, Frederick, *Telling the Truth: The gospel as tragedy, comedy and fairy tale* (HarperOne, 1977)

Carle, Eric, *The Very Hungry Caterpillar* (World Publishing Company, 1969)

Carson, D.A., *How Long, O Lord? Reflections on suffering and evil*, second edition (IVP, 2006)

Chang, Joseph, 'Recent common ancestors of all present-day individuals', Department of Statistics, Yale University, 1998

Collins, Francis, *The Language of God* (Simon and Schuster, 2007)

Cowman, L.B. (ed.), *Streams in the Desert* (Zondervan, 1997)

Dalrymple, William, *From the Holy Mountain* (Flamingo, 1998)

Dartnell, Lewis, *Origins: How the Earth made us* (Bodley Head, 2018)

De Botton, Alain, *The School of Life: An emotional education* (Hamish Hamilton, 2019)

De Botton, Alain, *Status Anxiety* (Penguin, 2005)

Diagnostic and Statistical Manual of Mental Disorders, fourth (revised) edition (American Psychiatric Association, 1994)

Dickinson, Emily, *Poems by Emily Dickinson: Second Series* (Roberts Brothers, 1891)

Dillard, Annie, *For the Time Being* (Vintage Books, 2000)

Dodds, C.H., *The Parables of the Kingdom* (Nisbet, 1935)

Dowden, Richard, *Africa: Altered states, ordinary miracles* (Portobello Books, 2008)

Duffy, Eamon, *Marking the Hours: English people and their prayers 1240–1570* (Yale University Press, 2006)

Edwards, Jonathan, *Images or Shadows of Divine Things*, ed. P. Miller (Yale University Press, 1948)

Ehrlich, Gretel, *The Solace of Open Spaces* (Daunt Books, 2019)

Emerson, Ralph Waldo, *Nature* (Penguin, 2008)
Fife, Janet and Gilo (eds), *Letters to a Broken Church* (Ekklesia Publishing, 2019)
Flinders, Tim (ed.), *John Muir: Spiritual writings* (Orbis Books, 2013)
Fox, Matthew, *Creation Spirituality* (HarperSanFrancisco, 1991)
Fry, Stephen, *The Ode Less Travelled* (Arrow, 2007)
Gissing, George, *The Private Papers of Henry Ryecroft* (CreateSpace, 2016; first published 1903)
Gros, Frédéric *A Philosophy of Walking* (Verso, 2015)
Hagberg, Janet O., and Robert A. Guelich, *The Critical Journey: Stages in the life of faith* second edition (Sheffield Publishing Company, 2005)
Hardman, Isabel, *The Natural Health Service* (Atlantic Books, 2020)
Hardy, Thomas, 'The Wound', from *Moments of Vision* (Ryburn Publishing, 1994; first published 1917)
Hendricks, William, *Exit Interviews: Revealing stories of why people are leaving the church* (Moody Press, 1995)
Hogan, Laura Reece, *I Live, No Longer I: Paul's spirituality of suffering, transformation, and joy* (Wipf and Stock, 2017)
Holmes, Richard, *Footsteps: Adventures of a romantic biographer* (Viking Press, 1985)
Horsman, Sarah, with Carl Senior and Alena Nash, 'Emerging findings from independent academic research commissioned by Sheldon and conducted by Aston University in collaboration with Sheldon', Sheldon Community, 2020
Hoyle, Carolyn et al., *The Impact of Being Wrongly Accused of Abuse in Occupations of Trust: Victims' voices* (University of Oxford Centre for Criminology, 2016)
Hugh of St Victor, *Eruditionis Didasalicae*, in *Patrologia Latina* ed. J.P. Migne, vol. 176
Hutchinson, Thomas (ed.), *Wordsworth: Poetical Works* (Oxford University Press, 1975)
Inge, Denise, *A Tour of Bones* (Bloomsbury, 2014)
Jefferies, Richard, *The Story of My Heart: My autobiography*, eds B. Williams and T.T. Williams (Torrey House Press, 2014; first published 1883)

John of the Cross, *Dark Night of the Soul*, trans. E. Allison Peers (Dover Publications, 2003)

Joyce, James, *Stephen Hero* (Jonathan Cape, 1956)

Julian of Norwich, *Revelations of Divine Love*, eds H. Backhouse and R. Pipe (Hodder and Stoughton, 2009)

Kendall, R.T., *Total Forgiveness: Achieving God's greatest challenge* (Hodder and Stoughton, 2001)

Kitamori, Kazoh, *Theology of the Pain of God* (SCM Press, 1966)

Lennox, John, *Where is God in a Coronavirus World?* (Good Book Company, 2020)

Lewis, C.S., *The Problem of Pain*, CS Lewis Signature Classics edition (Collins, 2012)

Lewis-Stempel, John, *Where Poppies Blow: The British soldier, nature, the Great War* (Weidenfeld and Nicolson, 2017)

Lotz, Anne Graham, *Wounded by God's People* (Hodder, 2013)

MacDonald, Gordon, *Rebuilding Your Broken World* (Highland Books, 1998)

Macdonald, Helen, *H is For Hawk* (Jonathan Cape, 2014)

Marriott, John, *A Recipe for Disaster: Four ways churches and parents prepare individuals to lose their faith* (Wipf and Stock, 2018)

Mayne, Michael, *This Sunrise of Wonder* (Darton, Longman and Todd, 2008)

McLaren, Brian, *God Unbound: Theology in the wild* (Canterbury Press, 2019)

Merton, Thomas, *New Seeds of Contemplation* (New Directions, 1972)

Mitchell, Edwin Valentine, *The Pleasures of Walking* (Vanguard Press, 1979)

Morgan, Alison, *Something Understood* (The Mathetes Trust, 2017)

Morgan, Alison, *The Word on The Wind* (Monarch, 2011)

Niemann, Derek, *Birds in a Cage* (Short Books, 2013)

Nouwen, Henri, *Making All Things New and Other Classics* (HarperCollins, 2000)

Pannenberg, Walter, *Toward a Theology of Nature* (Westminster John Knox Press, 1993)

Patterson, Christina, *The Art of Not Falling Apart* (Atlantic Books, 2018)

Rahner, Hugo, *Ignatius the Theologian*, trans. Michael Barry (Geoffrey Chapman, 1968)

Ralph, Peter and Graham Coop, 'The geography of recent genetic ancestry across Europe', *PLOS Biology*, 2013

Richardson, Rosamond, *Waiting for the Albino Dunnock: How birds can change your life* (Weidenfeld and Nicolson, 2017)

Rohr, Richard, *Falling Upward: A spirituality for the two halves of life* (Jossey-Bass, 2011)

Rothenberg, David, *Why Birds Sing* (Allen Lane, 2005)

Rousseau, Jean Jacques, *Reveries of The Solitary Walker*, trans. Peter France (Penguin, 1979)

Rutherford, Mark, *A Brief History of Everyone Who Ever Lived* (Weidenfeld and Nicolson, 2016)

Spirn, Anne Whiston, *The Language of Landscape* (Yale University Press, 1998)

Spufford, Francis, *Unapologetic: Why, despite everything, Christianity can still make surprising emotional sense* (Faber and Faber, 2012)

Steiner, George, *The Deeps of the Sea and Other Fiction* (Faber and Faber, 1996)

Stott, John, *The Birds our Teachers: Essays in orni-theology* (Angus Hudson, 1999)

Suurmond, Jean-Jacques, *Word and Spirit at Play* (SCM, 1994)

Swindoll, Charles, *The Grace Awakening* (Word, 1990)

Taylor, Barbara Brown, *Learning to Walk in the Dark* (HarperCollins, 2014)

Taylor, J.V., *The Go-Between God: The Holy Spirit and Christian mission* (SCM Press, 1992)

Tedeschi, R.G. and L.G. Calhoun: 'Posttraumatic growth: conceptual foundations', *Psychological Inquiry*, 15:1 (2004)

Thomas of Celano, *The Lives of St Francis of Assisi by Brother Thomas of Celano*, trans. A. G. Ferrers Howell (Methuen, 1908)

Ullathorne, William, *The Little Book of Humility and Patience* (Burns and Oates, 1860)

Usher, Graham, *The Places of Enchantment: Meeting God in landscapes* (SPCK, 2012)

Van der Toorn, Karel et al., 'Dragon', *Dictionary of Deities and Demons in the Bible* (Eerdmans, 1999)

Von Arnim, Elizabeth, *Adventures of Elizabeth in Rügen* (Virago Press, 1990; first published 1904)

Watson, Andrew, *Confidence in the Living God: David and Goliath revisited* (BRF, 2009)

Williams, Rowan, *A Ray of Darkness* (Cowley Publications, 1995)

Wohlleben, Peter, *The Hidden Life of Trees* (William Collins, 2017)

Wolfe, L.M. (ed.), *John of the Mountains: The unpublished journals of John Muir* (University of Wisconsin Press, 1979)

Wright, David (ed.), *Recollections of the Lake Poets* (Penguin, 1970)

Wright, Tom, *Surprised by Hope* (SPCK, 2007)

Xenophon, *The Memorabilia: Recollections of Socrates*, **gutenberg.org/ebooks/1177**

Zimmer, Carl, 'Charlemagne's DNA and our universal royalty', *National Geographic*, 2013

Zohar, Danah, *The Quantum Self* (Flamingo, 1991)

Zohary, Michael, *Plants of the Bible* (Cambridge University Press, 1982)

Tony Horsfall and Debbie Hawker encourage us to develop our resilience and to prepare ourselves for the challenges that life throws at us in an increasingly difficult world. Through biblical wisdom and psychological insight, they show us how to understand ourselves better, appreciate our areas of strength and strengthen our areas of weakness. Read this book if you want a faith that persists to the finishing line.

Resilience in Life and Faith
Finding your strength in God
Tony Horsfall and Debbie Hawker
978 0 85746 734 8 £9.99

brfonline.org.uk

Where do we turn when our world is falling apart? It takes courage to hope; to stand in our confusion and grief and still to believe that 'God is not helpless among the ruins'. Guided by Habakkuk and his prophetic landmarks, we are drawn on a reflective journey through the tangled landscape of bewildered faith, through places of wrestling and waiting, and on into the growth space of deepened trust and transformation. As you read, discover for yourself the value and practice of honest prayer, of surrender, of silence and listening, and of irrepressible hoping.

God Among the Ruins
Trust and transformation in difficult times
Mags Duggan
978 0 85746 575 7 £8.99

brfonline.org.uk

Many sincere followers of Jesus are secretly disappointed, dissatisfied and quietly desperate for more than they are currently experiencing. That more is found as we respond to the invitations of Jesus, which hold out to us the hope of dynamic change, of a truly vibrant, transformed life – a better song to sing. Each chapter explores one specific invitation, drawing out its possible implications for our lives, and suggests a spiritual practice or reflection to help us ground that invitation in our present-day reality.

A Better Song to Sing
Finding life again through the invitations of Jesus
Mags Duggan
978 0 85746 876 5 £8.99

brfonline.org.uk

GUIDELINES

BIBLE STUDY FOR TODAY'S MINISTRY AND MISSION

MAY–AUG 2023

INCLUDED IN THIS ISSUE

Psalms Book I (1—41)
Bill Goodman

Intercultural Bible reading
George Wieland

Matthew 19—23
Andy Angel

Refugees and the Bible
Rosie Button

Minor prophets
Alison Lo

A typology of shame
Sally Nash

Romans 9—12
Stephen Finamore

Ruth
Steve Walton

Deuteronomy
Ashley Hibbard

2 Peter
Michael Parsons

Philippians
Rosalee Velloso Ewell

Guidelines is a unique Bible reading resource that offers four months of in-depth study, drawing on insights of current scholarship. Its intention is to enable all its readers to interpret and apply biblical text with confidence in today's world. Instead of dated daily readings, *Guidelines* provides weekly units, broken into six sections, plus an introduction and a final section of points for thought and prayer.

Guidelines

Bible study for today's ministry and mission

£4.95 per issue, or subscriptions available both for print and app

brfonline.org.uk

Enabling all ages to grow in faith

Anna Chaplaincy
Living Faith
Messy Church
Parenting for Faith

BRF is a Christian charity that resources individuals and churches. Our vision is to enable people of all ages to grow in faith and understanding of the Bible and to see more people equipped to exercise their gifts in leadership and ministry.

To find out more about our work, visit
brf.org.uk